AT ODDS:
GAMBLING AND CANADIANS, 1919–1969

Using a rich variety of historical sources, Suzanne Morton traces the history of gambling regulation in five Canadian provinces – Nova Scotia, Quebec, Ontario, Manitoba, and British Columbia – from the First World War to federal legalization in 1969. This regulatory legislation, designed to control gambling, ended a long period of paradox and pretence during which gambling was common, but still illegal.

Morton skilfully shows the relationship between gambling and the wider social mores of the time, as evinced by labour, governance, and the regulation of 'vice.' Her focus on the ways in which race, class, and gender structured the meaning of gambling underpins and illuminates the historical data she presents. She shows, for example, that as 'Old Canada' (the Protestant, Anglo-Celtic establishment) declined in influence, gambling took on a less deviant connotation – a process that continued as charity became secularized and gambling became a lucrative fundraising activity eventually linked to the welfare state.

At Odds is the first Canadian historical examination of gambling, a complex topic that is still met by moral ambivalence, legal proscription, and volatile opinion. This highly original study will be of interest to the undergraduate history or social science student, but will also appeal to the more general reader.

SUZANNE MORTON is an associate professor in the Department of History at McGill University.

SUZANNE MORTON

At Odds:
Gambling and Canadians,
1919–1969

UNIVERSITY OF TORONTO PRESS
Toronto Buffalo London

© University of Toronto Press Incorporated 2003
Toronto Buffalo London

Printed in Canada

ISBN 0-8020-3564-7 (cloth)
ISBN 0-8020-8441-9 (paper)

Printed on acid-free paper

National Library of Canada Cataloguing in Publication

Morton, Suzanne, 1961–
At odds : gambling and Canadians, 1919–1969 / Suzanne Morton.

Includes bibliographical references and index.
ISBN 0-8020-3564-7 (bound)   ISBN 0-8020-8441-9 (pbk.)

1. Gambling – Social aspects – Canada – History – 20th century.
2. Gambling – Moral and ethical aspects – Canada – History – 20th
century.   3. Gambling – Government policy – Canada.   I. Title.

HV6722.C3M67 2003   363.4'2'0971   C2002-902524-9

University of Toronto Press acknowledges the financial assistance to
its publishing program of the Canada Council for the Arts and the
Ontario Arts Council.

This book has been published with the help of a grant from the
Humanities and Social Sciences Federation of Canada, using funds provided
by the Social Sciences and Humanities Research Council of Canada.

University of Toronto Press acknowledges the financial support for its
publishing activities of the Government of Canada through the
Book Publishing Industry Development Program (BDIDP).

For my sister, Janet Morton,
who works very hard for her good luck,
and for my parents, Anne and Garry Morton,
who never gamble but taught me
to be conscious of good fortune

Contents

Illustrations follow page 148

Preface

My family background includes both gamblers and anti-gamblers. Family tradition has it that one of my great-grandmothers was an occasional bookmaker, but as a poor widow with a large family to support she was left alone by the Hamilton police. My father tells stories of discreetly – behind the back of his anti-gambling Baptist mother – lending money to his grandfather for trips to the Fort Erie racetrack. In the early 1970s, my father's service club – under the federal legislation of 1969 – annually sold raffle tickets on a Cadillac. As a Presbyterian minister, he would not sell tickets himself, so instead did his share of the work by moving the luxury car to different suburban malls.

I don't buy lottery tickets or visit casinos (well, only when I'm travelling), but I reflect the ambivalence towards gambling for which I argue in this book. This ambivalence provides an interesting contrast to the more widespread (and at least temporarily successful) movements against alcohol of the first part of the twentieth century. While teaching, I have been guilty of making easy jokes at the expense of those whom I imagine to be the humourless men and women who formed the temperance movement, but the issue of gambling is not so clear to me. I am enough of a late-twentieth-century/turn-of-the-millennium libertarian (and moral relativist) to recognize the failure of prohibitive laws and to accept diverse ethics, yet I retain profound unease around the role of government in promoting and operating gambling for its citizens. I reject the classism and racism of many of those who opposed gambling and I find distasteful their righteousness and sanctimoniousness. However, in an age dominated by pragmatic utilitarianism, I also find their idealism appealing. Despite the anti-gamblers' tendency to make exaggerated claims concerning gambling's destructive potential,

I also agree that excessive gambling has destroyed and continues to destroy real individuals and families.

This book is not the definitive history of gambling in Canada, nor is it a version that emphasizes the experiences of people who gambled. It conveys not enough of the humanity of the gamblers and too much of the bravado of various inquiries and critics. What this volume does, however, is try to explain what I originally perceived to be the dramatic change in attitudes towards gambling between the end of the First World War and the federal government's revision to the criminal code in 1969 that permitted lotteries under certain conditions. What I found was not so much change as ongoing ambivalence towards various forms of gambling. Attitudes towards gambling in fact reflected the 'big' issues of society, such as work, property, democracy, gender, religion, governance, and definitions of community.

Now that my cards are on the table, I have a pile of people to thank. National history is expensive, and I could not have undertaken this project without the generous financial support of Quebec's Programme nouveau chercheur, Fonds pour la Formation de Chercheurs et l'Aide à la Recherche (FCAR). Some of my original thinking about this topic occurred during a postdoctoral fellowship supported by the Social Science and Humanities Research Council that I held at Queen's University. I also benefited from research undertaken by Kate Boyer and Don Fyson as part of the Montreal History Group's 'Power, Identity and the Law in Urban Quebec, 1800–1939,' Programme soutien au Équipes de Recherche FCAR grant.

Like all publicly funded institutions in the 1990s, archives and libraries were under increasing pressure, and I am appreciative of the high level of assistance that they continued to offer. I want to thank especially the Inter-Library Loan staff at the McLellan-Redpath Library at McGill, who processed seemingly endless rolls of microfilm with professionalism and good humour. In addition, I would like to acknowledge assistance from the staff at the British Columbia Archives and Records Centre, McMaster University Archives, the National Archives of Canada, the Nova Scotia Archives, the Ontario Archives, the Provincial Archives of Manitoba, the United Church Archives, and the city archives of Vancouver and Montreal. I owe a particular debt to Ranald Lesieur of the Archives nationale du Québec – Québec.

Research assistants did yeoman's service, and I am grateful and proud to have worked with Michael Boudreau, Tanya Gogan, Mary Matthews, Tamara Myers, Ann Perry, and Sarah Schmidt. Belinda Huang and Kelly Johnson prepared challenging translations. My colleagues and students at McGill and especially the Montreal History Group provide a stimulating community of scholars in which I continue to learn how to be a historian. It is a pleasure to be able to thank publicly the support staff in McGill's History Department, especially Mrs Georgii Mikula, whose dedication and many talents have helped free up time for me to teach and write. As department chair, I benefited personally from her generosity. I am also grateful to the History Department at Dalhousie, which generously gave me space and support during a sabbatical leave that saw me revise this work.

I am obliged in particular to Denyse Baillargeon, Colin Coates, Karen Dubinsky, Don Fyson, Andrée Lévesque, Bob McDonald, Ian McKay, Greg Marquis, Cecilia Morgan, Des Morton, Tamara Myers, Ian Radforth, Mike Szonyi, and Faith Wallis, who kindly offered suggestions, anecdotes, clues, computer help, clippings, citations, and language skills. Gerry Friesen, Janet Guildford, Karen Robert, and Shirley Tillotson generously took time from their own work to read various bits, and Tina Loo and Brian Young read an almost-entire first draft. Gerry Hallowell, formerly of this press, offered encouragement at a crucial stage. I hope that they will all recognize their formative influences on this work but will forgive the books that I did not write. I also want to acknowledge the cooperative and professional editorial staff at the University of Toronto Press; I am fortunate to have worked with Len Husband and copy-editor John Parry on this project.

West to east, Lynne Marks and John Blakely, Kirk Williams and Rob Skene, Di Hilton and Toby Lennox, and especially Janet Guildford extended gracious and warm hospitality to me during my research and, in the case of Beach Meadows, prolonged writing sessions. Nancy Forestell, Janet Guildford, and Tina Loo, three fine historians and good friends, sympathetically and with good humour put up with this project, willing to listen and respond to various preoccupations. My public acknowledgment of their encouragement, patience, and help is a small return.

AT ODDS:
GAMBLING AND CANADIANS, 1919–1969

Introduction

The lines at corner stores and ticket kiosks grow as cash jackpots reach record amounts. In the mall, one walks around a car parked in the aisle – the prize in local service club's draw. Television commercials inform viewers that they can win big prizes with specially marked boxes of a product or that they can escape from their daily routine with a visit to the local casino. Even banks present us with sweepstake enticements urging us to switch to self-service or to take out larger consumer loans. Meanwhile, newspapers advertise a large number of commercial bingo halls offering games on any given night, with proceeds going to charitable or non-profit organizations. Public-sector lotteries are among the major corporate clients for advertising agencies and plaster slogans such as 'Don't think for an instant,' 'Imagine the freedom,' and 'It's fun to be rich' on billboards, commercials, and print media. On reserves, native Canadians assert their limited sovereignty with gigantic bingo jackpots that exceed the set legal limit. Tabloids and pocket books at the supermarket offer astrology, numerology, and reincarnations of nineteenth-century dream books to forecast lucky numbers. Everywhere we look in modern-day Canada, we see games of chance that lure us to purchase a specific product, to be entertained, to help raise funds for non-profit organizations or charities, and to finance the welfare state.

Every aspect of society looks less normal, less natural, or less inevitable when we scrutinize it from a historical perspective. The particular circumstances of time and place create situations and assumptions that we can easily take for granted as eternal practices or truths. The ordinariness of gambling today is one such example. The lottery tickets and scratch prizes available at the grocery checkout, the television commercials that urge us to visit a casino, and the promotional sweepstakes sponsored by various businesses become almost invisible when they are so much part of our daily lives. Yet until 1969 virtually all forms of public gambling were illegal in Canada; only a generation ago, what we take for granted today was a source of public debate and moral ambivalence.

It is clear that the legislators of 1969 who amended the Criminal Code and made it possible for governments to license and sponsor their own lotteries severely underestimated the impact of their actions. A report prepared for Quebec's Bélanger Commission in the 1960s anticipated that a government-operated lottery in that province would contribute only 0.55 per cent of required provincial revenue.[1] In 2000, Canadians spent a total of $20 billion on legal government-operated gambling, and the provinces cleared a profit of $5 billion, which contributed up to 4 per cent of their respective provincial revenues. It is now a cliché to note that there is no one more 'addicted' to gambling in Canada than our provincial governments. For example, by 1995 Manitobans spent more money at their government gambling enterprises than they did on groceries.[2] In the year ending March 2000, the casino in the economically depressed community of Sydney, Nova Scotia, raised $54.3 million before taxes – and while some of this money stayed in the community in the form of winnings and wages, much of it either went off to Halifax as government revenue or was exported out of the country by its American operators – ITT Sheraton. The cash spent at the Sydney casino was largely local money not spent at other community businesses.[3]

Today we may be experiencing another period of moral concern (not quite a panic) about gambling. Newspapers report stories of gambling-related suicides and children being abandoned in casino parking lots by negligent parents whose compulsive behaviour hurts their children. Community activists organize referendum campaigns to prohibit video lottery terminals (VLTs). Researchers in Canada, the United States, and Britain suggest that we are creating a generation of adolescent gamblers – reportedly one in five teenagers has a serious gambling problem, compared to approximately 4 per cent of the adult population.[4]

This book seeks to contribute a historical perspective to contemporary debates by exploring the ambivalent attitudes that Canadians held towards gambling over the first half of the twentieth century. Between the end of the First World War and 1969, when amendments to the Criminal Code largely decriminalized it, gambling underwent a trans-

formation from a stigmatized minor vice to an acceptable activity regarded as appropriate and perhaps necessary to fund the Canadian
welfare state. Yet a historical survey shows us that this simple narrative
description belies the fact that cultural contradictions surrounded the
entire process.

As a predominantly Protestant country in the first half of the twentieth century, Canada shared the approach towards gambling with other
Protestant societies that one 1940s' sociologist characterized as unofficial toleration and official condemnation.[5] But it would be a mistake to
ignore the steady public lobby looking for reform and liberalization of
the law. During the 1930s, three pro-lottery bills were presented to
Parliament, and between 1959 and 1963 a total of eleven were introduced.[6] In 1953–4, the question of lotteries went before a joint committee of the House of Commons and Senate.

I argue that the regulation of gambling was not about gambling itself
but about how it related to a whole set of fundamental matters such as
work, property, family, and faith. Its regulation exposed cultural contradictions about understandings and definitions of such basic structures as capitalism, gender roles, and community. For instance, public
debate in the first half of the twentieth century reveals evidence of an
economic system that prized speculation and production, merit and
luck, thrift and consumption. The book looks at the ambivalence surrounding gambling via an exploration of behaviour, policing, laws, and
public discourse.

Gambling could be considered positive and state-sanctioned or criminal, depending on the participants, their motivation, and where proceeds were going. The respectability of gambling was situational –
based largely on the class, race, and gender of the participants. Historian Kevin Wamsley has noted that the presence of gambling in private
clubs meant that gambling occurred without comment in such respectable establishments as the Rideau Club in Ottawa, a favourite meeting
place for members of Parliament.[7] The rhetoric against gambling not
only focused on economic values but also was permeated with contemporary attitudes towards gender, class, and ethnicity. Opponents of
gambling held it responsible for family disruption and corruption within
such civic institutions as local government and the police.[8]

The consequences of gambling for individuals were also significant as opponents believed that it enticed men and occasionally women
into criminal behaviour. Nineteenth-century morality tales of young
men with access to other people's money who stole from employers

and customers to cover their own gambling debts survived into the twentieth century.[9] The apocryphal stories of the ruined lives of bank tellers, office bookkeepers, and retail clerks were complemented less frequently by tales of young women who turned to prostitution as 'the easiest way to make up for losses sustained at the tracks.'[10] But over the first seventy years of the twentieth century, the construction of gambling as deviant activity became increasingly difficult to maintain with the decline of 'old Canada,' as represented by the Anglo-Celtic, Protestant middle class and its traditional institutions such as churches and patriarchal control.[11] The secularization of charity and expanding expectations of the state opened the door for the rationalization of government-operated gambling as the state assumed the traditional role of charitable fundraising.

Gambling as a Vice

While there is a long tradition of raising funds through gambling for charitable and religious causes, gambling with less altruist goals was associated with vice. 'Vice' is a strangely old-fashioned term used to describe both criminalized and non-criminalized moral offences. It survived the shift from social reformers to modern police work when police adopted the term 'vice squad' for units assigned to enforce laws relating to prostitution, narcotics, and gambling. Today, vice and its regulatory enforcement conjure images of illicit drugs, prostitution, pornography, and the overzealous policing of big-city gay and lesbian bars. Although 'vices' have frequently been criminalized and prohibitions encoded in the law, they also have social, moral, spatial, and political dimensions. For example, a gendered understanding of vice made assumptions about appropriate behaviour connected to cultural expectations of male and females roles and their respective responsibilities in society. Gambling, as a predominantly male activity, was often associated in practice with other minor vices such as alcohol, swearing, and smoking, and it occasionally overlapped spatially with prostitution.[12] Although men composed the vast majority of gamblers, women also gambled. In particular, while women played bingo, they also bought lotteries and sweepstakes tickets and by the 1920s were visible at racetracks.[13] When the *Vancouver Daily Province* published winners of the Irish Sweepstakes in May 1932, eight of the twenty names that were not obvious aliases suggested women ticket holders.[14] The understanding of vice and its reification in the Criminal Code reflected Judaeo–Christian tenets, especially the dominant Protestant culture. Its strain of puritanism influenced attitudes towards gambling, sex, alcohol, recreational drug use, and Sunday observance. It is clear that the loss of hegemonic control by this culture has led to what one American historian has referred to as 'a significant inversion of cultural values in the twentieth century,' as non-normative behaviour lost much of its deviant status.[15]

All manifestations of vice were not considered equal, and within the hierarchy there were varying levels of sanction. In the 1950s, when Canadian society was liberalizing its laws on alcohol, Sunday observance, and censorship, a federal committee recommended that Parliament not legalize lotteries and sweepstakes. Lotteries and sweepstakes remained a vice, a form of gambling that, along with homosexuality, prostitution, and use of recreational drugs, the state would not legitimate, despite their widespread occurrence. While there are parallels between attitudes towards gambling and those towards other 'vices,' historians know and understand gambling least.[16] This lacuna is in part the result of ambiguity about gambling itself. People considered gambling variously a vice, an inevitable aspect of human nature, a 'minor' transgression, or a legitimate activity associated with charity and churches. Rather than entering a historically based discussion of human nature or instinct, this book explores the public debate concerning gambling and both the attempt to suppress it and the campaign to legalize it.

U.S. historian T.J. Jackson Lears has noted that gambling offers insights 'not merely about changing definitions of vice and virtue; it is about different ways of experiencing the world.'[17] Gambling is one of the place where belief and values systems met with economics. Moral issues intersected the market as public debate over the regulation of gambling swirled around major issues such as capitalism, consumption, productive labour, and human passions.

A Long History

Gambling games have existed throughout recorded history.[18] With Europe's colonization of North America, lotteries became a method of raising funds and distributing land. Harvard and Yale universities were partially endowed with monies raised by this method, and lots on Prince Edward Island were assigned this way. In a colonial society with little access to capital, large economic projects also depended on lotteries to raise money. The first Welland Canal became possible through a lottery operated by American capitalists.[19] Lotteries flourished in the United States until the Civil War, but by 1878 they were prohibited in all states except Louisiana.[20] The last legal nineteenth-century U.S. lottery took place on 1 January 1894, by which time there were federal restrictions and constitutional prohibitions in thirty-five states.[21] Lotteries were not as popular in Canada as they had been in the United States, but they did exist and were subject to regulation in Lower and Upper Canada. Raffles that offered goods instead of cash prizes flourished until 1856, when the Province of Canada outlawed draws and forbade the selling of tickets. Canada East, under pressure from the Catholic church, amended the law to permit lotteries for charitable purposes as long as the prizes were not money. Loopholes in this law permitted private lotteries, and in 1890 – before the 1892 revisions in the Criminal Code – Quebec even instigated a provincial lottery with a cash prize.[22]

But lotteries in various forms also existed outside Quebec. From the mid-nineteenth century on, the Calcutta Sweepstakes, for example, had attracted Canadian money abroad. In sweepstakes, entrants drew tickets, and the prize was awarded according to some additional contest, usually a horse race. In a domestic example, Harry Salmon's sweepstakes in Victoria operated with the tacit support of British Columbia's attorney general, who instructed local police not to prosecute.[23] In contrast, Chinese lotteries, which appear to have operated in every Canadian city with a Chinese population, were frequently the focus of severe enforcement campaigns.[24]

Forms of gambling such as card games were a normal aspect of frontier life, especially in the male frontier resource communities that dotted the west and north. Cockfights were a popular source of entertainment in rural communities. Horse racing, of both elite thoroughbreds and the more democratic trotters, played a central role in settler communities' celebrations. Technological innovation and new patterns of leisure and consumption fostered varieties of gambling that ranged from the syndicated North American wire service, which distributed betting information, to more mundane manifestations such as slot machines, punchboards, and commercial contests. Slot machines at times were in an ambiguous position as distributors went to imaginative extents to circumvent the law. These machines often dispensed inferior gumballs or small packages of mints to create the legal pretence that goods were exchanged for payment.[25]

Before 1969, all forms of gambling were subject to the attention of reformers. The critics of gambling are impossible to ignore, for as historian Ross McKibbin has pointed out in his study of working-class gambling in Britain, nearly all that we know about the topic comes from their perspective. In Canada, there was no real equivalent in organizations to the British National Anti-Gambling League, although gambling was an enduring issue for the Moral and Social Reform Council of Canada, the Woman's Christian Temperance Union, retail associations, and the Protestant churches.[26]

Perhaps not surprisingly, in the light of the religious origins of the modern work ethic, Canada's most vocal opponents of gambling that rewarded winners with 'something for nothing' were the Protestant churches, especially the Methodist church and after 1925 its successor, the United Church of Canada. Although there was not one monolithic position, most mainstream Protestant churches opposed gambling on the basis that it encouraged selfishness, denied providential control over human life, and undermined the stewardship of resources.[27] In its report to the federal Joint Committee on Capital Punishment, Corporal Punishment and Lotteries in 1956, the Anglican church claimed that 'the desire to get something for nothing is a denial of honesty and industry.'[28]

Cultural historians have noted how the complementary forces of Protestantism and liberalism reoriented authority from external institutions to what Jackson Lears has described as 'an internalized morality of self-control, and enshrined the autonomous individual whose only master was himself.'[29] Given increased emphasis on individual self-control and reason, the state in dominantly Protestant, liberal societies paradoxically demonstrated greater willingness to intervene in morality. But there was always tension between libertarian impulses and the perceived need for social regulation. Conversely, the rigid institutional regulation associated with the Catholic church corresponded to political cultures less interested in criminalizing 'sin.' Within Catholicism there was theological and cultural space to recognize passion and to accept that loss of control was part of human nature.

This discrepancy in how the two religious cultures addressed the regulation of morality had political significance in Canada. It frequently led to a clash of values between what we might characterize rather crudely as Anglo-Protestant Canada and French-Catholic Canada, concentrated in Quebec. As a minority culture that generally did not view gambling with so much disapproval, Quebec was subject to federal criminal laws on morality, created by and tending to reflect the values of the Protestant majority. The schism between Protestants and Catholics placed the federal government in a difficult position as to how far it could reform or enforce the law. Tolerant stances frustrated English-speaking Protestant reformers opposed to gambling, while many francophone Quebecers saw the existence of a criminal law that reflected Anglo-Protestant morality (if not practice) as a colonial imposition of values. Catholic minorities outside Quebec and most non-Protestant communities felt the same way, but Quebec's Catholic majority made it a particularly contentious issue there. Because gambling was a section in the Criminal Code originally under 'Offenses against religion, morals and public convenience,' the highest courts consistently held it a federal responsibility and granted the provincial legislatures no jurisdiction in the area.[30] Notwithstanding cultural differences and frequent opportunities for conflict between Quebec and the rest of Canada, the federal criminal law against gambling was enforced irregularly. The general observation of distinctiveness between Quebec and the rest of Canada does not deny any similarities. Some francophone Québécois, such as the Comité pour la moralité publique in the 1950s, joined in common cause with anglophones elsewhere in Canada opposed to gambling. Common notions of liberalism and capitalism, and even a Catholic version of puritanism, meant that some minority elements of francophone Quebec shared similar worldviews with English-speaking reformers in the rest of Canada.

The Law

Gambling has never been completely illegal in Canada except on Sunday. Courts ruled that informal private betting between fewer than ten people was legal. So while the law did not prevent any individual from making a bet with another individual, it did intervene in any situation where a third party might profit from the wager. In a sense, the law embodied ambivalence towards gambling, which was not in itself illegal, although participating in anything much more than a 'gentlemanly' bet or card game contravened federal law.[31]

Before 1969, Canadian law permitted three other exemptions. The Criminal Code of 1892 permitted raffles in the restricted setting of a charity or religious bazaar if permission had been granted by a municipality, the article being given away was not valued at more than $50, and it had first been offered for public sale. The propagation of lotteries, raffles, and assorted games of chance, including bingo, during the First World War led to further amendments in 1922 that forbade disposal of any object or amount of money 'by any mode of chance or mixed chance and skill where the participant was required to wager money or something of value.'[32]

Although the charitable and religious exemption became a regular topic of debate, two further exemptions were more controversial, as they contradicted the spirit of the law. The first was the exception in the 1892 law offered to carnival games of chance at agricultural fairs and exhibitions. The revenue generated thereby financed the educational objectives and prizes of the local associations that organized these annual events. The second, also in the original legislation, was the operation of betting at government-chartered racetracks. After Parliament imported British legislation regarding gambling, the state awarded gambling privileges to private, incorporated turf clubs.[33] Racing associations in Canada were joint stock companies, and until the First World War their primary source of revenue was the sale of bookmaking rights at their tracks.[34] The existence of such legal betting reminds us that Canadian historians have ignored the ongoing presence of a powerful, real, and self-styled gentry in Canada that continued well into the twentieth century. The colonial elite did not disappear with Confederation in 1867 and continued to rival members of the non-Anglican, Protestant middle class for control of Canadian society. Although the middle class gained control of the economic and political structures, it never succeeded in attaining complete cultural and moral dominance.[35]

The best racetracks in Canada could boast the patronage of the governor general and regal connections such as the annual running of the Queen's or King's Plate. The Ontario Jockey Club in Toronto brought together members of colonial elites such as Sir Casimir Gzowski, railway builder and honorary aide-de-camp to Queen Victoria, T.C. Patteson, former editor of the *Toronto Mail*, and Sir Frank Smith, former federal minister of public works, alongside successful status-conscious capitalists such as Adam Beck, William Hendrie, and Joseph E. Seagram. In Montreal, the Jockey Club, under the leadership of Sir H. Montagu Allan, Alfred Baumgarten, Sir Mortimer Davis, Sir Herbert Holt, Major Herbert Molson, Lord Shaughnessy, George W. Stephens, and Commander J.K.L. Ross, could claim equally illustrious supporters.[36] The elite's unique perspective was evident not only in its dismissal of puritanism but in its belief that thoroughbred racing not only was a class-appropriate leisure as the 'sport of kings' but also served military

and imperial objectives. This imperial worldview regarded the breeding and racing quality of Canadian thoroughbreds as a vital contribu-
tion to the British Empire's military superiority. The illusion (or at least
the rhetoric) that a strong cavalry remained relevant to modern warfare
continued even after the brutal lessons of the First World War and
formed a central justification for continued legal gambling in testimony
before a royal commission in 1920.[37] The explicit link between the male,
upper-class Canadian colonial gentry and the imagined requirements
of British military imperialism was sufficiently powerful to create an
exemption vis-à-vis gambling that stood outside the general thrust of
the Criminal Code.

By 1914, the track bookmaker had given way to the parimutuel
machine, which calculated odds strictly according to the distribution of
bets and eliminated bookmakers. The existence of this state-sanctioned
form of gambling suggests that betting at tracks was not regarded as
harmful for all citizens, since it was acceptable for Canada's elites.
Accusations of blatant class discrimination were associated with this
exemption – gambling was acceptable for elites that possessed both
money and 'self control' but was dangerous for working-class Canadians. The law provided a means for people to bet legally on horse races
at the racetrack for those who were able to be there in the daytime and
use the government-approved parimutuel machines (whence federal
and provincial governments took their share of revenue). Those who
could not leave their place of work during the day broke the law when
they placed bets with a local bookmaker. It is not surprising that most
working-class gambling took an illegal form, since this legal double
standard left dedicated gamblers who were wage earners with no legal
option. A Halifax labour newspaper in the 1930s reminded its readers
that 'if it was wicked and frightfully wrong for Mr Workingman to
gamble a dime on "Bingo," it was equally wicked and wrong for Mr
Leisure-Class to gamble ten or twenty-five dollars on a horse via the
gambling machines known as the "parimutuels."'[38]

The exemption for parimutuel betting became the focus of those who
wanted more liberal gambling laws as well as those who criticized
gambling. Ontario Attorney General W.E. Raney, one of the country's
most prominent critics of gambling in the 1910s and 1920s, used an
argument almost identical to the Halifax labour editorialist's – legalized racetrack betting created 'confusion of the moral standard produced by an immoral law, and by the support of that law by people of
high social and political standing. People reason, "how can it be wrong

if it is approved by the law? How can it be wrong if it is approved by Sir This and the Honorable That?"'[39]

The class dimension and dynamics surrounding gambling were extremely complicated, and, unlike the characterizations made by historians in Australia and New Zealand, gambling in Canada was not strictly an example of working-class culture that occasionally found common cause with elite conventions against the middle-class reformers. Gambling was an aspect of Canadian working-class culture, but at least some working-class Canadians were ambivalent towards gambling as it undermined the ethos of productive labour on which skilled craftsmen asserted their status. For example, in 1922 the Toronto District Trades and Labor Council supported the provincial government in its fight against the elite Ontario Jockey Club.[40] In New Zealand and Australia, Labour parties in power liberalized gambling laws, and their position was understood as a manifestation of class interests. The Canadian case followed more closely the British Labour Party's anti-gambling tradition, as leaders saw gambling as undermining respectable working-class self-help and moral uplift and offered a more radical critique – that it distracted workers from the possibility of real political change.[41] Canada's Co-operative Commonwealth Federation (CCF) had its origins in socialism, a religiously based reform movement, and rural populism – currents at the heart of the anti-gambling movement. Within the CCF and its successor, the New Democratic Party (NDP), there was ongoing tension between so-called class interests and Protestant puritan values, but many members of both parties had no problem reconciling the two traditions.

The Lobby for Reform

Although Canada's Criminal Code was clearly a matter of federal authority, attempts at legal reform were not restricted to this level. Citizens of Vancouver, in a municipal plebiscite in 1932, heartily approved establishment of a provincial lottery to support underfunded hospitals by a vote of 25,735 to 9,777. Although BC popular opinion strongly supported legal reform, the most consistent organized opposition to the federal prohibition on lotteries came from Quebec. Even before the crash of the stock market in 1929, the mayor of Montreal, Camillien Houde, had unsuccessfully attempted to establish a lottery to eliminate the city's municipal debt.[42] When insufficient government funds in 1934 threatened the construction of new facilities for the

Université de Montréal, a lottery bill passed unanimously through both houses of the Quebec legislature, with the proviso that this lottery would be conducted only when obstacles in the Canadian Criminal Code were removed. When Quebec Premier L.-A. Taschereau proposed a national lottery for charitable and educational purposes, he gained the support of his Ontario counterpart, Mitchell Hepburn, and of the Union of British Columbia Municipalities, the Saskatchewan Association of Rural Municipalities, the national Red Cross, and the Trades and Labor Congress. Its proceeds would be distributed on a per capita basis among the provinces.[43] The Quebec legislature in 1950 again adopted legislation creating a provincial lottery, but, like the earlier legislation, the act could not be implemented until federal law changed. Finally, after the expense of Expo 67 Mayor Jean Drapeau of Montreal introduced a lottery in the form of a 'voluntary tax.' This lottery was declared illegal and abolished just before federal legislation finally changed the legal status of lotteries.[44]

Although the anti-gambling forces appeared to have had the exclusive ear of federal politicians, it was quite another matter to have the laws enforced at the local level. It appears as if some prominent officials, such as the district superintendent of the Quebec City post office, were confused about the law. This public servant believed that the laws of Quebec permitted 'some scope' when lotteries were organized for charitable purposes and therefore was 'sympathetic' when the mail was being used for this 'commendable work.'[45] Such misunderstanding also occurred in Victoria, for in May 1920 the *Victoria Daily Times* and the *Colonist*, along with two prominent local businesses, were prosecuted when that city began 'a new crusade against the war time practice of charitable raffles.'[46] Local moral reformer Clarence Harris laid charges after the newspapers promoted a raffle of a car for the benefit of the Victoria Jubilee Hospital. Earlier that spring, charges had been laid against a downtown tobacco shop, for raffling a Prussian helmet, the war trophy of an invalid veteran. The tobacco store believed that it had complied with the law, since it displayed in the window, beside the helmet, a permit signed by the mayor. The cooperation of Victoria's mayor and its major hospital in both these enterprises suggests how acceptable these activities were in the local community. However, criminal law in Canada is a federal matter – a position supported by the courts, which consistently held that provincial legislatures had no jurisdiction in the area; yet enforcement of this law was a provincial matter, under the attorney general.[47]

This separation of powers explains in part the periodic and uneven enforcement of the law. Many people who participated in minor forms of gambling, such as the buying and selling of lottery tickets, were left alone. When Victoria police intimated in 1931 that they were considering prosecution of any sweepstakes ticket holder, Attorney General R.H. Pooley vetoed the plan. But in 1936, Vancouver police began a period of careful enforcement of the law against the sale of Irish Sweepstakes tickets, making twenty-five arrests and disrupting the supply of these tickets in the entire region. This cleanup was only temporary, and tolerance was the norm – by March 1938 tickets for the June race at Epsom were 'selling like hotcakes on the streets of Vancouver.'[48] A similar period of intense police enforcement in Halifax in May 1938 and in Montreal in November 1951 briefly closed lottery operations there. These occasional crackdowns continued until 1967, on the eve of introduction of legislation to change the law.

Periodic crackdowns were also enforced against other forms of gambling. In February 1935, Premier Taschereau, in his role as Quebec's attorney general, ordered provincial police to close down all gambling houses and directed that people convicted receive jail sentences, not the usual fines. At the time gambling houses were said to be flourishing in Montreal and its western suburbs and operating openly in Hull, Trois-Rivières, Sherbrooke, and Quebec City.[49]

Before the change in the law in 1969, lotteries placed local police and provincial attorneys general in a difficult position, given the wide gap between the law and public opinion. The president of the Chief Constables Association of Canada complained in 1954 that it was 'no easy matter to enforce an unpopular law.' The judiciary also had problems sentencing people found guilty under the law, and one Montreal judge noted the irony of sending a man to a jail that had been constructed with the proceeds of an eighteenth-century lottery. A British historian, Andrew Davies, has concluded that gambling exposed the 'weakness of police as an agency of control' and the limited 'capacity of the state to define or enforce acceptable patterns of behaviour.'[50]

It is not always easy to determine what motivated the periodic enforcement of the law, despite what at times had seemed almost universal disregard. Some instances were evident, such as the political partisanship that prompted action against the merchant operating a commercial lottery from his Montreal clothing store. The merchant had acted as campaign organizer for an opposition party in the previous election, and a letter of complaint placed this political argument ahead of the harm that the lottery was inflicting on other local, legitimate enterprises. Likewise, a Liberal backbencher pointed out to Premier Taschereau that instigating proceedings against 'nos bons partisans' in Rivière-du-Loup would create many enemies.[51] While political partisanship no doubt played a role elsewhere, the authority of the law, supported by the vocal minority of gambling opponents, could also prompt action. Moral reformers who attacked games of chance at agricultural fairs in the 1920s were dismissed by their opponents as stirring 'up mischief in the direction where they would get the most publicity.' Bewildered Edmonton Mayor K.B. Blatchford complained in March 1924 to the federal minster of justice, Ernest Lapointe, that 'no objection has been offered to them until recently.'[52]

Blatchford's protest reminds us that no sustained anti-gambling campaign was constant across time, and all must be understood in their specific historical contexts. The advent of gambling as a public issue in the late nineteenth and early twentieth centuries reflected reformers' concerns about economic and family values, specifically their notions of productive labour, thrift, and property. The worldview of gambling opponents was embodied in the Criminal Code but conflicted with relatively new ways of gaining wealth, such as speculation on the stock market. This tension between productive labour and speculation was not even shared by all influential Canadians. It had little resonance within francophone Catholic Quebec or among the remnants of colonial gentry found at Canada's 'best' racetracks.

Historiographical Context

The time frame of this book – 1919–1969 – covers a period of change in every aspect of life and exposes the residual strength of Victorian values well into the twentieth century. The First World War created a climate sympathetic to patriotic and philanthropic lotteries and raffles and introduced bingo to Canadian soldiers while in transport and in the trenches. With the armistice in 1918, social reformers, particularly those associated with the social gospel, sought to create a nation free from sin (their definition) by enforcing and expanding legal restrictions around a variety of morality offences. The re-entry of soldiers into civilian life, in particular, caused them to believe that gambling was a serious problem.

Change over time is often difficult to capture, as the rhetoric of anti-gamblers and the law remained relatively constant throughout the entire period. Recent work by American historian Peter Stearns has noted that the usual practice of locating the end of Victorian culture in the 1920s misses the extended period of changes that lasted several decades more.[53] My conclusions are similar. A notable aspect of the opposition to gambling was the almost static nature of its arguments. In addition, Canada's political leaders remained demographically stable for a remarkably long time. Pierre Trudeau, born in 1919 and chosen prime minister in 1968, was the first twentieth-century head of government who was not shaped by a Victorian upbringing. Public attitudes and practice, however, did not coincide with this remarkable stability. Both the 1920s and 1950s saw noticeable shifts in public opinion, as more liberal attitudes towards gambling went hand in hand with increased tolerance concerning alcohol and sex. This general parallel between attitudes towards gambling and those vis-à-vis other 'minor vices' exists, except that those on gambling had a more direct relationship to general economic conditions. During the 1930s, the Depression simultaneously expanded and restricted gambling's popularity. Change over time is perhaps more apparent in the minority groups most associated with gambling. Part of the criticism levelled against gambling was its association with certain groups – a prejudice that did not reflect practice, as there was evidence of gambling everywhere. While present-day stereotypes link gambling to Aboriginal peoples, in the first half of the twentieth century gambling was linked prejudicially to a relatively small (and predominantly male) Chinese-Canadian community. Indeed, before 1969, except in the north, I found no mention of Aboriginal Canadians in any writing against gambling.

In order to show these elements of change and continuity, I organize chapters in terms of both chronological periods and specific themes. I begin with a discussion in chapter 1 of the moral concerns about gambling expressed by its opponents in the first seventy years of the twentieth century and then in chapter 2 examine the context of gambling activities between 1918 and 1945. The middle three chapters explore specific themes of masculinity (chapter 3), femininity (chapter 4), and ethnicity (chapter 5) as they related to concerns about gambling. The final two chapters combine chronological periods and specific themes by examining both the post-1945 panic about gambling and its links with organized crime (chapter 6) and the postwar move to amend the Criminal Code and the linking of gambling with both the welfare state and charitable fundraising (chapter 7).

From the beginning, I envisioned this work as a 'national' project. I began research with the assumption that I would find major differences by region. I selected five provinces as my focus, since the federal Criminal Code was enforced (or not enforced) at the provincial and municipal levels. Nova Scotia, Quebec, Ontario, Manitoba, and British Columbia provided examples of diverse ethnic and religious compositions, various rural and urban distributions of population, and distinct economies that might affect attitudes and practices according to place. Sex demographic ratios also mattered, since resource economies in the north and British Columbia were predominantly male before 1950, suggesting a greater occurrence of a largely male activity. Therefore provincial differences were significant, and I argue that they impeded any efforts by the federal government to achieve a consensus to amend the criminal code.

I am acutely aware (as were federal politicians) of what Karen Dubinsky has referred to as the 'moral geography' of Canada in terms of both diverse values and constructed notions of danger. Moral geography was based on perceptions that associated place with depravity. An obvious example would be the widespread assumption by many English-speaking Canadians that Montreal was a city of vice. Montreal was not alone in this reputation, as this label was applied to frontier and resource-town settings. In 1920, a Methodist minister, distraught about gambling at a fair in his southern Ontario farm community, wrote that, based on his experience of years in northern Ontario among miners where illegal gambling was prevalent, 'it remains for Old Ontario to give an example of the toleration of open gambling right under the noses of authorities.'[54] This clergyman clearly had different expectations of the community standards of the male, multi-ethnic communities of the north and of the homogeneous families of the rural south.

For purposes of this study, Quebec, Manitoba, and British Columbia provide examples of more tolerant jurisdictions vis-à-vis gambling than the more restricted environments of Ontario and Nova Scotia. Cities, especially Montreal and Vancouver, receive greater attention than small towns and rural districts, and this bias reflects probably not the presence of more gambling activities but merely the urban-based records available to historians. Notwithstanding the urban slant, within each province and each community, as the above example illustrates, there was no universal standard. In British Columbia, where public opinion polls were the most sympathetic, after Quebec's, to liberalization, Attorney General Robert Bonner was one of the most outspoken opponents of change in the 1950s and 1960s of change.

My interest in tackling the 'big picture' springs in part from recent historiographical debates in Canada. These discourses have bemoaned the loss of a national perspective, the increasing tendency of English-Canadian scholarship to exclude Quebec from studies of Canada, and the simultaneous recognition that much of the distinctiveness of regional history has become lost (or at least less visible) as social historians apply 'universal' categories of analysis, such as class, race, and gender to our studies. As a social historian who believes these 'universal' categories essential in our coming to grips with the past, I have come to regard national studies as an opportunity to highlight diversity and address commonality rather than providing 'one big picture.' There is a disproportionate amount of material on gambling available for Vancouver and Montreal compared to Toronto (let alone Winnipeg or Halifax). The overview approach reveals the diversity of experience and the complexity of discussing a 'Canadian' experience. Since comparative case studies and local investigations are the norm in Canadian social history, this book attempts to frame the topic in a larger context, even if the results are complex and sacrifice nuanced local texture.

This study is the work of a social historian exploring themes and topics often associated with cultural and intellectual history. Although it contributes, I hope, to an understanding of moral regulation, this is not its primary framework. While most scholarship on moral regulation focuses on promotion of and resistance to such regulation, or, as Joan Sangster has put it, 'the process,' I look more at why and how a specific moral issue – gambling – posed such a problem for a powerful group of Canadians.[55] The book interrogates the multiple constructions and responses to gambling to show how that activity posed a dilemma that reflected a wide range of fundamental concerns and to see what we might learn about Canadian society as these anxieties dissipated. While I examine some forms of regulation by state agencies, Parliament, the churches, medical professionals, and police and consider the persistence of enthusiastic players, my central preoccupation is with the meaning, maintenance, and negotiation of competing social values. The result is, I believe, an attempt to balance both experience and meaning.

This study deals much more with the relatively few anti-gamblers than with the millions of Canadians who took part in this popular form of play and leisure. Police, the justice system, churches, and reformers left us many records of their activities, while the gamblers left few surviving traces of their actions and enjoyment. This book draws on sources generated by governments, churches, public inquiries, and police commissions. Not surprisingly, these documents offer few accounts of the fun, sociability, and relaxation that gambling offered its participants. Gamblers such as bookmakers were notorious for never writing anything down, flushing evidence down the toilet, or using 'flash' paper, which ignited at the touch of a match. All too rarely, glimpses of gambling's appeal appeared in parliamentary debates and newspapers. Newspaper discussions identified by the invaluable BC newspaper subject index reveal passionate gamblers openly criticizing the law. The nature of the sources not only tilts strongly in favour of those who opposed gambling but also highlights urban voices at the expense of the rural experience. Commercial gambling actually may or may not have been more prevalent in cities, but it was certainly observed more there than in rural and small-town contexts.

Individuals themselves, however, gambled for a wide range of reasons. While critics concentrated on economic and moral motivations, they were not the only reasons why individuals participated in games of chance. For many people, gambling took the form of a hobby, and they extracted a great deal of pleasure from the action itself. British historian Ross McKibbon argued that the activity attracted some people because 'it produced thrills, risk, excitement, stimulation, and they did so because their working lives were monotonous and uncreative.'[56] Gambling could also be the site of forms of sociability from the homosocial male environments of poker games or bookmakers' parlours to the dominantly female world of bingo games. For other participants, it provided an invaluable escape from the drudgery of ordinary lives and something on which to base dreams, no matter how improbable.

Writing history is a political activity. History is also a way to explore morality: to understand the way in which people and societies construct morality, structure rhetorical arguments, and establish legitimacy. The conflicting attitudes in Canada towards gambling between 1919 and 1969 may not only shed light on a specific current dilemma but may also move us towards an awareness of the profound ambivalence in the Anglo-Protestant culture, which was responsible for much of the morality imbedded in Canadian criminal law and that underlay and shaped other social forces such as wealth, sex, and physical violence. It is by placing attitudes and responses to gambling in the context of a particular time that we can define and confront fundamental changes in values. The revelation of tensions, paradoxes, and contradictions within this value system may also allow us to discover new and different responses.

PART ONE

Critics and Gamblers

CHAPTER ONE

The Critics' Views, 1919–1969: The Economic, Moral, and Social Costs of Gambling

The punch line in many Canadian jokes plays on the notion that English-speaking Canadians are unusually adherent to the law. The image of a country of obedient citizens patiently awaiting a light to turn green in the middle of the night, however, does not conform to Canadians' actual behaviour in gambling. During the first seventy years of the twentieth century, most Canadians participated in some form of illegal gambling, yet there was a great reluctance to legitimate what people were actually doing via legal reform. This dissonance between law and behaviour exposed both the widespread ambivalence towards gambling and the disproportionate power held by middle-class, Anglo-Celtic Protestants, or 'old Canada,' in creating and maintaining cultural hegemony through the criminal law. The criminalization of gambling reflected particular nineteenth-century beliefs and worldviews about social organization and related economic, moral, business, and social concerns. These views persisted long into the twentieth century, and 'Victorian' Canada did not really end until perhaps the federal Omnibus Bill of 1969 that decriminalized many morality charges, including transforming gambling into a regulated activity.

Although many people enjoyed gambling, it also served as a source of anxiety, and the debates about its place in society allow us to observe the overlapping and interconnection of economic, moral, and social concerns. These anxieties were not universally shared and often had little resonance in French, Catholic Quebec or in English-speaking elite circles that modelled themselves on traditional British gentry. However, a vocal and powerful section of the anglophone Canadian middle class fairly consistently opposed gambling and held that it challenged the basic rational premises that underlay economic order and that it threatened the family. An Australian study concluded that gamblers received so much criticism because they 'attacked the twin pillars of civilization, the Protestant work ethic and the ideal bourgeois family.'[1] The debates about gambling remind us of the fundamental relationship between Protestantism, work, and family as anti-gamblers negotiated the tension within an economic system that prized both production and speculation, merit and luck, thrift and consumption.

The Work Ethic, Thrift, and Liberalism

The economic organization of twentieth-century society required a set of virtues and 'common sense assumptions' to support it. The sanctification of work, thrift, and liberalism created a powerful ideological framework that was just as important as more material components of the economy, such as labour, technology, and capital.[2] The challenge that gambling posed to its opponents was that it contravened this ideological framework and often highlighted its internal contradictions. Ann Fabian, in her study of nineteenth-century U.S. attitudes towards gambling, summed up the problem in her observation that 'the split between virtuous speculation and vicious gambling could never be maintained with absolute precision: gambling contained too much of capitalist virtue to stand exalted as unalloyed vice.'[3] Risk-taking behaviour in the capitalist market was both essential and potentially disastrous to society. This tension led to a definition of gambling as something lacking in any practical economic purpose.[4] Gambling and economic speculation both involved taking risks, and considering them simultaneously reveals simultaneously extremely complex and perhaps contradictory attitudes about chance. Opponents of gambling could never conceive of it as a form of work, although they could so characterize speculation.

The evolving debate on gambling reflected changes in the Canadian economy over the twentieth century. With economic reorganization came not only new ways of making a living, but also new manners of thinking about work. The shift away from most people extracting, making, or producing transformed notions of work, as mass values supporting the intrinsic value of production for its own sake became redundant. Similarly, as Canadians entered a stage of capitalism that depended on mass consumption to sustain general prosperity, there was a gradual reorientation away from thrift towards spending. To understand the twentieth-century debates on gambling, we must begin by thinking about labour and thrift.

During the 1930s, the House of Commons debated and easily defeated several private bills proposing a legal lottery. Across the political spectrum consensus emerged as political adversaries articulated a worldview that perceived lotteries as a threat to productive labour, perseverance, and self-discipline. The arguments advanced by the former Conservative prime minister, Arthur Meighen, that 'gambling is an attempt to get by chance what should be earned by industry, to obtain the rewards of doing well by doing ill,' were remarkably similar to those made by the founder of the socialist Co-operative Commonwealth Federation (CCF), J.S. Woodsworth. Woodsworth argued that 'lotteries divert attention from real values and suggest that only those who get something for nothing succeed.'[5]

The similar assessment of these political opponents alert us to the status of the work ethic. That principle justified both the distribution of wealth in society and patriarchal power by elevating the position of the male breadwinner within the household. Economics was intertwined with religious thought, as the Protestant Reformation had postulated that faith in God called everyone to some productive work. Writing on the work ethic in the nineteenth-century industrial United States, historian Daniel Rodgers states that while the Reformation struck 'down the Catholic rhythm of sin and confession, folly and remorse, Protestantism required that the believer ceaselessly analyze, rationalize, and forge his life into a systematic service to the Lord.' Adherents of the work ethic regarded labour as the chief source of human fulfilment, a perspective shared with a wide assortment of unlikely bedfellows, who ranged from union leaders and radicals to industrialists and businessmen. In addition to offering a purpose for life, labour also cultivated moral rewards in itself and therefore was often extolled in the programs of reformers and educators. Although this broad coalition of labour and capital valued hard work, members could extract dramatically different meanings from its significance.[6]

By the nineteenth century the so-called Protestant work ethic was clearly a secular ideology and was connected to economic organization as much as to any particular creed. Industrializing economies required workers to accept low wages. The prospect of lottery prizes, so one argument went, would encourage idle labour. Moreover, workers who gambled undermined the economic stability that contemporaries thought necessary to ensuring public welfare and personal well-being. By contravening the work ethic, gamblers sought profits when they produced nothing, offering nothing in exchange for the money that they made. The almost scientific relationship between labour and remuneration was regarded as the cornerstone for a stable society.[7]

The intensification of paid work under industrialism spawned the rational-recreation movement, which emphasized individual self-improvement, personal health, and values that would complement and reinforce the behaviour and qualities required in the workplace. Although rational recreation was not universally adopted and was fiercely resisted by many workers who found great enjoyment in the tavern, the movement shaped dominant ideas about class-appropriate leisure. In particular, recreationalists despised working-class gambling because it threatened the work ethic by severing the links between labour, skill, and compensation.[8]

Aspects of the work ethic became codified in provisions of Canada's Criminal Code regarding gambling. In the justification of unequal distribution of wealth in society, skill or merit became a major rationale. Workers who possessed specialized and valued skills could demand more than their 'unskilled' subordinates, which stance equated skill with merit. Therefore, in the definition of a gambling game, the presence of any degree of skill that might form a component of the task ameliorated the offence. This tendency surfaced most regularly in discussions about games at carnival midways, early pinball machines, and slot machines that had plungers to stop the barrels from spinning. Because of the possible role of skill in winning at slot machines, during the 1920s practically every new model introduced had to be found illegal as a game of chance, not of skill.[9] The role of skill or merit remains today in the requirement of 'skill-testing questions' that Canadians must answer to claim their prizes in random contests.

The creation of an ideal of rational economic action was also essential to the operation of a liberal political economy, since the role of skill or merit in justifying wealth brought together economic and political convictions. One of the primary political tenets of twentieth-century Canada was liberalism, an ideology founded on strong defence of private property. The sanctity of private property could be upheld best under a consensus that the means by which the property was acquired was legitimate and just. Gambling and its connection to luck and chance undermined the logic of the status quo, as it weakened the rationale behind the so-called legitimate right to private ownership, because chance and luck replaced skill, effort, and inheritance. Into the 1950s, the Christian Social Council of Canada (the scion of the Moral and Social Reform Council of Canada), when arguing against any relaxation of the criminal law on gambling, asserted that 'labour or human effort is the natural basis of the right of property.'[10] In an orderly, stable society based on rational action, rightful wealth should derive not from a fortuitous accident but rather from human reason, effort, or at the least divine providence.

Liberalism sanctified not only private property but also individual consciousness, the primacy of reason, and a scientific view of the world. For humans to be civilized, reason must prevail over passion. The progressive ideology of secular and religious reformers embodied this belief in their celebration of 'self-control and social efficiency,' which, according to Jackson Lears, saw 'society as a smoothly functioning system, with no room for randomness or unpredictability.' To promote a modern view of society was to eliminate the role of chance. The threat that gambling posed to this perspective was evident in the words of Senator George E. Foster, who in 1931 asked what 'advantage' lotteries offered 'the civilized as against the uncivilized man' if they discounted 'all judgement, all reason, all experience.'[11] Random outcomes contravened a worldview that promised rational order. Yet there were contradictions even within the liberal critique, which could not balance a legislated notion of common good with individual autonomy and liberty.

Ideas about skill helped entrench the deep morality of production for some observers. The economy was imbued with moral values, although they were seldom universal. As finance capitalism triumphed in the 1920s, there was a move away from the idea of a 'just' profit for corporations towards that of any margin of earnings being legitimate. Indeed, it is clear that many people did not distinguish between gambling and economic speculation. This modern and contemporary construction of (non-)difference has confounded economists such as Reuven and Gabrielle Brenner, who in their 1990 book on the international economic history of gambling and speculation concluded that even legal scholars have confused gambling with speculation, resulting in areas of legal ambiguity.[12] Surely legal scholars, rather than being confused themselves, reflected the profound ambivalence that prevented complete separation of gambling and speculation.

Gambling and Speculation

At different points in time, life insurance, trading in commodity futures, land speculation, and the stock market would all have appeared as forms of gambling to at least some part of the population. For example, until the mid-nineteenth century, life insurance held connotations of gambling on death or misfortune. The popular association between gambling and insurance was maintained in the term 'numbers policy insurance,' which referred to the small daily lotteries held in American cities.[13] By the end of the nineteenth century, critics of gambling defended participation in insurance schemes as an appropriate form of taking risk. In his 1898 critique of gambling, Briton John Ashton described insurance as 'gambling proper' but ultimately beneficial, since it prompted stability rather than challenged it. The respectability of life insurance in late-nineteenth-century Canada was evident in the remarkable link between prime ministers and this industry. Before 1920, five of Canada's eight prime ministers had been presidents of major insurance companies, and a sixth was a director.[14]

In a political system that gave disproportionate weight to rural voters, land speculation was an important political issue. Farmers saw that land speculation increased the cost of land with no relation to labour and thereby hurt their interests and national agricultural development, as it placed acquisition of more land beyond the means of many farmers. The National Farmers' Party platforms of 1916 and 1921 proposed a direct tax on unimproved land values to address this problem. Many middle- and working-class city dwellers also had expressed concern about land speculation, and this formed part of the appeal of Henry George's single tax movement, which aimed to tax landowners.[15] Moreover, the farmers' critique of land speculation condemned the non-productive labour of speculators while it celebrated farmers' own productive work, which improved the land. The moral authority that farmers felt accompanied their labour was also evident in the political views of skilled workers, who expressed a '"producer" consciousness' in the flexible political ideology of labourism. Though not connected directly to concerns about land speculation, criticism of other forms of speculation emerged during the First World War. In 1917, the Trades and Labour Congress of Canada demanded an end to 'gambling in foodstuffs by speculators,' which exploited consumers and obtained profits without labour.[16]

The most enduring and common link forged between gambling and speculation touched on the stock market. Both opponents and proponents of gambling adopted this line of argument. Both sides objected to the hypocrisy or at least the double standard in the state's sanctioning some forms of gambling, such as parimutuel bets at the racetracks and penny stocks at the stock market, while forbidding others, such as lotteries and bingo games. While both sides used this critique, they proposed radically different solutions.

Supporters of the legalization of lotteries and perhaps even of a government lottery to fund social services objected to the double standard. An editor at *Saturday Night* called in March 1922 'for a reasonable gaming code' to end the 'absurdity' of small raffles' being illegal while the law tolerated the 'Stock Exchange and mercantile gambling.' In Victoria, an editorial employed a biblical metaphor to satirize legislators' straining at the gnat of lotteries 'while swallowing the Wall Street camel.'[17] Gamblers were also quick to make the connection. After the 1929 crash the radical One Big Union used the link to encourage participants to enter its subscription contest with slogans such as 'The Stock Market Is Shot – Take a Chance on the Weather [Contest]' or 'Here's Something That Will Help You Forget the Depression.' When a reporter asked an Irish Sweepstakes winner of 1935, Clyde Horne of Dartmouth, Nova Scotia, what he would do with his winnings, he responded, 'None of your stock market speculation for me ... I'm going to invest the money in some good bonds that will secure a steady income.'[18]

Opponents of gambling objected to what they saw as the moral dishonesty of investing in stocks and shares while condemning gambling. One 1926 letter to the editor noted that both kinds of 'investments' were made to increase wealth. He held out in disdain the 'narrow minded people' who were 'horrified if one mentions horse-racing as a source of revenue, but ... put their money in stocks and shares and wild cat schemes if they will get a return of their capital with interest.' Vancouver Mayor Lyle Telford used a more diplomatic approach when he urged in 1939 that critics of lotteries be consistent so as not to 'deprive people of the right of taking part in a sweepstake while you yourselves gamble on the Stock Exchange.'[19]

Opponents noted also the class bias implicit in the double standard for gambling and speculation. A letter to the editor of a Halifax newspaper in 1938 denounced legislation that permitted some 'who can afford to spend thousands a year in stock markets for personal gain but if I, who wish to spend a mere 25 cents a week with the hope that I too may win economic independence, I am informed immediately that I will be prosecuted.' As late as 1965, an outraged Vancouverite objected to the closure of local bingo games: 'It is downright silliness, when you bestow your official blessing on gambling on the stock market ... but will not allow me to gamble on bingo.'[20]

The connection between gambling and stock markets was not the impression solely of the ordinary, marginal, and perhaps economically unsophisticated onlooker; men familiar with both arenas also made the comparison. E.B. Osler, vice-president of the Ontario Jockey Club and member of the executive board of the Toronto Stock Exchange, argued in 1909, in his defence of racetrack gambling, that 'more men are hurt yearly in the stock market than on the Woodbine track.' During debates of the 1930s on a proposed national lottery, Senator George Lynch-Staunton, a supporter, noted that opposition made little sense when 'a man may gamble to his heart's content on the stock exchange.' In the House of Commons a Quebec member, A.L. Beaubien, argued that 'gambling on the wheat market and on the stock exchange is far worse than buying a sweepstake ticket because you only buy a sweepstake ticket once in a while.'[21]

Politicians representing a working-class constituency emphasized the class discrimination embodied by the current legislation. MP J.S. Woodsworth, founder of the CCF, opposed all forms of gambling but noted that there were 'a great many institutions carrying on a species of gambling. In the business world we have our real estate exchanges and grain exchanges and stock exchanges, on which there is practised what is in my judgement virtually gambling.' Woodsworth criticized the prosecution of minor participants in gambling such as the holder of a sweepstakes ticket or the Chinese fan-tan player while 'these larger and much more dangerous forms of gambling should go on unchecked.' BC Conservative MP John Fraser claimed that while 'speculators have the stock markets and exchanges for gambling in stocks and shares ... I contend that it is harsh discrimination that the day labourer on the farm, forest, mine, or high seas, is the only one who is to be legislated out of the opportunity for indulging in this mild form of gambling.'[22] During the 1950s, testimony before the parliamentary Joint Committee into Capital Punishment, Corporal Punishment and Lotteries cited the class bias of the law, where the 'ordinary worker who has not too much money to purchase stocks with on the market' can participate in lotteries and bingo.[23]

Parallel to frequent use of the stock market in discussions of gambling, deliberations on the stock market occasionally invoked the notion of gambling. Legislation to restrict commercial speculation was introduced in Canada in 1888 as part of the Criminal Code. It became an offence to gamble on the stock market, for it became illegal to buy or sell stock without the intention of obtaining or selling actual shares. Christopher Armstrong, in his history of Canadian securities, described the law as both 'ineffective and easily evaded.' He notes a few cases where this law was employed against stock promoters, yet, according to an Ontario report, this offence was not common knowledge by 1961.[24] In another example, a 1938 editorial in the *Halifax Herald* asked if 'stock-gambling' had become so widespread that 'it has become "respectable" – so deeply entrenched [sic] that it is impregnable?' The editorialist then contrasted 'stock-gambling' with the illicit nature of other forms of gambling. Indeed, he held the stock market responsible for encouraging the gambling spirit of participants. In an address to a Halifax service club, a long-time social reformer compared the stock market to the provincial government's recent decision to sell alcohol in its own stores. Rev. Neil Herman argued that 'the stock markets may be sanctioned by the statutes of the government, but that does not make them respectable, any more than government controlled rum is more respectable than the bootleg product. Both will make you drunk if you take enough.'[25] Likewise, in a sociologist's discussion of modern society and gambling in 1928, an examination of bookmakers in Montreal suddenly digressed into a description of a respectable broker's office on St James Street. Finally, after the Second World War, zealous gambling opponent J.R. Mutchmor, secretary of the United Church of Canada's Board of Evangelical and Social Service, wrote philosophically that the moral issues of gambling went beyond legal definitions and that any condemnation of gambling by the church 'should include in their condemnation a reference to stock market gambling.'[26]

Some commentators celebrated the connections between gambling and the stock market as something positive. An editorial appeared in *Saturday Night* in 1909 during the debate on the Miller Act, a parliamentary amendment intended to restrict legal gambling at racetracks. The magazine supported gambling at tracks and argued that 'when we come to get to the very bottom of the gambling habit it is surprising how it reaches out into all conditions of life.' After noting the gambling aspect of wheat sales, stocks and bonds, land speculation, and insurance, the editor concluded that 'the very soul of trade and commerce is impregnated and infused with the gambling spirit.'[27] In 1923, Ontario

Attorney General W.E. Raney, renowned for his opposition to all forms of gambling, also attempted to curtail excess speculation on the stock market with a 'blue-sky law' that appointed a provincial securities commissioner and regulated the sale of securities, salesmen, and brokers. The United Farmers of Ontario government placed the act on the statute book, but it was never proclaimed into law.

The next attorney general, Conservative W.H. Price, did not concur with Raney's rigid attitude and articulated a more tolerant position 'Investment and Speculation,' a speech to the Canadian Life Insurance Officers Association in 1927. Price began by stating that Canada had reached a 'stage of investment ... on the border line between investment and speculation.'[28] He acknowledged that people desired to make money 'without too much effort' and that this impulse needed only to be regulated 'in a way that will not do harm to our country, that will not do harm to established business, but will give an opportunity to the men who want to adventure, to the men who build up the country as much as any other class of people, to the men who want to risk some of their money, and even protect them when they risk a fair amount of their money.' Price's understanding of economic growth and prosperity included a role for speculators, as he credited them with nation-building at their own expense. Thus he regarded them as neither a threat to economic order nor a moral problem.

This form of praise also appeared again in the 1960s as part of the Canadian Chamber of Commerce's campaign to legalize lotteries. After a survey of its membership, the organization concluded that 'in fields such as stockmarket speculation and business ventures ... in fact the Canadian economy has been largely built up by risktakers who in many cases have taken chances with their investment money.'[29] The need for high-risk funds to finance technological innovation and infrastructure development for resource extraction in general and for mining in particular meant that speculators were simultaneously posing a threat to the status quo and providing an essential economic service.

There were periods when some people attempted to create a clear demarcation between speculation and gambling. In the search for culpability that followed the 1929 collapse, rampant blame fell on stock speculation. One *Saturday Night* contributor, however, argued that 'all business is speculative' but that 'speculation as distinct from gambling, is the act of judging the future,' not taking foolish risks. Rev. H.J. Cody, rector of Toronto's St Paul's Anglican Church and later president of the University of Toronto, differentiated between gambling and participation in commerce and the stock exchange, which latter activities required judgment and were based on reason, not chance.[30] The argument assumed a component of skill in economic speculation that was distinct from the role of luck in gambling – a distinction hard to discern in the frenzy of stock trading in the late 1920s.

Generally, Canadians were more anxious to differentiate between speculation and gambling during periods of economic prosperity. The depiction of the basis of successful speculation in skill and reason served to justify the entitlement to wealth obtained without labour. As well, gambling always took place for individual gain, while some forms of financial speculation served the community. The author of the entry for gambling in the *Encyclopaedia of Religion and Ethics* (1954) concluded that the gambler 'subserves no need of the community. The merchant's whole policy is to eliminate risk as far as possible. The gambler desires risk.'[31]

The designation of gambling as purposeless reflects the constructed relationship between work and leisure. As we saw above, critics believed that gambling challenged the work ethic because it undermined the concept and practice of productive labour. Rewards were not the result of skill or physical effort. Gambling was therefore play rather than labour because the participant 'got something for nothing.' But the division between labour and leisure was not actually so rigid. Gambling was often an aspect of workplace male culture: on the shop floor it took place simultaneous with work, and for many Canadians it provided employment. Certainly, such a simplistic division based on work and play exaggerated the difference between gambling and economic speculation. But the same link was present even in financial speculation – someone who purchased stock *played* the market.

Children at Risk

Gambling's potential to undermine the work ethic led to concern about its potential to interfere with the proper socialization of labour in the next generation. Critics cited the bad example that games of chance held for children, especially boys. When a Montreal company released a chocolate bar called Try Your Luck, that included two bars with nickels placed randomly in every case of twenty-four, the candy bar was immediately criticized and prohibited. Critics feared that it taught children to gamble.[32] Gumball machines that distributed an unpredictable number of pieces also were banned, since they removed the stability of a cash transaction for candy. The Big Brothers organization was among the opponents of mint-vending machines because they taught 'young chaps' to expect something for nothing, since they did not dispense a regular number of mints. When the town clerk of a Montreal suburb wrote Premier Taschereau to request that no licences for slot machines be issued for St Lambert, he did so in the name of improving youths' morals. MPs who opposed the legalization of lotteries also stated their position in terms of the harmful effect that legal lotteries and sweepstakes would have on youths. Samuel Gobeil, MP for Compton, warned in 1934 that 'if sweepstakes are legalized in Canada I think we shall see every schoolboy and schoolgirl trying to save five cents in order to be able to buy a sweepstake ticket.'[33] Children had to learn to value labour and its corresponding benefits if society was to reproduce a co-operative and dependable labour force. Lotteries, raffles, and candy prizes upset an order based on worth and earned rewards.

In the 1950s, the Women's Missionary Society of the United Church also addressed the fear of acquiring something for nothing and placed the implications of this danger firmly in the context of its effect on children. Spokesperson Mrs Rolland Garrett argued that 'Children should not be led to believe in luck or chance,' as lotteries were 'an enemy of personal integrity, of family welfare and hurt the character of the individual.' She concluded: 'Lotteries create the element of uncertainty in life and nothing is so injurious to children as the feeling of insecurity and the idea of one's gain being dependent upon the loss of others and the winner becoming the possessor of property that has not been earned. The idea of something for nothing is not a wholesome way to raise a family.' Rev. D.B. Macdonald of the Canadian Welfare Council's Delinquent and Crime Division also stressed gambling's detrimental effect on young people. Like his counterparts in the Protestant churches, he worried particularly about the implication of individuals' 'obtaining wealth without giving anything in return,' as it taught the 'young to look for an easy way to earn a living rather than by hard work, and in this way can undermine habits of thrift.'[34] The prominence of children in these arguments suggests that opponents of gambling imagined an uncertain future should the young not learn to extol labour.

The Business Lobby

While much of the public discourse against gambling came from a moral or religious perspective, 'legitimate' businessmen contributed their own perspective. H.H. Stevens of the Reconstruction Party in 1935 argued against sweepstakes solely on the basis that they 'have been shown to be one of the most uneconomic, costly, and foolish ways of raising money.'[35] There was obvious self-interest on the part of those who protested against any form of gambling simply because it was bad for their own business. When the United Church's J.R. Mutchmor wrote in 1945 to a minister in Amherst, Nova Scotia, with suggestions for a sermon against raffles, he suggested a two-pronged attack – raffles were a form of stealing, and they would turn youngsters away 'from all the basic factors in the free enterprise system, such as work, honest dealing, payment of debts, etc.' The clergyman admitted that 'the second argument is from expediency, but I regret to say that in my pulpit work I find it more effective than the first ... When I point out that teaching people that they can obtain something for nothing, is undermining the capitalistic system, then I note my business friends in the congregation really listening.'[36] This argument about lotteries' weakening the capitalist ethic appeared to make sense to some listeners.

The postulated threat to capitalism would have met with considerable sympathy from some businessmen, particularly small-business owners who believed that lotteries inhibited operation of the free market. In 1925, the 'continuing' Presbyterian church had cited diversion of money from legitimate businesses in its opposition to any form of gambling. While some owners of small businesses operated lotteries as members of service clubs, others probably opposed all forms of gambling and perhaps found the cause of the Depression in rampant gambling in the stock market.[37] Ideological opposition was grounded in real business concerns, practices, and experience. Commercial lotteries disadvantaged small business owners, who found it difficult to compete with the offers of larger enterprises because of their limited market. The argument that gambling interfered with the work ethic and dispensed something for nothing was applied to consumption and was appropriated by those critical of commercial sweepstakes. While retail merchants admitted that commercial lotteries were expensive to run and brought additional cost to the consumer (or cut into the merchant's profit), much of their criticism related to the product given away. Retailers noted that the prize, bonus, or premium was usually different from the article or product being promoted, and once an item was given away, its market value was harmed. These prizes included silverware, radios, automobiles, and television sets. BC merchants went so far as to claim that frequent giveaways permanently injured commercial sales of General Electric irons and electric floor polishers. Other retailers complained that prize distributers bought items wholesale and bypassed the retail level altogether.[38]

Lotteries and sweepstakes could divert substantial funds from local business. In June 1922 a lawyer for the Manitoba Employers' Association estimated that the One Big Union's popular contest was draining $75,000 a week from legitimate businesses in Winnipeg. A local movie theatre operator claimed that the contest was costing his business between $15 and $20 a day, since it hit recreational spending hardest.[39] The vulnerability of recreational businesses meant that movie theatre operators and their associations were frequently the most persistent opponents of lotteries, especially bingo. The argument that lotteries diverted money from legitimate enterprises continued after the war.

Horse races were also blamed for taking money from legitimate commercial enterprises. In 1925, the Retail Merchant's Association of Winnipeg and the Winnipeg Board of Trade had expressed concern about the number of days on which local tracks were operating. The six weeks of operation was reduced, but in 1930 a group of businessmen was still campaigning to limit racing to one week a year. Their arguments often began with concern about the money and time wasted at the racetrack in the light of local poverty and culminated with worry about diversion of money from 'legitimate channels of trade.' Landlords complained that some tenants did not pay rent and dismissed notions of general hard times with the argument that in 1930 Manitobans had spent $17 million on liquor, cosmetics, and horse racing. The Retail Merchants Association of Canada submitted a brief to the 1954 parliamentary joint committee and based its opposition to legal lotteries on its experience with racing: 'There is always a sharp rise in unpaid accounts when the races come to town. The reduced spending power continues for weeks after they are gone.'[40] Money spent at the track left fewer dollars available to support legitimate business.

Public and Private Costs

Critics related the public aspects of gambling and its imagined consequences for society at large to private threats to individual morality and family stability. Some argued that gambling assaulted the principle of thrift. Concern about thrift is complex and perhaps unfamiliar to today's sensibilities. To dispense money on gambling was, to some, a waste of resources. It contravened ideas of self-help, individual autonomy, and self-control, but, most important, it placed family assets at risk and posed the threat of poverty. Since gambling was primarily a male diversion, and since men were more likely to have access to funds, critics painted the picture of the husband's failing in his duties as family breadwinner, with sad consequences for wife and children. The social cost of gambling was family disruption. Tellingly, Manitoba's grade-eight curriculum in the 1920s dealt with 'the evils of betting and gambling' under the general topic of thrift.[41]

Critics here were making a number of assumptions about the nature of the household and its operation. They assumed a family, financially dependent on the regular income of an adult male breadwinner, who was able to earn enough to support a wife and children. They seemed unaware that a single wage might not support a household, that wages were not necessarily regular, and that a house might not have an adult male present. While the adult male engaged in productive labour, the adult female managed the household, practised thrift, and transmitted values about the worth of hard work and thrift to the next generation.[42] Obviously, not all households conformed to this model, and reality was less ordered and rigid than experts portrayed. The incredible vulnerability of many households only heightened the potential danger of gambling.

The work ethic justified both the overall distribution of wealth in society and patriarchal power within the household. There was supposed to be some connection between material wealth and merit, and the work ethic, by privileging labour, which was rewarded by wages or the generation of investment revenue, supported the elevated position of the male breadwinner within the household. Like lottery and raffle winners, women in a rather a perverse way 'got something for nothing' when financially maintained by a male breadwinner. Of course, women could escape the evils of idleness, but their unwaged work was seldom recognized as labour. If the household was supported not by honest labour but by chance, how could the male breadwinner claim the moral legitimacy of household head?

Not only did gambling threaten the legitimacy of the male breadwinner, but opponents of gambling focused on its diversion of resources away from the household, which caused both material hardship and domestic tension and conflict. Money spent on a sweepstakes ticket, at a bookmaker's, or at a bingo game took funds from the family budget. Sweepstakes and lotteries diverted any surplus household wealth from more productive uses, such as savings. Parliamentarians questioned the wisdom of the state's playing any role in encouraging 'men who ought to be spending their money in providing for the wants of their families, men who are perhaps themselves on relief, to spend the few dollars that may come into their hands in buying sweepstake tickets.' The wife of a 32-year-old unemployed garage mechanic who 'bawled out' her husband for spending $2 on a sweepstakes ticket in 1950 may have agreed with the concerns – until the ticket became worth $15,500.[43] The claim that lotteries pauperized the poor dated back to the eighteenth century. Protection of the poor was a theme that suggested some degree of continuity in the discourse on lotteries, but in the twentieth century concern for the poor more often took a gendered form, and the object of pity was the female.

It would be a mistake to dismiss the suffering linked to some gambling as merely the invention or hyperbole of reformers. Desperate wives and mothers regularly wrote local police chiefs, mayors, and provincial attorneys general to inform on their husbands (and sons) or on the establishments or individuals who operated the illegal games that prevented wages from arriving home. Usually these letters were anonymous and signed with a *nom de plume*, such as '*une mère éprouvée*' or 'a penniless mother.' One woman from Gaspé explained her anonymity in terms of the personal danger that she risked in reporting a local card game, 'for if my husband knew it is me that informed on them there would be murder in my house.' Another Quebec woman, writing in French to Premier Taschereau, explained that she had long suffered as a result of her husband's passion for gambling. She requested the premier's help for the sake of her fellow female citizens who were in the same position but unable to complain about their husbands without jeopardy.[44]

Conclusion

Previous to the post-1945 transition of the Canadian economy into one that was consumer-driven and service-based, the North American labour market was ideologically supported by a strong work ethic that valued and attached moral worth to labour, thrift, and merit. While upholding the work ethic, capitalism also required certain individuals to invest money in often highly speculative schemes that might lead to financial returns or losses. Economic values celebrated both prudent productive labour and intrepid financial risk-taking.

The Criminal Code's prohibition of most forms of gambling reflected these beliefs and condemned gambling for threatening the status quo, upsetting an economic order based on merit, and encouraging the abandonment of honest work through acquiring 'something for nothing.' These values were central not only in the performance of the economy but also in the construction of the dominant political ideology of liberalism and prevailing gender identities. An examination of the opposition to gambling provides an opportunity to observe overlapping of economic and moral concerns and exposes ambivalence and contradictions in capitalism. The confusion about gambling reflected the difficulty in reconciling dynamism, growth, and risk-taking with stability and healthy productivity. The various mythologies or ideologies of a 'respectable' and 'rational' market reflected the participants involved and their motivations. Definitions hinged on circumstances and cultural differentiations as subtle as those between gambling and speculation. Although gambling was segregated as a leisure activity, and as something that took place outside the market and beyond the law, many observers could not help but notice its similarities with legitimate economic activities.

CHAPTER TWO

For Richer, for Poorer: Gambling, 1919–1945

Faced with economic, political, and social uncertainty between 1919 and 1945, Canadian men and women expressed their vulnerability in a variety of forms, including the active pursuit of luck in gambling. Canadians in their thousands broke the law enthusiastically as they purchased illegal tickets; organized unlawful lotteries, raffles, and sweepstakes; bet on horse and dog races; operated slot machines; and attended illicit bingo. The widespread nature of these activities cut across class, sex, age, region, and race. In a society marked by its lopsided distribution of wealth, uneven access to consumer goods, and periods of high unemployment, many people chose alternative strategies to seek the material rewards supposedly offered by capitalism and work. Participation in gambling appeared to involve rejection of rational economic action. Some observers' fears that many Canadians were spurning sound financial decisions and hard work were heightened by what they saw as concurrent dramatic changes in social, economic, and moral order in the interwar period. In this era of change and uncertainty, the proposed link between rational actions and stability possessed a particular poignancy.[1]

Practice, participants, and public debate about various forms of illicit commercial gambling between 1919 and 1945 (a later chapter examines criminal activity) permit us entry into a world in flux. Public debates reflected the perception that social, political, moral, and economic instability had expanded the opportunities for 'commercial' and charitable gambling, especially among the working classes. With the adoption of the attributes and infrastructure of modern communications, technology, business organization, and commercialized popular culture, gambling increased its visibility and organization at the same time as

the 'Victorian values' of 'old Canada' were under assault. In the debates about gambling, both ends of the spectrum were forceful in their
cause. As the 1920s' 'rebellion against Victorianism' and the economic
vulnerability of the 1930s popularized the practice of gambling among
one part of the population, criticism of speculation and its place among
the causes of the Great Depression simultaneously reinforced anti-
gambling arguments. The Depression had not only obvious economic
consequences but also a powerful ideological impact, as the economic
collapse undermined the validity of a worldview based on self control,
productive labour, and thrift.[2]

Some people came to believe during the First World War that a
rational, comprehensible, or predictable world no longer existed, and
the economic devastation of the Depression strengthened that theory.
The boom and bust of the economy made it difficult for many Canadians to believe that the market was rational, any more than there was an
underlying logic or pattern to how individuals were affected by economic change and collapse. This incomprehensiblity flew in the face of
a heavily rationalist culture. The belief in luck, never far from the
surface among the Canadian working class, rose to the level of observ-
able popular culture and spread to other groups. Observers believed
that all Canadians were gambling more.[3]

The perceived increase in gambling in Canada was originally blamed
on the First World War. During that conflict, authorities at home turned
a blind eye to illegal fundraising methods adopted for worthy wartime charities. This proliferation of illegal raffles and lotteries under the
guise of patriotism and philanthropy was matched by the epidemic of
gambling taking place among Canadian soldiers stationed in Europe.
Historian Desmond Morton has identified gambling as 'a soldier's
chief pastime,' for it filled empty hours, fought boredom, and provided
entrepreneurial opportunities for men who spent a great deal of their
time 'hanging around.' Even the military hierarchy sanctioned perhaps
the most mundane form of gambling when troops staved off boredom
with games of bingo during crossings of the North Atlantic.[4] Officially,
gambling and bookmaking on any military property contravened regulations. Certainly one of the most ignored duties of a commanding
officer was to 'discountenance any disposition in his officers to gamble.' Canadian soldiers responded violently to the arrest by military
police of men operating a gambling syndicate in one of the camps in
England after the Armistice. This crackdown sparked one of the infamous demobilization riots of 1919.[5]

The postwar reintegration of veterans into Canadian society saw increased levels of visible gambling. Reformers explained that veterans returned to a civil society with their new vices after the experience of having 'gambled their lives' in Europe. One pamphleteer even claimed that a psychological legacy of the battlefields of France and Belgium and the upheaval at home was rejection of the 'plodding ways of peace.' The connection between war and gambling was not always negative. A member of Parliament, James Murdock, connected the overwhelming 'spirit of gambling' in the 1920s with the typical veteran who returned home 'with the hope and belief that he could take a chance in the ordinary affairs of men and make up for the time he had lost and the sacrifices he had made.'[6]

With the Armistice, Protestant social reformers directed their full attention to domestic concerns, particularly the lowering of moral standards allegedly brought on by the war. Sexual promiscuity, alcohol, and recreational drug use were more sensational concerns, but gambling was also on their agenda. Anti-lottery editorials reappeared in *Saturday Night*, and the Evangelical Board of the Methodist church resumed its anti-lottery crusade in response to the increase in all forms of gambling, 'especially in the English-speaking provinces.'[7]

North Americans were shocked by the role that professional gamblers played in 'fixing' the 1919 baseball World Series. While many Canadians saw this as another example of the moral corruption of their neighbours to the south, the preoccupation with American gamblers and the threat that they posed to 'morally superior' Canadian society was a constant theme. In the general effort to put a lid on societal unrest, authorities in many areas tried to place gambling safely back in the pot.

In this chapter I look at the range of gambling institutions: for the rich – racetracks (where the well-to-do evaded the law) and private (elite) clubs; and for the working classes – 'penny gambling' in punchboards, pinballs, and slot machines; agricultural fairs, with their games of chance; and lotteries, sweepstakes, and contests. The chapter concludes with consideration of changes in attitudes engended by the Depression and the Second World War.

For Richer

Racetracks

After the war, the most vocal gambling debate rekindled a pre-war discussion on the law and the future of horse racing. In 1909, H.H.

Miller, Conservative MP for the Ontario rural riding of South Grey, introduced a private member's bill to criminalize bookmaking at racetracks, intending thereby to close the exemptions in the criminal code that permitted legal gambling. The *Canadian Annual Review* noted that this, next to the Naval Bill, was the most discussed piece of legislation for the year. Miller was supported in his actions by the Moral and Social Reform Council of Canada, a coalition of Protestant reformers and religious organizations in which the Methodist church was prominent.[8] While the original bill was defeated by a single vote – with Quebec members of the House unanimously against the measure – it resulted in a compromise that limited racing in any given locality to no more than seven consecutive days twice a year. All off-track betting was now against the law, and so-called respectable tracks, which did not cater specifically to an American or working-class clientele, voluntarily eliminated the bookmakers at their tracks and adopted parimutuel machines. Miller's bill parallelled the American Hughes Act of 1907, which had criminalized all forms of racetrack gambling and pushed many professional American gamblers and enthusiastic patrons north.[9]

The respectable tracks had anticipated pressure to reform and had in 1908 created a national governing body, the Canadian Racing Association, in an attempt to self-regulate the industry. Owners and track directors hoped to legitimize certain racetracks and intended their introduction of parimutuel machines and elimination of bookmakers to attract the 'average citizen' to their grandstands.[10] Generally, track owners were successful in their objective, and by the 1920s racetracks, along with other forms of commercial leisure such as cinemas and vaudeville, attracted the full range of Canadian society. Francophones in Montreal patronized the Dorval track, while at other tracks women placed bets without fear of 'social ostracism' and only occasionally in separate women's 'betting rings.'[11] Tracks such as the Ontario Jockey Club in Toronto and the Montreal Jockey Club were constantly having to differentiate themselves from less reputable counterparts, with their American and working-class patrons. A *Saturday Night* editorial in 1909 claimed that the Fort Erie track and Toronto's Dufferin Park had 'no excuse for existence,' in contrast to the Ontario Jockey Club, which was 'managed by the first citizens of Ontario with the object of exploiting a fine old British sport.'[12] But the number of tracks continued to expand. In Windsor, the rapid expansion of tracks was aimed specifically at the American market. Before the war, Windsor and its neighbour across the river, Detroit, had supported one track, the Windsor Jockey Club. In 1916 two additional tracks opened in Windsor after entrepreneurs purchased dormant charters and established new tracks across the river from the booming Detroit market. Toronto operator Abram Orpen opened Kenilworth Park three miles south of the Windsor Jockey Club, using a charter originally issued to the Manitoulin Island Gore Bay Riding and Driving Park Association in 1899. The location of the new track was selected solely for its convenience for American patrons. The suitability of its location was recognized by rival Grant Hugh Browne, a stockbroker and boxing promoter from New York, who opened the third track, Devonshire Park, directly across the road from Orpen's operations.[13] Genteel-sounding names did little to convince gambling opponents of the tracks' respectability.

The rapid expansion in the number of Ontario racetracks was halted not by reformers but by the First World War. By 1917, concern about 'thrift and economy' on the home front led to a federal order-in-council that rescinded the Miller Bill under the War Measures Act and put a halt to thoroughbred racing for the duration of the war and 'immediately thereafter.' Only the King's Plate ran at the Ontario Jockey Club in 1918 and 1919, and no legal betting took place.[14]

The government's belief that betting at racetracks could interfere with 'thrift and economy' and with the country's capacity to fight the war reminds us of how closely notions of gambling were mixed up with attitudes towards productivity. The wartime ban on legal betting preceded by several months the prohibition of alcohol, which was articulated in much more concrete terms – the wasteful diversion of potential food products into alcohol manufacture. The vague general economic argument against gambling did not specifically invoke employees' absenteeism or the misallocation of resources by horses 'being transported or track workers' engaging in non-essential labour. Rather, the arguments were part of a larger notion of honest labour, which contrasted it with economic speculation.

The wartime order-in-council continued in effect after 1918, but the debate resumed. Ottawa established a royal commission in August 1919. Prime Minister Robert Borden favoured continued operation of certain elite racetracks and appointed as chair J.G. Rutherford, the veterinary director general and livestock commissioner of Canada, who had been a prominent witness against Miller's bill during 1910 hearings.[15]

Horse racing was the most organized form of gambling and, as a big business, had supporters beyond racetrack owners, professional gamblers, and horse breeders. Among its most powerful allies were newspapers. In March 1923, the sports editor of the *Montreal Herald* wrote to Senator J.P.B. Casgrain explaining that a proposal to restrict the type of racing information allowed in newspapers would reduce his paper's circulation. He estimated that the *Herald*'s noon edition, with its racing information, along with the 'sporting extra' that appeared in the late afternoon with the day's results, accounted for the sale of nearly 10,000 extra papers each day.[16]

Domestic debates about horse racing always took place in a clearly North American context. American progressives had been extremely successful in eliminating horse racing as part of their extensive pre-war morality campaign. However, under Canadian law the ability to place bets at racetracks remained the most glaring exemption in a Criminal Code that prohibited nearly all other forms of public commercial gambling. Proponents of thoroughbred racing fought hard for this continued exemption, as they believed that their sport had no future without the betting component and was necessary for Canada's economic and military well-being. Supporters linked their sport to the development of agriculture, although thoroughbreds were never farm horses. The supposed importance of Canadian thoroughbred horses for the British calvary during the First World War and their alleged ongoing military role seem to have held persuasive powers.

Supporters of thoroughbred racing in turn faced vigorous opposition from most Protestant churches. Horse racing and its corresponding link to betting at tracks were the subject of an annual resolution by the Ontario and Quebec Convention of the Canadian Baptist church. Presbyterian activist Rev. John G. Shearer argued that Canadians building a new peacetime society should not be forced 'to choose between the breeding of good horses and the developing of good men and women.'[17]

Part of the mandate of the Rutherford Commission of 1919 was to determine 'the general effects of such race meets and betting upon the community or any particular class or classes or the community.' The commission held hearings in Ottawa, Montreal, Toronto, Windsor, Winnipeg, Regina, Calgary, Vancouver, and Victoria. As there was no thoroughbred racing in eastern Quebec and the Maritimes, the commissioners did not visit these areas.[18] They found a proliferation of racetracks across Canada since the six in operation in 1910. Ten years later, there were twenty-seven in operation, with eight in Quebec, nine in Ontario, three in Manitoba, one in Alberta, and six in British Columbia. According to the commission's final report, most tracks had switched to parimutuel before 1917, except for 'tracks controlled and operated by professional book-makers.' Under the parimutuel system, bettors wagered against each other rather than against the bookmaker and the odds that he established. (In 1928 an electronic totallizer, capable of immediately calculating and adjusting the odds on each horse according to the amounts bet, was introduced.[19]) Rutherford was satisfied with the more rudimentary machines of 1920 and found the environment much improved, since the 'touts, jail-birds, tipsters and other unprincipled purveyors of supposedly secret or stolen information, are but rarely in evidence where ... the element of personal profit to the professional layer-of-odds no longer exists.' He concluded: 'Persons of this class are not only in themselves, and in many different ways, a menace to decent society on and off the race course, but were often instrumental in inducing young and unsophisticated individuals to make bets, when, if left to themselves, they would never have thought of doing so.'[20]

Rutherford's conclusions conformed with the pre-war practice of differentiating between good and bad racetracks, based on class and ethnicity. For example, he singled out two Quebec tracks, Blue Bonnets in Montreal and Connaught Park across the river from Ottawa, as operated by 'gentlemen' apparently interested more in the sport than in the monetary returns. He contrasted these well-run tracks with the track in Hamilton, Ontario, controlled by a professional American gambler. The active presence of such people proved a lightning rod in reformers' campaigns to make the 'business of betting on race tracks ... a crime.' It exploited fears of moral contamination, with racetracks bringing together 'Canada's elite and America's scum.'[21] In Montreal in 1923, *Le Canada* claimed that there were more than 3,000 resident bookmakers in the city and linked their illegal enterprises with the presence of U.S. gangsters. BC Attorney General A.M. Manson expressed concern to the federal minister of agriculture about the 'undesirable characters' who entered Canada from the United States to follow the meets. The respectable Black community of Montreal also disapproved of certain African Americans who followed the races north each summer.[22]

Although proponents attempted to differentiate between respectable and notorious tracks based on clientele and ownership, the presence of thoroughbred horses themselves helped to offer the air of legitimacy. Legal restriction of parimutuel betting to horses only excluded the greyhound, sometimes called the 'workingman's racehorse.' Critics closely associated dog racing with Americans when it was introduced in Winnipeg during the summer of 1932. While dog races had been popular in Montreal in the 1920s, local attitudes in Winnipeg were much more ambivalent. One concerned citizen saw it as 'an American organization, American Dogs and under American management and Americans brought in to do the work and who do not give a "rap" about the welfare of our Boys.' The Manitoba Greyhound Racing Association dissolved after one short season, and in September 1932 the dogs were returned to Chicago.[23]

Following Rutherford's report, in June 1920 the federal government introduced legislation to limit gambling at racetracks to the parimutuel machine system and reduced the track owner's percentage of the wager on each race. It sought to reduce 'the number of race tracks operating in Canada and keep undesirable gamblers out of the game' without hurting legitimate operations. *Saturday Night*, one of the strongest supporters of elite racing, criticized the day limits on track meetings and favoured simply closing what it considered inferior courses.[24]

One of the most prominent opponents of horse racing was Ontario's attorney general, W.E. Raney, elected with the United Farmers of Ontario (UFO) in 1919. A lawyer and a Presbyterian Sunday School teacher, Raney had acted as counsel for the anti-gambling Social Service Council of Canada in the 1910 hearings on the Miller Bill and in the first two sittings of the Rutherford Commission, before he resigned after the UFO's election. As attorney general, he convinced his government that if it could not abolish racing it could limit racing through provincial taxation powers.[25]

Raney soon fell into the murky water of federal – provincial conflict, as he denied provincial licences to tracks that permitted betting and attempted to annul existing track charters. Ontario legislation aimed at eliminating published betting information was declared *ultra vires* by the Judicial Committee of the Privy Council. The province, however, possessed the right to tax, and the UFO government increased the licence fee required to operate races from $1,250 per day to $7,500. In 1922, it expanded the Ontario Corporation Tax Act to include a 5 per cent fee on parimutuel winnings.[26]

Ontario was not alone on the margins of opposition. As an anti-gambling campaign heated up in British Columbia in 1924, the British Columbia Woodworkers Association, an organization affiliated with the Canadian Manufacturers' Association, was joined by a local Orange lodge, the Vancouver Local Council of Women, the British Columbia Woman's Christian Temperance Union, the Native Sons of Canada, and the New Westminster and the Fraser Valley District branches of the

Retail Merchants Association of Canada. This diverse group was united in opposition to racetrack gambling, on the basis that 'moneys spent constitute a serious drain on individual and family funds.' Winnipeg retail merchants were perhaps more candid in their concern over the total six weeks of racing in the city, since 'it takes too much money out of the regular channels of trade.' In 1927, nearly $48 million was bet legally at government-regulated parimutuel machines in Canada, almost 65 per cent of it wagered in Ontario. This amount was but a fraction of the sums placed with bookmakers by Canadians for both domestic races and meets in the United States and as far south as Tiajuana in Mexico.[27]

Private Clubs

Although horse racing was the most popular form of gambling, and not always illegal, Canadians practised other kinds of gambling. Another type of commercialized gambling to be defined as a problem by critics was the private gambling club. Except for Chinese clubs, these institutions often operated under legal federal or provincial charters of defunct or fictitious social clubs.[28] In Montreal they were typically called bridge clubs, although this game would never have been played. In urban Niagara Falls, one gambling club operated under a charter that promised 'to provide and maintain facilities for its members to carry on hunting and fishing.' Its operators decorated it with 'two fishing rods hanging on the wall and one net was behind a cigarette machine.'[29]

These private clubs permitted registered members to play games of chance as long as the club was not seen to profit from the private betting between individuals. In 1932, the Supreme Court of Canada overturned a lower court conviction against the Brunswick Sports Club of Vancouver, declaring that 'no part of the stake is taken by the club although a charge is made for use of facilities.'[30] The club had 12,000 members and hardly conformed with the exclusivity or elitism expected from a private club. Since it charged only for the use of facilities, police were powerless against what Vancouver's chief constable referred to as 'one of the worst menaces to the city.' In the mid-1930s, with thirty-two card tables in operation, the Brunswick Sports Club declared annual earnings of $155,000.

By 1938, the growth and profits of such private clubs prompted federal legislators to close the loophole under which clubs operated.

The pressure originated in British Columbia, where the Vancouver press had campaigned against the 'exorbitant rents' that charter clubs collected from players for the privilege of sitting at the gaming tables. Thereafter, the legal definition of a common gaming house included any place where 'any direct or indirect fee is charged to participate in a game.'[31]

Private clubs during the interwar years included facilities that ranged from a neighbourhood shack in Halifax, where men played cards and listened to the radio, to the chain of highly organized clubs operated by the Conn family in Vancouver, where veterans of the Spanish civil war passed time with lumbermen from the province's interior.[32] Clubs were often elaborate enterprises. The Brown Derby, later renamed the Combine Club, situated just outside Toronto's city limits in Etobicoke, could hold 700 or 800 people at a time. It was built specifically as a club, with false windows and doors and discrete landscaping to provide as much privacy as possible and unobstrusive parking for 150 cars. In another, more exclusive Toronto club, gamblers enjoyed the tasteful furnishings of plush velvet and polished chrome and were entertained with food and drink. One interwar gambler nostalgically recalled the white-meat–only chicken sandwiches served *gratis* to patrons.[33] Games in such clubs ranged from poker, through roulette to location-specific pastimes such as the Montreal dice game *barbotte*.

For Poorer

Penny Gambling, Punchboards, Pinballs, and Slot Machines

There was a great gulf between exclusive private clubs and the penny gambling that expanded particularly among the working classes during the 1930s. Both forms of gambling shared general commercialization and great potential for profit. Contemporaries stressed the 'escapist' nature of leisure consumption in the 1930s, especially for working-class Canadians. It was as if poverty increased the need for luxury and as if gambling offered the opportunity for escape, increased status, decision-making, and, above all, the chance to gain 'money that was otherwise unattainable.'[34] It was in this context that gambling opportunities became omnipresent. Local stores and restaurants in every part of the country appeared to have access to punchboards – sheets of cardboard perforated with usually a thousand holes, in which tickets had been placed. For a nickel and later a dime, the player could punch out one of the tickets, which might specify a cash prize of $1 or some trinket. Prizes confiscated from a punchboard in Halifax in 1944 were mere trinkets indeed and included eight boxes of chocolates, sixteen grey hankies, two cookie cutters, two packages of lemon-pie filling, and one package of toothpaste.[35] The profit for retailers and punchboard manufacturers was great, as the board and prizes cost nowhere near the $50 that each board generated.

The pinball and the mechanical games introduced after legal reform in 1932 represented a more complex form of amusement. The earliest games involved players' shooting marbles into holes protected by pins (somewhat like a version of croquinole), and it was difficult to argue that there was more skill than luck to success.[36] Winners received a number of 'free game tokens,' which they could redeem for a nickel.

Slot machines, which awarded prizes based on stopping a series of revolving barrels in a set pattern, antedated the 1930s but their numbers increased in this decade despite their illegal status. Before the First World War, a few cafés and poolrooms had introduced them to attract customers and earn extra revenue. Various new provincial laws restricted or banned them before the federal government forbade them in amendments to the criminal code in October 1924. However, Canadian courts continued to have a difficult time determining the legality of particular variants before further federal legislation passed in 1938. Courts in Ontario and Quebec had acquitted owners with slot machines on their premises, while in Alberta the courts convicted a proprietor for keeping a common gaming house.[37] In an attempt to evade the law, early machines dispensed gum so as to support the fiction that there was a cash transaction for goods. The legacy of these 'gum machines' continues to this day, in the fruit symbols of lemons, cherries, grapes, and plums, once the flavours of gum available. Candy slot machines that appeared in Winnipeg and Toronto in 1928 dispensed a low-grade confectionery (usually mints) and were conflated by opponents with gumball machines, since there was always a chance of getting more than an exact measure of candy. Critics claimed that these machines exploited children, but the dispersal of poor-quality mints was an attempt to get around the law, since the player always received a minimal prize, if not a token to be redeemed for cash or goods. Critics in Halifax emphasized that these machines siphoned money out of the local community to the machines' owners in Montreal or Chicago. None the less the devices were extremely popular. In 1936, Vancouver police estimated that there were between 3,000 and 5,000 slot machines in that city alone.[38]

Agricultural Fairs

The sort of legal grey area around slot and pinball machines and the need for the law to respond to practice were also evident in carnival midways. In the legislative fervour after the First World War, agricultural fairs lost their exemption from operating raffles and games of chance on midways. Many fairs found these lucrative activities essential to financing their educational and agricultural dimensions, such as furnishing prize money, and this loss was particularly resented in western Canada.[39] In an astonishing example of political candour, federal Agriculture Minister W.R. Motherwell asked the minister of justice to amend the Criminal Code to exempt *bona fide* agricultural societies, since 'the Agricultural societies and associations all over Canada were very hard hit by an amendment to the Criminal Code made last year, and which went through without my noticing it.' Despite attempts to block any weakening of the legislation, and efforts by the Protestant Social Service Council and newspapers such as the *Saskatoon Daily Star*, to forbid raffles or games of chance sponsored by religious organizations, agricultural fairs were again exempted. Rather spectacular abuses followed, such as the Ottawa-area case where a bingo game took place in front of a single loaf of bread and a chicken, in the hope of claiming the agricultural privilege.[40]

Members of fraternal organizations pushed unsuccessfully for the same rights. The Elks led the most organized and persistent campaign, often with public support.[41] The fraternity claimed 20,000 members, with 165 of its 194 lodges in the four western provinces, and had both Catholic and Protestant adherents; many Elks belonged to other fraternal organizations, including the Knights of Columbus and the Masonic Lodge.[42] MPs who were also Elks argued that fraternal organizations had raised money in the past by annual fairs that included games of chance and that their charitable work was essential in many communities. Carnivals served as a welcome alternative to other means of raising money, such as tag days and personal subscriptions, which offered no entertainment value in exchange for charity offered.

Furthermore, those who supported extending rights to fraternal organizations pointed out that while local agricultural organizations usually contracted out the midway concessions to professional carnival or exhibition companies, which in turn paid the local society a bonus but took large sums of money out of the community, all funds raised in fraternal carnivals stayed where it was spent.[43] In 1929, the Elks launched a concerted drive that resulted in 120 lodges' sending petitions to Ottawa. The same petition form was also received from sympathetic branches of the Canadian Legion, western Gyro Clubs, the Manitoba Independent Order of Foresters, the Fraternal Order of Eagles of Medicine Hat, and the Calgary Branch of the Loyal Order of Moose. These western-based, non-partisan organizations, however, were not able to effect change. In May 1930, the Elks claimed that they had sixty-three MPs in support of an amendment to the criminal code, yet Minister of Justice Ernest Lapointe did not act, convinced that such a 'contentious' amendment 'would meet considerable opposition in the House' and that it would do the government no good in proposing it. Perhaps the Elks were hopeful after the election of a new government in July 1930, since the new prime minister, R.B. Bennett, was an Elk himself and had promised that 'if the opportunity offers, I will do all I can to see that the legislation is enacted.' Commitments of support from the former opposition, however, were difficult to translate into action by the government on such a delicate issue. The severity of the Depression, particularly in 'Elkdom's' stronghold of Alberta and Saskatchewan, placed additional demands on the resources of prairie fraternal organizations and increased their need to run carnivals and bazaars, yet they could not do so within the law.[44]

Certainly there were local variations in attitudes towards exemptions to the law. The Toronto-based magazine *Saturday Night* saw a regional flavour to the protest, claiming that carnivals were more important in western Canada for fundraising, for the promotion of community spirit, and also for entertainment in places 'where entertainment is not too plentiful.' In Nova Scotia, Protestant 'reformers' acquired provincial legislation to do what the federal government would not. In 1936 the Provincial Exhibitions Act was amended to prohibit 'all kinds of gambling and all games of chance, including wheels of fortune, dice games, pools, coin tables, draw lotteries ... at the place of holding the Exhibition, or within three hundred yards thereof,' thereby doing away with even the federal agricultural exemption.[45] Critics noted the hypocrisy of a midway shorn of games of chance adjacent to the government-operated parimutuel machines for the harness races at the exhibition track.

Lotteries, Sweepstakes, and Contests

Lotteries were among the most common and widespread forms of gambling. Except for bingo, they were rarely considered in spatial terms. Unlike other forms of gambling that might be associated with spatially defined 'vice' districts, illicit clubs, racetracks, or even the slightly dangerous (or at least exciting) fair midways, lotteries in their many forms entered households, churches, and even the House of Commons, since many MPs felt it politically useful to support various constituency fundraising causes.

Organized sweepstakes existed in Canada before the First World War. One of the largest lotteries operated out of British Columbia, where two Vancouver hotelkeepers founded it around 1905. The awarding of top prize to one of their own employees brought public pressure to bear, and police closed down the contest. Jewish retailer Harry L. Salmon, who had been its agent in Victoria, honoured his patrons by providing his own money for prizes and took over the entire operation. The sweepstake, whose tickets cost a dollar and bore the name Salmon in the shape of a fish, operated five times a year and was largely restricted to British Columbia. A distribution system was never set up beyond the province, as Salmon feared that police toleration would end if the sweepstake grew too big. The cautious owner suspended operations during the war, since it might be considered 'impolitic,' but he resumed it with peace. In 1924, after several warnings, Harry Salmon was fined $500 for operating a lottery. Even such a stiff fine betrayed public support for this 'reputable' sweepstake, as it was estimated that Salmon's 15 per cent commission brought him $12,000 per draw. He appears to have soon departed the lottery business, when his operation was taken over by two Victorian tobacconists, C.A. Steele and E.A. Morris, who operated it, despite frequent prosecution, until the mid-1930s.[46]

In the 1920s, new, larger lotteries opened, such as the Army and Navy Veterans' Association, which operated out of Quebec City until a crackdown necessitated its move to Newfoundland. Prior to 1921 all lotteries had been illegal in Newfoundland, although they operated openly. The annual seal fishery lottery offered prizes as high as £1,000. As of 1921, lotteries held in connection with bazaars for charitable, social, educational, and athletic causes could operate with the permission of a magistrate. St John's became a centre for offshore promotion of Canadian lotteries; by 1929 there were a number of professional operators, and Newfoundland was collecting a large amount of income tax from prize money. In 1932 the government set up a Lotteries Licensing Board and tighter regulation, and so most professionals moved elsewhere.[47]

Since all lotteries more than $50 were forbidden by Canadian law, many of them were fraudulent, distributing only a portion of the advertised prizes, awarding fictitious winners, and retaining a majority of the proceeds for the operators. Promoters also took advantage of the public's willingness to support good works. Operators of a 1927 lottery preyed on public sympathy with the claim that proceeds would aid families who lost children in the tragic fire at Montreal's Laurier Palace theatre. It had made no contact with any of the families when the provincial police stopped this fraudulent draw.[48]

Among the new lotteries brought about by the war was the first Irish Sweepstakes – a fundraiser for families of Irish sailors drowned at sea. In 1930 a professional consortium called the Irish Free State Hospital Subscription Fund reorganized the sweepstake to raise money for the Irish National Maternity Hospital and immediately capitalized the stakes on a worldwide distribution network. Three times a year, it matched selected tickets with the names of horses running in British races, and winnings depended on whether the horse assigned in this preliminary draw ran and on how it placed. Despite its illegality in Canada, winners were widely publicized, with names or aliases and addresses appearing on the front page of many local newspapers.[49] In the first draw, held in November 1930, just as depression conditions were settling in for many Canadians, a lucky Art Dawe of Vancouver won £83,517 as a second prize. Because of the publicity surrounding his success, within a year an estimated $250,000 from British Columbia alone was going to Ireland, and by 1938 approximately one-third of Torontonians bought Irish Sweepstakes tickets, priced between $2.50 and $3.00 each, an estimated total of $3 million. This, along with the French National Lottery, represented a tremendous amount of money leaving Canada and thereby shaped one of the primary arguments of those who supported lotteries.[50] A form of economic nationalism began to have resonance here, even though it had little force in other political contexts at this time. Based on the residences of Canadian winners throughout the 1930s, tickets appear to have been available everywhere in Canada, from Nova Scotia to British Columbia, and from the cities to the oldest agrarian communities and the newest frontier resource camps of the north.

Commercial enterprises from supermarkets to movie theatres also adopted sweepstakes and various games of chance as a promotional tool to attract customers and dollars to their product. Commercial lotteries or advertising sweepstakes therefore expanded rapidly when businesses attempted to attract more customers and boost sales. Movie theatres operated bank nights, when they distributed gifts and money prizes to lucky ticket holders in the audience, until explicit provincial bans came into effect in the early 1930s.[51] At least eleven small towns across Ontario in the 1920s participated in commercial lotteries organized by a Toronto company. This plan established customer clubs and awarded tickets for each dollar spent at participating merchants. The Toronto firm received 3 per cent of the net in exchange for providing prizes, which, depending on the location, included cars, electric stoves, sets of silver, radios, or a trip to California.[52]

The advertising objective was perhaps more obvious when nationwide companies such as Bovril and Imperial Tobacco used mass-circulation magazines and newspapers to publicize their contests. In 1937, Bluebird Diamonds promoted the chance to win a free honeymoon or $1,000 and Royal Yeast offered four years' tuition, room, board, and expenses at any university in Canada as top prize in its contest. On a smaller scale, local merchants such as Lynch Electric Appliances of Timmins, Ontario, offered less glamorous prizes, such as an ice tray and tongs, a toaster, and a silver water jug to lucky customers.[53]

Women, who made the specific brand choices in most households, were special targets for this type of sales promotion, and the kinds of prizes given away reflected this connection. Domestic accessories and labour-saving devices appealed to women who would benefit from prizes yet rarely could afford such items. Women who purchased goods or selected brand choices based on contests were taking advantage of a potential economic opportunity beyond the regular cash transaction for goods. The success of contests and commercial sweepstakes testified to the power of the consumer – she was not simply being influenced in her brand or store selection, but was helping to shape modern advertisement. But women were frequently reproached for participating in commercial sweepstakes, which allegedly made them irrational and thus unfair consumers. Prizes and contests supposedly interfered with rational consumer choices and penalized producers and retailers who stood by traditional marketing strategies.[54] Contests disadvantaged smaller stores and passed on added costs to all consumers, thereby undermining fair competition, which was supposed to foster a stable market.

The One Big Union (OBU) operated a subscription campaign out of Winnipeg to save its weekly newspaper, other publishers promoted their newspapers or magazines with similar contests, and some created papers solely for this purpose.[55] The collapse of the post–First World War labour revolt left the radical syndicalist organization the OBU and the operation of its weekly newspaper in a difficult financial position. During a financial crisis in 1920, when the newspaper was 'strenuously fighting for existence,' the *OBU Bulletin* responded with a modest $100 raffle. A more permanent solution was proposed in November 1921, when the idea of operating a weekly contest to increase circulation was brought before the Central Labour Council. Supporters of the proposal admitted that 'it might be thought objectionable to encourage the sporting instinct in the workers, yet they would gamble anyway.' The staff of the *OBU Bulletin* hoped that a contest would increase circulation by several thousand.

Influenced by the OBU's British leadership, they chose a contest modelled on the English football pools. Subscribers could clip coupons predicting the results of the overseas football matches from the *OBU Bulletin* and submit them with their subscription payments.[56] The offer placed no limit to the amount of subscription money that could be sent in one week. Every 25¢ subscription earned one entry; $1.00, seven; and $5.00, forty-two. This modest raffle quickly expanded into the largest weekly lottery in Canada, with prizes as high as $8,000, divided among as many as 292 first-, second-, and third-prize winners. Post Office officials estimated that by May 1922 circulation had soared to 190,000 and that for the week of 8 June 1922 225,000 copies of the newspaper were printed. From an economically fragile position and a subscription list of less than 1,500, the *Bulletin* now had a permanent staff of thirty and a bank balance of $30,000.[57]

Throughout the 1920s, the *Bulletin* regularly transformed its contest to avoid prosecution. Charges were initially laid as a test case in 1922, but the contest was declared not to be a lottery, and charges were dismissed. In 1925 the *Bulletin* stopped its British football pool and began a contest based on guessing or predicting temperatures in North American cities on a given date.[58] By avoiding any connection to sports, it did not induce the readers to 'foretell the result' of any contest. The temperature contest, however, did not attract huge numbers, and so four months later, the *Bulletin* risked prosecution by introducing a baseball pool, followed by a football pool again one month later.

During the early 1930s, the *OBU Bulletin* was in constant conflict with the law, as authorities tightly policed its contests. Raids on its office in April 1931 temporarily halted distribution of prize money and set a pattern of harassment that continued through October 1933. At this time, continual disruption of the contest and confiscation of entries led the *Bulletin* to discontinue its Subscription Prize Contest – an action that led to the paper's folding in May 1934. The *OBU Bulletin* realized that the contest had financed its radical paper, and editor R.B. Russell explained its closing in terms of the loss of 'readers who had previously procured the paper through the contest.'[59]

One of the issues raised by the *OBU Bulletin*'s contest was the matter of policing. It would be difficult to believe that this contest did not receive particular attention as a result of the paper's radical political views. When the Employers' Association of Manitoba wrote to the federal minister of justice in 1922, its president urged immediate action, since 'aside from the evils of the gambling feature, the publications operating these are of a radical labor type and are spreading their socialistic propaganda, tending toward exploiting industrial unrest and to over-throw our present social system.'[60]

The challenge posed by the old adage that the law must not only be fair but must be seen to be fair is evident in the prosecutions against forms of gambling that did not result in individual profit, such as activities sponsored by the Canadian Legion and local service clubs. With some unease and a great deal of political delicacy, Ontario's attorney general ordered cancellation of an automobile raffle in 1922 by 'a well known patriotic society' just a day or two before the draw and ordered all money refunded. One factor that affected the police's willingness to overlook the law was the scale of the infraction. In 1928 a draw by a Vancouver branch of the Legion for a $75,000 mansion in Port Grey could not be ignored; the police brought it forward as a test case, and the contest was declared illegal. In the same year, Ontario Deputy Attorney General E. Bayly admitted that he did 'not like to interfere with respectable organizations, but the trouble in all these lottery matters is that the Code provisions are there and respectable persons should not be allowed to "get away" with things that outsiders of less repute cannot.'[61] In practice, however, when the Niagara Falls police brought forward the problem of a wheel of fortune operating at a local Lion's Club fair, the same official advised them that 'if the people are respectable and the bazaar is a charity bazaar, allow these matters to run.' He was supported by the attorney general, who in a similar case involving a church noted that 'if it is for religious purposes than no very great harm can be done.'[62]

Labour frequently noted the class bias. The Communist Party's newspaper, *The Worker*, stated that while the attorney general of Alberta dropped charges against a local branch of Elks for operating a wheel of fortune at its carnival in 1927, and churches and service clubs regularly operated lotteries and raffles with the authorities turning a blind eye, other groups were not as fortunate. A southern Ontario Trades and Labor Council was prosecuted for sweepstakes that it operated throughout 1928–31 to provide relief for the unemployed. Politicians feared public scandal and popular backlash, as the reality of prosecuting 'respectable citizens' or, worse, parish priests was far more complicated than the hypocrisy of the law.[63]

Even in a climate of uneven enforcement, ordinary people used the law to their own advantage. When large sweepstakes 'took off' in the 1930s, an old and forgotten federal statute was rediscovered which declared that anyone who informed on someone who had gained money by illegal means was entitled to the ill-gotten gains. Immediately, sweepstake winners were informed on by prearranged friends and relatives, who in turn received a small cut of the winnings. The federal government responded by declaring that all money acquired through illegal means should revert to the crown, but this produced a jurisdictional battle between provincial and federal governments, and no province, despite the appeal of cash in the treasury, was willing to accept the political ill-will that would result from seizing winnings of the widely celebrated and well-publicized winners.[64]

During the 1930s, legislators at all levels of government found themselves debating the legality and the appropriateness of state involvement in lotteries, sweepstakes, and raffles. Despite minor setbacks, the success of these illicit fundraising efforts encouraged cash-strapped governments to turn to lotteries. In Montreal, Mayor Camillien Houde attempted unsuccessfully to establish a lottery to raise revenue without increasing taxes.[65]

The actions of pro-lottery politicians met with some grassroots support. Vancouver politicians such as Mayor L.D. Taylor played on the support that a provincial lottery for underfunded hospitals had received in a 1932 municipal plebiscite. As I noted above, popular opinion in Quebec was strongly 'pro-lottery.' The success of international lotteries in the 1930s pointed out a further appeal, as politicians recognized that there was a large group of French Canadians living in New England, who, like the Irish in North America, would gladly remit money back to their native land in the form of lottery revenues. Clearly many of the illegal sweepstakes that operated out of Quebec in the 1930s were aimed directly at Americans, and a post–First World War

U.S. thesis claimed that Canada's 'lax gambling laws' meant that it 'provided a home for more illegal schemes plying the American trade than any other single country in 1930s.'[66] One such example appeared in 1930, and the tickets were decorated with a combination of the Union Jack and the 'Stars and Stripes.' This particular operation capitalized on a post office address called Blue Bonnets, which participants would have surely confused with the established Montreal racetrack of the same name. After a 1936 article appeared in *Reader's Digest*, the Quebec attorney general's office was swamped with letters from Americans querying whether or not the Quebec tickets they held or had distributed were fakes. The existence of fraudulent lotteries in Quebec prompted Montreal's Better Business Bureau to request action from the province's attorney general, as Montreal and Quebec were gaining 'widespread unfavourable publicity.' The thousands of ticket receipts and American-addressed envelopes seized by Quebec Provincial Police in one 1933 Sherbrooke raid reflected this market.[67]

An alternative to these illegal (and occasionally fraudulent) private lotteries was the promotion of legal state lotteries and regulated, open legal gambling. Legal state lotteries and tolerant gambling laws were the subject of debate in both the United States and Britain at this time. Nevada legalized gambling in 1931 and laid the foundations for a major post-1945 tourism industry. Other U.S. states introduced unsuccessful proposals for lotteries, and some eastern states, such as Massachusetts, decriminalized bingo.[68] Similar economic pressures and the popularity of the Irish Sweepstakes and football pools led the British government to examine gambling in its Royal Commission on Lotteries and Betting, 1932–3.

None the less, in Canada there remained an ambivalence about gambling, even among its most successful practitioners. The OBU, during its phenomenally successful football pool, expressed unease about encouraging the 'sporting instinct' in workers. In a building that was purchased with revenue from its contest, the library committee approached the Central Labour Council in 1924 regarding permission to play cards on OBU premises. This pastime was approved only on the 'understanding that no gambling would be allowed.' Outside Quebec, newspapers' editorial positions remained divided, even within the same city and region. In British Columbia, for example, the *Victoria Colonist* came out in favour of legalized sweepstakes in May 1931, the *Daily Province* opposed any change in the law, and the *Vancouver Sun* sat on the fence: 'If Canada is not going to tolerate sweepstakes, then some teeth and intelligence should be put into the law which purports to prohibit them.'[69] The critics of lotteries were successful, if not in eliminating lotteries, then certainly in keeping them illegal.

Changing Times

Depression

The impact of the Depression complicated understandings of gambling in myriad ways. Not only was the vulnerability of the economy exposed to investors who lost money, but all Canadians were affected by precarious economic conditions. In fact, the cause of the Depression was often expressed in terms of the consequences of wide-scale gambling. G.D. Stanley, MP for East Calgary, stated in 1933 that it was 'well understood that during the last several years, particularly in 1928 and 1929, gambling was the great evil of this country and the source of most of the troubles from which we are now suffering.'[70] In an interview that appeared in *Canadian Magazine* in 1934 University of Toronto economics professor Gilbert Jackson explained the speculation frenzy of the 1920s as the result of 'faults of character' as North Americans became overcome with 'the desire, at all risks, to get rich quick.' The consequence of this 'mass action' was the destruction of 'the business equilibrium of the whole world.' Jackson believed that there was an economic lesson to be learned from the Depression, and whether it had been understood could be determined by ' scrutinizing our individual and our collective reactions to the gambling opportunities of the present.'[71] General understanding of the connection between luck, speculation, and gambling may have been further enhanced by the phenomenal popularity of the game Monopoly, introduced in 1935.

While the debate about the relationship between the cause of the Depression and gambling continued, other observers claimed that the money wasted by gambling worsened its impact. One Vancouver newspaper opined that 'there could be no surer and no quicker way of bringing prosperity back to this city than by putting the lid on all gambling and clamping it down.' According to this view, money spent at bookmakers and lotteries could revive the entire economy if it was funnelled to legitimate local storekeepers.[72]

This perception overlooked the underground economy that gambling fostered. While some profits undoubtedly left the country, gambling was a source of employment, especially during the 1930s. In Montreal, Harry Ship, the real-life model for Jerry Dingleman in Mordecai Richler's *The Apprenticeship of Duddy Kravitz* had left Queen's University and in his early twenties got his start working as a clerk at a St-Urbain Street bookmaker, which also employed two of his brothers.[73] Various forms of gambling not only provided permanent and full-time employment but could also supplement an inadequate income or relief payment. Thousands of people sold Irish Sweepstakes tickets to their friends, family, and workmates, while solitary entrepreneurs proliferated, such as a Montreal man who made a checkerboard and then raffled it off amongst interested neighbours. Raffles also were turned to as acts of desperation. When in 1931, the family of country singer Hank Snow found itself completely destitute, with no food in the house, Snow took his mother's 'treasured' Hawaiian guitar into Liverpool, Nova Scotia, and went door to door, trying to sell ten-cent tickets on it.[74]

Even more than the First World War, Depression conditions appear to have promoted the popularity of various forms of gambling. A letter from a Vancouver municipal employee, which instigated a 1936 inquiry into that city's police force, claimed that 'thousands of dollars paid out in Cash Relief every month, finds it way to the numerous gambling dens and clubs' and that it was 'a great temptation to a large number of persons forced on Relief owing to conditions over which they have no control, to try and augment their financial resources by a lucky session at the gambling tables or lotteries.'[75] In Windsor, Ontario, track operator Abram Orpen feared a backlash against legal horse racing when the 1932 attendance and betting volume set records. He was particularly uneasy with the publicity given to unemployed men who won at the track, for although these were happy stories, the general public would realize its most extreme fears as non-working men were betting with unearned money. Unlike his competitors, he did not introduce special tickets for women to attract female patrons, since he would not 'take the household money from women by staging "Ladies days."'[76]

In contrast with the relative success of the Windsor tracks stood the difficulties experienced by the tracks in Montreal. In a letter to the Quebec attorney general, the area jockey clubs blamed their heavy deficits not on general economic conditions but on illegal competition from the many bookmakers operating in the city and its suburbs. They cited an American trade publication which claimed not only that Montreal was the bookmaking centre in Canada but that the city's proportion of bookmakers to population exceeded even Chicago's. Montreal's bookmakers were not the former 'sporting gentry,' but 'bold chisellers' who accepted bets as low as five cents.[77]

The ordinariness of nickel bets with a local bookmaker found parallels elsewhere in the volume of lottery and sweepstake tickets available. There was a ready market of willing customers for the many fraternal service clubs across Ontario that organized car raffles for causes as diverse as building an Orange Hall in Oshawa and veterans financing their 1936 pilgrimage to Vimy Ridge. The crown attorney in one northern Ontario town declared that during the summer of 1935 'raffling has been so prevalent that at times ... there were as many as three cars standing in front of the Post Office and individuals selling tickets for the same.' Similarly a Protestant minister claimed that it was impossible to walk down the main street of an eastern Ontario city 'without having men step out from store doors calling "ticket on a new car, sir."'[78] Other items that surpassed the limit on the value of any prize included a number of complete houses. In 1939 a Toronto area service club sold 25,000 $1 tickets for a house in the new subdivision of Leaside that resulted in the prosecution of both the club's president and its secretary, although the mayor of Toronto himself had selected the lucky ticket.[79]

The Second World War

The increased conspicuousness of charitable gambling during the Depression expanded further with the advent of the Second World War. The exigencies of war created tolerant conditions for lotteries that raised money for war-related charities.[80] Once again, the powerful mix of patriotism and philanthropy justified worthy causes' resorting to lotteries as an effective means to raise funds. The war in fact helped consolidate the clear distinction in public opinion and tolerance that had emerged between commercial and non-commercial forms of gambling. Raffles and bingo were more acceptable, but a get-tough attitude had emerged on organized commercial vice. The former were seen to help the war effort, while the latter harmed it. One of the new criticisms of commercial vice was the costly drain of Canadian money going to the United States through an organized continental vice syndicate. Wartime currency regulation could not intervene in the illegal informal economy. As early as 1940, Vancouver Mayor Lyle Telford encouraged the federal government to increase policing on bookmaking in order to stop the exportation of scarce Canadian dollars to the United States through American-based syndicates. J.-O. Asselin, chair of Montreal's municipal executive committee, made a similar plea to the dominion appraiser in February 1942. On 26 December 1944, after the United States banned all horse racing for the duration of the war, pressure increased for Canada to follow suit.[81] No such drastic measure was taken, as supporters argued that the Canadian racetracks were already more tightly regulated, with their extremely limited racing season. Some adaptations had taken place early in the war as associations in the same city were permitted to operate out of only one track to save on transportation and gasoline. Race times were altered so as not to interfere with traffic patterns, and twilight racing was introduced 'so that tracks could be manned by employed persons in their spare time.' Operators of racing associations in Winnipeg claimed that 98 per cent of their employees were steadily engaged in other businesses.[82] The continuing functioning of Canadian racetracks at a time when their U.S. counterparts were closed recreated a situation similar to what had occurred during the First World War. American gamblers invaded Canada for the 1945 racing season.

While wartime conditions elevated concern about commercialized gambling, community groups capitalized on a potent mixture of philanthropy and patriotism to promote and extend toleration of other forms of gambling. Vancouver in particular seemed to be saturated with this type of large-scale fundraising. In 1943, lotteries there collected enormous sums through unobstructed raffles for homes that capitalized on local housing shortages. Vancouver Rotarians netted $71,000, with most of it going to a recreation centre for armed forces personnel, while city Kinsmen raised $55,000 in their 'milk for Britain' campaign.[83] As in the First World War, ordinary Canadians may have simply been gambling more. Soldiers once again tried to counteract boredom with cards and dice. An award-winning painting from an army art exhibit and a Coca-Cola advertisement from 1944 both depicted servicemen playing cards. The mass popularity of gambling extended to the civilian population. After the war the Wartime Prices and Trade Board faced a shortage in its blue meat tokens, which, the board suspected, were being used as poker chips.[84]

The universal perception of growth in gambling between 1919 and 1945 testified to its popularity, but the meaning of its status was complicated. It is difficult to differentiate between actual behaviour and imagined moral panics, as critics claimed Canadians gambled more in the speculative 1920s, the depressed 1930s, and the wartime 1940s. Uneven prosperity and the expansion of commercial leisure, Depression conditions, and war may all have fostered environments that tolerated gambling, but it is impossible to arrive at a single specific influence. The common thread of instability, whether caused by economic, political, or social uncertainty, meant that for a section of the English-speaking, Protestant middle class that had created and maintained the status quo, any change posed a threat.

The significance of gambling was also fraught with ambiguity. The popularity of charitable gambling as a means of raising funds made it possible to combine entertainment and potential gain for the support of worthy causes. The lure of some return for generosity made giving easier, especially during periods of great demand, such as the war, or of general scarcity, such as the Depression. But when 'respectable' fraternal, patriotic, athletic, and community organizations raised money through gambling, they broke a very unevenly enforced law. While gambling comprised a form of community service for some, it was associated with status for others, just as specific racetracks were linked with the country's elite. But the 'problem' of gambling most often focused on working-class Canadians.

Opponents of gambling feared that, particularly among the working class, gambling served as an expression of cultural resistance and a rejection of dominant values associated with diligence and thrift. In part, they were probably right. But it is not clear that gambling had this same significance for all its participants, all the time. Gambling could be not only a rejection of dominant values but also a celebration of the very values associated with entrepreneurial risk-taking in twentieth-century capitalism.

For working-class Canadians, gambling offered a way to combine entertainment with a creative means to obtain money or material goods. Proponents of gambling in its various forms celebrated the pleasant dreams that it provided, particularly in difficult economic times.[85] Certainly, winning could make a very real difference and held the promise of financial independence. A young Halifax businessman who distanced himself from any radical thought ('I am not a Red of any form') defended church card parties after he had won a small sum of money, which he considered 'a gift from heaven as it enabled me to meet bills contracted through illness and face the world "Square with the board."'[86]

Families in Vancouver in overcrowded wartime apartments rejoiced at their good fortune in winning a home of their own.

But critics of gambling who identified its potential role within an oppositional working-class culture had a point. Recognition of the role of luck challenged the legitimacy of power and wealth in society. Luck was something that could be possessed without regard to the usual constraints such as class, sex, race, age, language, marital status, education, skill, and geographic location.[87] A belief in luck did not necessarily mean a reciprocal belief in fatalism. The buying of a ticket on the Irish Sweepstakes or spending an evening playing cards at a gambling club was a demonstration of agency that involved decisions and choices to change the circumstances of one's life. Most people had a keen realization that they were living against the odds. Even if the economic system loaded the dice against most working-class Canadians, the act of visiting a bookmaker or sending money to the *OBU Bulletin* was an expression of hope. Men and women all over Canada who participated in these illegal activities were demonstrating that they were still playing the game of life, even if they did repudiate the myth that productive labour alone brought success. Anyone could win under capitalism, but the odds were terribly long. Buying tickets and placing bets made a great deal of sense for people who recognized that everyday survival meant taking chances, and at times the act of living required not only courage but a great deal of luck.

PART TWO

Masculine, Feminine, Other

CHAPTER THREE

Gambling, Respectable Masculinity, and Male Sporting Culture

Dominant twentieth-century masculine ideals held that men had to negotiate a space between the call to be daring, courageous, and audacious and at the same time to be stable, dependable, and responsible. This apparent contradiction within masculinity was frequently expressed as the tension between 'natural' male instincts and the uplifting influences of civilization. Gambling and the arguments of its opponents provide a means of exploring this paradox in opposing notions of masculinity and highlight its conflicting demands. Between the First World War and the legalization of some forms of gambling in 1969, the anti-gambling movement's arguments were premised on an unchanging definition of masculine domestic respectability that emphasized a man's responsibility for providing for his family. The tenacity with which a minority of Protestant clergymen, newspaper editors, and their political allies maintained their position, and obstructed any liberalization of the Criminal Code, reflected the powerful resonance of their rhetoric and their anxiety to keep masculine norms within this delicate balance.

Gambling celebrated and encouraged a 'bachelor' form of masculinity and the qualities of courage, audacity, and risk taking, as it simultaneously threatened the domestic version of masculinity and its emphasis on labour and thrift. To maintain and perpetuate the power relations in Canadian society, men had to be able to draw on both aspects of masculinity, and they preserved patriarchy under this incongruity. But there was always ambivalence. While the domestic ideal that saw men as breadwinners and responsible household heads was reified in the Criminal Code, the bachelor sporting culture was recognized in what many men actually did and in lax standards of law enforcement in many communities. This chapter's first section explores this ambivalence. The second suggests how each of these two opposing versions of masculinity – husband, father, employer versus the attractive, usually unmarried gambler of fiction – reinforced male power within society. In the last section, Montreal serves as a case study of male space because of its strong association with male sporting culture, at least in the imagination of Canada's English-speaking majority.

A Profound Ambivalence

Public gambling – in its various forms of bookmaking, cards, and dice games – was largely restricted to men. A female reporter who published a series of articles on Montreal gambling in 1946 stated that she had met with her informants in coffee shops rather than entering their establishments, since she did 'not think women were allowed.' The image of gambling clubs as male-only spaces was also supported by a longtime employee of one of Montreal's busiest downtown betting establishments, who claimed that he had never seen a woman in his place.[1] But there were many places where women gambled in public. In addition to a presence at the racetrack, women were also found in the most exclusive gambling clubs, usually on the arm of a man at the *barbotte* table or by the roulette wheel. Other forms of gambling appealed specifically to or incorporated women – namely, bingo and commercial sweepstakes. By and large, placing bets, playing cards, and rolling dice were activities that men engaged in with other men.

The close connection between gambling and men was a result of complementary material and ideological factors. Men were likely to have surplus money available for entertainment spending and had the most control about how this money was spent. In addition, at least in the early part of the twentieth century, men had access to the sometimes 'dangerous' public space where illegal forms of gambling took place. But gambling was not only about those who actually had money or about who had access to public space, for it also possessed characteristics associated with desirable traits of masculinity. Various forms of essentially competitive games capitalized on notions of 'macho risk taking,' aggressive behaviour, and courage.[2] Roger Lancaster, in particular, has noted that the North American (Anglo-American) ideal of masculinity held that a man took risks with bravado but always while maintaining some control through strategy or an understanding of probability. This factor, combined with a man's ability to conceal what made him vulnerable, made poker 'the quintessence of the North American idea of masculinity.' A similar argument could be made about horse or sports, where familiarity with the track record meant that betting was informed by expertise rather than by random selection. Certainly men and women bet differently. Studies comparing their behaviour show that men consistently took larger risks when betting, overestimated the degree of skill involved, and were more likely to bet to win than to show.[3] Their risk-taking behaviour was a requirement of both the dominant economic and gender systems, as both capitalism and masculinity balanced security and danger, stability and growth.

There was a strong, if under-examined connection between masculinity, *machismo* (by which I mean a form of hypermasculinity), and risk-taking behaviour. Courage, bravery, daring, honour, and audacity have been cultivated as desirable traits by which men demonstrated that they were not feminine. These so-called positive attributes of risk-taking behaviour have been associated with economic ambition, military participation, hazardous occupations, and full engagement in democratic citizenship through standing for office. But in another context, Jackson Lears has argued that risk-taking behaviour had a particular significance as a response to modern society. What he identifies as modernity's 'activist imperative' and its 'therapeutic self-absorption' Lears links to 'a fascination with "risk-taking" and "winning through intimidation" as ends in themselves.'[4] This risky side of 'modern' masculinity could and did conflict with the parallel and contradictory expectations of stability and security in domestic breadwinning and public citizenship. Perhaps not surprising, society resolved this contradiction in part by ascribing specific behavioural expectations based on race, class, and marital status.

The small, influential group of white, Protestant middle-class reformers of 'old Canada' who opposed gambling continued well into the twentieth century to adhere to the sorts of Victorian archetypes identified by historian Edward Rotundo. Rotundo isolated two masculine ideals reverberating throughout Canadian debates on masculinity and gambling. The first – 'the Christian gentleman' – 'controll[ed] his impulses to selfishness and vice through the power of inner will.'[5] Participation in even the most minor form of gambling such as lotteries defied these principles, as one man's success was another man's loss. The second model was embodied in 'the masculine primitive' type who repudiated the harnessing of his desires. The 'masculine primitive' was associated with violence, commercial sex, drinking, and gambling. He rejected the virtues of a respectable domestic masculinity, which the white, Protestant, middle-class reformers were quick to identify with themselves. Although in practice respectable domestic masculinity and unrespectable rough behaviour appeared across class and ethnic groups, influential representatives of 'old Canada' associated specific ethnic minorities, such as Chinese, Jews, and African and French Canadians, with gambling and other vices.[6] Illicit gambling within these groups seemed to the Anglo-Celtic middle class yet another way in which these usually working-class 'outsiders' failed to live up to their model of comportment.

The allure of gambling was much more powerful than its critics seemed to understand. Despite the attention focused on specific class and ethnic groups, its prevalence and persistence, according to one Montreal observer, 'extended to all classes, colors, creeds and nationalities.'[7] Gambling linked a diverse group of men, and despite particular class, race, or linguistic variations, the common sites of illicit gambling often demarcated public male space.

Studies undertaken to uncover the relationship between space and gender have concentrated on heterosexual women's or homosexual men's space. The work of American and British scholars such as Mary Ryan, Christine Stansell, Judith Walkowitz, and George Chauncey have altered the way in which we see the countryside and the city and the way in which women and gay men used spaces to create and reinforce their own identities.[8] This chapter borrows from these insights and applies them to an examination of heterosexual male spaces associated with gambling. Although male spaces could be and were further segregated by class, race, language, and marital status, they provided settings that preserved a male sporting culture in a period that historians have usually associated with the development of heterosocial or mixed-sex commercialized leisure. There was continuity with older same-sex leisure patterns. At the same time as marginal heterosexual women and gay men used urban space to forge identity for survival, semi-public male spaces in the city could also reinforce heterosexual male privilege, as this chapter shows. As historian Kevin White has suggested, the culture associated with these male spaces often contained a strong element of misogyny.[9]

Gambling was one of the activities most associated with what has been described as traditional male sporting culture. In the late nineteenth century, it, together with alcohol and commercial sex, according to Keith Walden, 'appealed to men of all backgrounds and ages, not just to bachelors.' Timothy Gilfoyle also linked various forms of gaming with communal drinking, commercial sex, and the celebration of male autonomy through sexual aggressiveness, promiscuity, and renunciation of connections with family. Gambling in particular and male sporting culture in general posed a direct challenge to respectable bourgeois Christian morality. Gilfoyle's study of nineteenth-century prostitution, Elliot J. Gorn's investigation into boxing during the same period, and Walden's examination of Toronto's Industrial Exhibition all argue that the nature of male sporting culture and its emphasis on masculinity diminished divisions based on class, ethnicity, and religion. This vision of a brotherhood of men, however, must be tempered with the recognition that the men brought together by sporting culture were never equal. Judith Walkowitz, in her investigation into late Victorian London, reminds us that it was a group that she referred to as 'privileged men' who traversed urban space without boundaries. This freedom and openness to go anywhere would not have been shared by their working-class or non-white brethren, for whom the class and ethnic borders were not so permeable.[10]

In the twentieth century, distinct male space persisted as a part of everyday Canadian life. Taverns were regulated by discriminatory provincial laws that permitted women only under specific conditions. Indeed the tavern, along with other examples of exclusively male space such as the locations of professional and amateur sports, and the culture surrounding brothels frequently overlapped with gambling activity.[11] Moreover, male segregation within the city was not restricted to leisure activities, since most occupations and many industrial jobs were in themselves gender-specific.

Although male sporting culture survived in Canada, by the early twentieth century it was often overshadowed by heterosocial forms of leisure, which brought together young men and women. The advent of commercialized forms of mass entertainment, such as amusement parks, nightclubs, roller rinks, dance halls, and movie theatres, popularized this new ideal. Facilities that originally attracted a working-class clientele quickly expanded to include middle-class patrons and helped to undermine a strong tradition of same-sex leisure.[12]

These new spaces and their particular association with youth were the source of anxiety for reformers. While the moral regulation of women had been preoccupied with their sexuality, the moral regulation of men had focused more on their role as economic and political actors. The emphasis placed on specific private and public masculine roles changed over time and was connected to concerns about political and economic stability. John Rosecrance has recently argued that gambling became 'legitimated' in the United States over the twentieth century as it became accepted by the middle class.[13] This insight is useful but needs to be refined to recognize the role of gender. We must relate the acceptance of gambling in Canada to general perceptions of middle-class masculinity. This connection becomes apparent when we examine the preoccupations of the opponents of gambling, who emphasized the threat that they believed it posed to the assigned roles of respectable middle-class men – namely, husband, father, employee, and citizen.

Although these categories were thought to be universal, the force of anti-gambling rhetoric was directed most explicitly at those men who were thought to be least able to afford it. Working-class gambling was policed more closely and thought to be more dangerous than its middle- and upper-class counterparts. A journal for social workers argued in 1934 that the temptation to buy lottery tickets fell 'much more heavily on the poorer man,' while 'the wealthy man is likely to invest an inconsiderable portion of his income this way.' Parliamentarians in the 1930s also questioned the wisdom of the state's operating lotteries that would encourage men, some without incomes, to spend the little money that they had on a ticket instead of on meeting household expenses. In Madge MacBeth's satirical novel *The Land of Afternoon* of 1924, a member of the National Council of Women argued: 'If we can prohibit the sale of liquor to a drunken man, I don't see why we can't restrict gambling to persons of a certain income.'[14]

For anti-gambling activists, and for the temperance movement, the object of suffering created by male behaviour was always the family, embodied in an impoverished wife or, worse, a destitute mother and family. An American expert witness who testified before a Canadian parliamentary committee in the 1950s cited an unnamed Illinois mayor who claimed that every morning his waiting room was filled with the wives and mothers of municipal employees who begged him to close the gambling establishments because their husbands' and sons' wages were not arriving home. Montreal anti-gambling crusader Pacifique (Pax) Plante depicted even the gambling operators themselves as remorseful for female suffering. Plante reported that Arthur Davidson, the 'king of gamblers' in Montreal during late 1930s and early 1940s, was not disturbed in his sleep by thoughts of the police, but rather was haunted by visions of the wives of unlucky gamblers. Plante claimed that Davidson told him, 'When they come and plead that their husbands had lost all in my establishment and that the family has nothing to eat for the week, I can never resist. I give them all $25, sometimes $50. But it is them who make me suffer most and harass me on long days.'[15]

Davidson's gestures of gallantry suggest that he shared the same chivalrous outlook as the police. Men policing a masculine activity found themselves in a difficult situation, because working-class policemen tended to share the same values as the men whom they were prosecuting.[16] This contradiction was understood or at least expressed in terms of chivalry; the police were not persecuting their manly brothers as much as protecting women who complained about the consequences of the behaviour of their husbands and sons. In a 1951 investigation into commercial gambling, the commissioner of the Ontario Provincial Police explained that many of its investigations were the result of appeals from women.[17] The ethos of chivalry, in which men on either side of the law placed a high value on protecting female victims, permitted some men to condemn this masculine behaviour without compromising their own manliness.

Men who gambled away money that they did not earn were subject to particular contempt and censure. An unemployed 'sober and serious married disabled veteran' in Montreal – someone who clearly conformed with a post–First World War notion of the deserving poor – informed on a municipally licensed beggar who gambled away his proceeds each evening. The unfortunate righteous veteran claimed that 'a sight such as this was disgusting to men in his position who have been trying their hardest to earn a mere subsistence.' This type of concern was also examined by Montreal's unemployment commission in the 1930s. This body stipulated that if a husband wasted his assistance cheque on drink or gambling, the registrar must be notified immediately, and a new registration would be made in the name of the spouse or society responsible for the family.[18] This was a rare case in which cheques could be made in the wife's name. We can link the concern directed at both men on relief and working-class gambling more generally to the belief that economic loss would interfere with men's duty to support their families.

Competing Visions of Masculinity

Husbands, Fathers, and Employees

Gambling could interfere with the ability of a husband to provide, but critics also believed that this economic stress could eventually destroy a family. Before a parliamentary committee in 1953–4 that considered liberalization of the laws on lotteries, the chief of police from Hull, Quebec, reported that gambling was a major cause of broken homes in his city. Imported U.S. expert Virgil Peterson, who admitted that he knew of no study on the matter, was none the less sure that 'without any question gambling is a very great contributing factor in many situations along that line.' Such claims echoed the belief of the Church of England in Canada that legalized lotteries would not promote 'stable family life.'[19]

Certainly a major part of a father's responsibility, like that of a husband, was providing financial support for dependants. But a father could also fail by setting a poor example for his children, principally his sons. Critics of gambling always concentrated on the bad example that games of chance offered to children, interfering with the socialization of the next generation of labour and its acquisition of the work ethic. Opponents were quick to publicize any opportunity that children had to buy lottery tickets, play bingo, or purchase candy through illegal gumball or mint-vending machines. Concern for the moral purity of young men was at the centre of arguments against gambling at agricultural fairs put forward in the 1920s by the Social Service Council of Canada, which drew attention to 'the evils' that might arise if young rural men were exposed to wheels of fortune and games of chance. In 1925 a Methodist minister concluded: 'It is highly pernicious that an effort should be made to bring in sometime 1,000 boys from over the country to receive what purports to be training for citizenship [at such exhibitions] and then to introduce them immediately to a carnival of gambling.'[20] The United Church Women's brief to the parliamentary committee of 1953–4, argued in a gender-neutral fashion that 'wholesome development of children does not take place in an atmosphere in which there is an element of chance.' Other male witnesses from policing were concerned primarily about boys. Hull's chief of police claimed that any place of gambling (including bingo!) attracted hoodlums and that there were 'youngsters who turned or became delinquent and later criminals on account of ... the behaviour in their own family.'[21]

An overt if unconscious reference to the preoccupation of exposing young boys to gambling was present even in those engaged in commercialized games of chance. In response to a 1957 complaint by the local Woman's Christian Temperance Union about the presence of pinball machines, a small-town Ontario proprietor noted that he had posted a sign warning *boys* under sixteen not to use machines.[22] In a world fraught with such dangers, the paternal example could discourage participation in lotteries, pinball games, raffles, and even the pursuit of candy prizes. Where fathers were not setting the proper example, the state was asked to do so.

The concern about a father's example was closely connected to opponents' general criticism of the way in which gambling subverted the character of a good employee – a primary quality of respectable manhood. Gambling might diminish the work ethic or even lead employees to use company material or time to pursue their interests. The Employers' Association of Manitoba was particularly perturbed by the OBU's large subscription contest in the 1920s. In urging the federal government to close down the contest, it cited not only the OBU's revolutionary politics but also its belief that the contest was distracting employees from work, as 'guesses are made out during business hours and stationery of their employers is employed.' It claimed as well that the government's own workers were acting in a similar manner and that 'the public interest requires that speedy action should be taken to check this evil.'[23]

Cooperation between employers and the police to control illegal gambling also affected the post–Second World War workplace. In Ontario during 1952, members of the provincial police's anti-gambling squad went under cover in ten private industrial companies to identify bookmaking operations and recruitment to play illegal games. Major employers such as Canadian General Electric, Dominion Stores, General Motors, Imperial Oil, Loblaws, and the Steel Company of Canada allowed placement of undercover officers.[24]

Employers' concerns went even further. Popular culture had long generated apocryphal stories in which honest young men from good families, tempted by the easy riches of gambling, became indebted and eventually ruined themselves and their family name by embezzling employers. Employers opposed to the OBU's contest tapped into this tradition when they claimed that their employees were stealing funds to play the 25-cent game. Similarly, the first General Assembly of the 'Continuing' Presbyterian church in 1925 lobbied the government to oppose any relaxation of gambling prohibitions at agricultural fairs, since these activities would constitute a 'strong temptation to employees, who are responsible for the proper care of money, to use trusted funds illegally.'[25]

But the expressed fears seem disproportionate to actual experience. Male workers participated in many social, recreational, and political activities that no doubt occasionally interfered with work and led to the use of employers' resources and letterhead. Yet their bosses did not complain about their membership in church choirs or fraternal organizations. Advertising, with its persuasive appeal to consumers' happiness, may have proved an even greater enticement to theft by employees, yet other forms of temptation were not targeted in the same manner as even the most minor forms of gambling. This situation suggests that there was something deeper at the root of employers' concerns.

Although employers spoke of waste and embezzlement, their primary concern was the erosion of the work ethic and the threat that lotteries might pose to the concept of productive labour. The cliché 'getting something for nothing' reverberated throughout all discussions of games of chance and referred by inference to the work ethic. Any erosion of the work ethic and productive labour among men might shake the very foundations of society and the meaning of membership in it.

The perceived connection between forms of gambling and a threat to a certain type of male citizenship explains the tenacity of anti-gambling opponents. Even after the Second World War, men were regarded as the primary actors in the capitalist and democratic system, and the concept of male citizenship had both economic and political components.[26] Gamblers simultaneously repudiated the virtue of productive labour and broke the criminal law. Gambling, in the most extreme argument, undermined the work ethic among men, interfered with the operation of the market, threatened the independence of the male judiciary, and jeopardized the integrity of elected male politicians. It was therefore more than a 'minor vice.' Opponents saw gambling as a threat to the fabric of the nation.

But this threat was also closely associated with such positive expressions of masculinity as sports. Anti-gambling reformers sometimes demarcated a fine line between appropriate and inappropriate male sporting behaviour. One such reformer, the Anglican canon and university president H.J. Cody, argued that gambling 'tends to degrade or kill what should be manly sport.' He contrasted the physical achievement of 'all manly and exhilarating amusements,' generated by either man or horse, and the noble and pure attitude towards athletics held by the ancient Greeks, who did not wager on outcomes, with the 'money getting' of gambling.[27]

Glamour and Danger versus Domesticity

Another tension surrounding male gambling was its association with sexuality and loss of self-control. The language about gambling itself was frequently saturated with sexual metaphors. In the 1920s a Protestant minister from a southwestern Ontario town claimed that service-club 'frolics' that included raffles were 'orgies of gambling.' The phrase 'a regular wide open gambling orgie' appeared in the staunchly Protestant *Toronto Telegram*, which described a fair organized by a Catholic parish in Hamilton and pointed out that the 'Roman Catholics of Hamilton were not molested by any officer.'[28] Although touching on the anti-Catholic strain that remained central to twentieth-century Protestant culture, the phrase evoked moral panic by bringing together the distinct threats of undisciplined sexuality and games of chance.

The association of gambling and sexuality was by no means strictly heterosexual. Psychologists in the 1920s linked gambling to 'sex-substitution' behaviour and used this insight to explain its popularity in homosocial environments, such as lumber camps and the military. As a substitute for sexual activity, gambling could be discreetly condoned, as it received credit for reducing general levels of tension and 'a certain amount of homosexuality.'[29] Other accessories of the gambling culture were aggressively heterosexual. A punchboard seized in Kemptville, Ontario, in 1957 was decorated with a hundred female names. The player punctured a desired 'girl's name' for a chance at a prize. The proprietor of a bookmaking and card establishment in Oshawa in the early 1960s decorated his walls 'with pictures of nude or semi-nude women in suggestive poses.' A similar motif was evident at the infamous Montreal clubs the Hawaiian Lounge and the Club Saint-Michel, where gamblers met in the 1940s.[30] But perhaps the most ubiquitous emblems of all links between gambling culture and heterosexuality were the packages of 'girlie' playing cards available everywhere.

Links between male sexuality and gambling were an element in the depiction of gamblers as seducers in nineteenth-century fiction, a characterization that survived in the twentieth century in the romantic leading men of stage and screen.[31] From Gaylord Ravenal, the riverboat gambler in the 1927 production of *Showboat*, through Robert Redford and Paul Newman's characters in *The Sting* (1973), there was a strong connection between sexually attractive men and gambling. James F. Smith has noted that American popular film has portrayed two versions of the male gambler – most frequently the romantic seductive gambler, but occasionally a darker, pathetic/tragic variant.[32] In Hollywood's portrayals, gamblers did not make good husbands, but they did comprise some of the most appealing, romantic leading men, who under the best circumstances renounced their gambling habit and reformed before marriage. Despite the screenwriter's efforts to shorten the four-hour movie, Clark Gable's Rhett Butler in *Gone with the Wind* (1939) partook in gambling scenes that did not exist in the original, lengthy book as a means to convey his masculine character to theatre audiences.[33] Humphrey Bogart's Rick Blaine lost Ilsa in Paris but continued to operate a roulette wheel in *Casablanca* (1942), while Marlon Brando's professional gambler Sky Masterson gave up gambling and won the demure Salvation Army missionary in *Guys and Dolls* (1955). At least one dashing romantic lead transmuted into a tragic figure: Omar Sharif's portrayal of real-life professional gambler Nicky Arnstein in *Funny Girl* (1968) followed the course of his failed marriage to comedian Fanny Bryce as he continued to gamble after their wedding. The audacious behaviour exhibited in all these characters was appealing only if it belonged to bachelors. Hollywood knew what the public also knew – sex was one thing, domesticity was another.

But of course many married men gambled, and the extreme position of anti-gambling 'reformers' left little space for the moderate majority who gambled. This dilemma was partially accommodated through emphasis on the difference between the evil world of illegal, commercial gambling and the more acceptable expression of masculine bonding that occurred in private, informal games or in contests. The spatial separation of commercial male-sporting behaviour away from the home meant that a bachelor-type subculture could survive and be maintained at the same time as the bonds of matrimony were protected. Respectability associated the home with consistency and permanence – attributes at odds with the excitement and risk taking of gambling.[34] Within the home, moderate risk-taking behaviour could be deemed appropriate if it was restricted to non-commercial leisure activities such as private poker games among friends.

The world of private single-sex male poker games was celebrated in numerous venues such as 'Penny Ante,' the American syndicated cartoon based on an ongoing friendly poker game that appeared in a number of Canadian English-language newspapers in the 1920s. The place of casual, informal poker games for working-class men was also evident in the Workers' Educational Association's attempt to sell tickets for the dream life that might accompany the lucky winner of its 1944 lottery for 'the model working man's home.' The promotional literature touted a kitchen-dinette arrangement that opened into a living-room 'so that [during] Saturday night parties ... men can play poker close to the icebox and still talk to the women folks sitting in the 15 × 16 foot living room.'[35] This benign working-class example of contained risk-taking behaviour (with men in the kitchen and women in the living-room) would have been acceptable and respectable for both single and married, middle- and working-class men. Significantly, the home did not appear to be corrupted by this kind of gambling, which was restricted to men but conducted in the proximity of their wives.

While private social gambling may have been an acceptable leisure activity among married men, there was a clear differentiation between this and commercial or professional gambling. Although many professional gamblers led seemingly ordinary lives – in Montreal a number of prominent gamblers lived in the suburbs and travelled downtown to work – theirs was not an appropriate occupation or form of recreation for respectable married men. Women, who were sometimes partners with their husbands in home-based book-making, became virtually invisible during police raids. While arresting home-based male bookmakers in what must have been family operations, police seemed to take women at their word when they denied knowledge of their husbands' activities and of the frequent telephone calls to their homes.[36]

While women were rarely seen as co-entrepreneurs, wives received credit for bookmakers' leaving their gambling businesses. The tension between marriage and a bachelor subculture was evident in the case of an Ontario man who claimed to have stopped taking bets voluntarily at his wife's request. He said that his wife was distressed by their children answering the telephone for incoming wagers and incorporating bookmaking terms into their daily speech. A prominent Montreal bookmaker also claimed to have quit taking wagers at the request of his new wife. Before a public inquiry in 1950, he explained, 'when you get married, you change.'[37] No one asked him to elaborate on his statement, suggesting a shared anglophone and francophone understanding in the courtroom of distinct masculine behaviour appropriate to married men and to bachelors.

Male Spaces: A Case Study in Montreal

Although some men ran gambling operations from their homes, the forms of illegal gambling that received the most attention from opponents were likely to be those that identified with male space and excluded women. One common characteristic of these spaces was their state of disrepair. In Montreal during the 1930s and 1940s, downtown bookmaking operations usually had lunch counters, actually licensed by municipal authorities, which sold sandwiches, soft drinks, coffee, and cigarettes to men while they waited for the results of the races. With no apparent irony intended, municipal sanitary inspectors would occasionally remove or threaten to remove lunch-counter licences for breaches of the municipal code of health, while ignoring the illegality of the primary business. For example, in June 1942 the operators of a large and permanent bookmaking establishment received a warning that unless rat droppings were cleaned up, rat holes were filled in, and a sink was installed, the lunch counter would lose its licence to serve food. Problems with cleanliness of lunch counters reveals a common characteristic of male spaces, which were often identified as dark and dirty. A photo taken during a police raid of another gambling joint clearly displays a sign requesting patrons 'not to spit on the floor.' These concerns inadvertently reveal a level of male sociability, particularly in bookmaking shops, which was distinct from the act of placing the bet itself. Customers clearly sat around at tables provided by owners, perhaps drinking a Coke and eating a sandwich, while they awaited results. At the Sportsmen's Club, there were often informal card games, for which owners did not receive any percentage of the money played. This form of comradeship overcame the physical conditions and probably added to the pleasure of the gambling experience. Participants were involved in an urban community subculture, not strictly a commercial business transaction.[38]

While versions of this subculture existed in the barbershops and poolrooms of small towns and the dormitories of lumbercamps and military barracks, it was associated most with large urban centres. In the minds of English-speaking Canadians, the city with the richest male sporting culture was Montreal. While francophones may hold memories of that city as a devout and religious city, Montreal in the 1940s marketed itself to English-speaking tourists as a sportingman's city. Guides such as *Montreal Confidential* directed tourists and businessmen to the city's most exciting clubs and districts, while the short-lived American tabloid *Pic: The Magazine Men Prefer* offered a photo essay on 'Montreal: Booming Paris of the West,' featuring gambling clubs and the famous burlesque performer Lily St Cyr of the Gayety Theatre.[39] The English-language North American press played on the fantasy element that Montreal offered by drawing attention to the city's exotic nature: as a bit of Paris in North America it was touted as one of the most vital centres of male sporting culture to survive on the continent. Its tolerant history vis-à-vis liquor made it a popular destination for parched tourists during prohibition. Moreover, unlike other Canadian and eastern U.S. cities, it was not dominated by the culture of a Protestant elite that demanded enforcement of legislated forms of morality. Montreal's reputation for glamour and excitement, as an island of Latin freedom in a generally repressive Protestant continent, was widely incorporated into North American popular culture in examples that ranged from early Harlequin romances to Damon Runyon's short stories.[40]

In the 1940s, Montreal was still Canada's largest city, with approximately one million people. This population was divided by many factors, including language, with approximately 65 per cent of the population speaking French. So, in addition to its North American pattern of urban division along class and racial lines, whether in the wealthy districts of Westmount and Outremont or in the concentration of visible minorities in Chinatown and Black districts, language divided the city along an east–west axis identified as St-Laurent, or 'the Main.'[41]

In 1945, before any serious attempts to enforce the laws on gambling, Montreal reporter Ted McCormick wrote, 'The gaming houses are scattered like raisins through the loaf of the town.' While this was an appealing image and suggestive of abundant sites, it was not quite true. The location of betting and gaming establishments was not random, and although there was no single 'men's district,' gambling activities were often associated with specific neighbourhoods or districts.[42] The Caron Inquiry of the 1950s heard of 248 addresses as locations of repeated raids between 1942 and 1950. Not a single address connected gambling to the wealthy municipalities of Westmount or Outremont, and only one was listed in the middle-class, English-speaking neighbourhood of Notre-Dame-de-Grâce. Instead, the locations were concentrated in several areas – the red-light district around Ste-Catherine and St-Laurent, the areas next to the main train stations, the downtown theatre and nightclub district, and the precincts centred around the working-class commercial streets of Mont-Royal and St-Laurent. In addition, prominent bookmakers and gaming houses also operated close to places that employed large numbers of men, such as the Angus railyards, the munition factories, and the Tramway depot.

While the downtown core was a major area for illegal male leisure activities, an investigation into gambling challenges our understanding of suburbs as only domestic space.[43] Elite gambling clubs catering to a generally male clientele often operated just outside municipal police jurisdictions – a strategy that began in the late 1920s, when the White House Inn operated in Lachine, and continued into the 1940s, when the 'swankiest' gambling club in Montreal attracted patrons to the Mount Royal Bridge Club in the upper-middle-class suburb of Côte-St-Luc. A crackdown in Montreal policing in the 1940s also drove the city's largest and most important dice games – the *barbottes* – to the fringe areas of Côte-St-Luc and Côte-St-Michel. Specially commissioned taxis linked all Montreal gambling districts together through the transportation of clients.[44] The presence of gambling clubs in areas generally associated with family life and respectability prevented any rigid or strict denotation of Montreal's moral geography.

The places associated with illegal gambling shared not only spatial concentration but the common legal pretence of legitimate businesses. The city directory shows fifty-four 'bridge clubs,' fourteen billiard parlours or pool halls, eleven barbershops, eight bowling alleys, and five tobacco stores at addresses where raids took place. These businesses were occasionally even combined, so that cigar stands also had their own pool tables.

In a day and age when men had their hair cut more frequently and cigarettes were more acceptable but as yet not available in food stores, barber and tobacco shops appeared on almost every corner. Their high customer turnover and male clientele made them perfect screens for collecting bets on races. An address on Ste-Catherine ouest, where a bookmaker operated for at least fifteen years, appeared in the city directory as a barbershop. A witness testifying before the provincial Caron Inquiry in 1950 stated that clients entered through the front of a barbershop that led to a larger room upstairs. The shop itself was large enough for three or four chairs but held only one for show. In every city examined, gambling was associated with cigar stands, tobacco shops, and pool halls. Much more conspicuous to police in Canada, but extremely rare, were those that did not have such effective covers. Although a bookmaker in Brantford, Ontario, was finally caught in a local men's beverage room in 1964, he had been running his operation out of a beauty parlour and lingerie shop.[45]

The link between barbershops and a male gambling subculture had been long established in Montreal. In the report of the 1925 citizen's inquiry into municipal policing, Judge Louis Coderre cited the example of a gambling house at the corner of Ste-Catherine and Peel 'camouflaged, and very poorly, as a barber shop.' Coderre continued to draw the connection between betting houses and barbershops and tobacco stores, noting, 'Their doors are open to all, which shows how safely they can be operated.'[46]

Even if barbershops themselves were not the site of illegal gambling, they could be a good source for men looking for information about where to find some 'action.' When reporters for La Presse were seeking a barbotte game, they successfully approached the barber across from the Mount Royal Hotel. These networks went beyond information and could encourage personal relationships. Montreal gambler Harry Ship stated that he had first met some of his later gambling colleagues hanging about the same barbershop on St-Laurent.[47]

A specific barbershop and the type of gambling associated with it usually catered to a particular ethnic, neighbourhood, or class-based clientele. Except for the richest and the poorest clubs, organized commercial gambling could also bring together men from across the class spectrum. Crowded around a barbotte table might be 'businessmen, servicemen, playboys with their girlfriends, clerks, theatre ushers, taxi drivers, workers and so on down the line to just plain rummies.' While Montreal police dismissed accusations about the vast numbers of returned soldiers and working-class family men who lost their pay envelopes in the city's illegal clubs, this denial contradicted frequent depictions. Devotees loved the extreme upward (and downward) mobility associated with the practice. Prominent Montreal gamblers often came from working-class backgrounds and occasionally claimed that they lost everything as quickly as they had gained their wealth. Reports after the murder of prominent gambler Harry Davis dwelled on his impoverished childhood.[48] This unstable world of quick wealth and sudden poverty contrasted with the more rigid conception of status in the respectable world and made cross-class mixing possible, especially for those with money in their pockets.

Gambling could also bring together men across other divisions such as ethnicity and language. Certain clubs catered to specific ethnic groups such as the Jewish clients attracted to the Laurier Bridge Club's pinochle games and the almost exclusively Italian and Syrian clientele of the Montsabre Club on rue St-Denis.[49] These ethnic male enclaves were at least a partial reflection of residence patterns, as particular clubs served neighbourhood men. The homogeneity of these clubs may have also reflected the likelihood of debts being honoured within a distinct community. But, in the light of the multi-ethnic character of Montreal, it is remarkable to see how gambling brought different men together. Male sporting culture in Montreal occasionally mixed together French, English, Jewish, Italian, Black, and Greek men, but rarely the Chinese.

The gambling clubs that served the Chinese were most likely to be segregated, with racism compounded by the isolation of language. In the petitions to establish the Caron Inquiry before 1950, the French- and English-speaking Montreal reformers were strangely silent on Chinese clubs, although they were the most diligently policed in the city. The same situation, with perhaps even less fraternization, appears to have existed in Vancouver, where in clubs outside Chinatown white and Black loggers played together but did not mix with the Chinese gamblers.[50]

Time of day intersected with location to create distinct male space. Locales with a more gender-neutral function such as small groceries, confectionery shops, and lunch counters could be transformed by the hour, the day, and the season. Bookmakers and gambling clubs in the downtown area, which catered to both nightclub clients and daytime employees in offices and small manufacturing, often shared expensive rental space. Bookmakers and their agents would open at ten in the morning and would be busiest between three and six in the afternoon. Bookmakers were most active on Saturdays, which coincided with free time, the racing schedule, and a new pay cheque. In the evenings, *barbotte* or card games would begin after the last race had been run, around eight, and would operate until four or five in the morning.

Daytime betting on horses complemented the hours of small businesses, such as barbershops and taverns, which were supposed to close at ten p.m. However, pool halls and bowling alleys, with their later closing times, and private social clubs, with no time restrictions attached, were ideal for cards and *barbotte*.[51] The around-the-clock facilities available to men show that at least some men were free to move around the city day or night. Specific places could adopt different functions at different times.

Although male sporting culture was still spatially defined in Montreal through the 1940s, it was a world in decline. Steven Riess attributes its demise to the rise of suburbia, as the relocation of many families from the city core interfered with easy access to separate male spaces. He might also have recognized the increased comfort that the domestic sphere offered, as most homes became less crowded, and television brought commercial sports such as hockey into the home. The entrance of larger numbers of women into the paid workforce and public urban space would also have played a major role. By the early 1960s, the Ontario Provincial Police would observe that 'the cigar store and pool room is [sic] vanishing.' Illegal gambling continued to be a male activity, but its space-specific culture diminished as anonymous telephone contacts relayed bets to the suburbs, where bookmakers operated out of ordinary-looking houses.[52]

But what did it mean to create and maintain urban space that excluded women? The persistence of male sporting culture permitted the survival, reproduction, and reinforcement of a particular version of masculinity. Men, and in particular white middle-class men, continued to 'own' the entire city in a way that was not possible for women. Enclaves associated with male sporting culture appeared to be crucial for young men – bachelors – who were learning about masculinity. Bookmakers' establishments, pool rooms, bowling alleys, cigar stands, and taverns allowed them to socialize with other men in an environment removed from the domestic sphere and the pressures of heterosocial leisure activities. In doing so, they strengthened notions of participants' masculinity, as they recreated a network of privilege and power. Although space could be valuable to the marginalized and the oppressed such as Chinese Canadians, those who had power used it effectively to perpetuate their position and preserve a form of masculinity that existed outside the bourgeois ideal. The practice reinforced and celebrated male privilege, aggression, and competitiveness. There were divisions in class, ethnicity, and sexual orientation, but the examination of gambling spaces in one particular city in the 1940s suggests that men with a variety of identities shared the same physical space and a similar male-sporting culture. There were limits to this commonality, as the exclusion of Chinese men reminds us, but placing a bet, staking a hand, or rolling the dice attracted, in the words of Montreal novelist Ted Allan, 'men of various sizes, shapes, odours and auras.'[53]

Conclusion

This image of the wide amalgamation of men into all-male preserves returns us to the core dilemma surrounding masculinity and gambling.

Gambling and the debates of its critics create insight into the dual models of masculinity available to heterosexual men for the first half of the twentieth century. The 'masculine primitive' elicited courage, audacity, and risk taking; the 'Christian gentleman' embodied self-control. Obviously, these were not typically two distinct kinds of men but rather typified the complicated balance that many men lived daily. There was both ambivalence and tension within masculinity, and sheer numbers suggest that most men lived with their feet in both worlds. While the domestic ideal was fiercely upheld in the Canadian Criminal Code, the bachelor sporting culture was recognized in the endemic participation by Canadian men in various forms of illicit gambling, and it was celebrated in popular culture and aided by indifferent policing practices in many communities. Although the argument in this chapter has focused on gambling, it is clear that attitudes towards alcohol, commercial sex, and physical violence reflected the same ambivalence.

The tensions surrounding this paradox also waned not only as a distinct male sporting culture declined, but also as a new ideal emerged for a middle-class man in the 1960s. The most obvious characteristic of this new ideal was a diminished emphasis on breadwinning. This in part responded to a new economic reality in which by 1971 one-third of women in the Canadian workforce were married. If Barbara Ehrenreich is correct when she situates the decline of the male breadwinner ethic in the United States in the 1950s, we can see a corresponding change at that time in the discourse by opponents of gambling about the failure of men to provide for families to a much more general apprehension about gambling and poor citizenship.[54] In the public inquiries that proliferated in both countries after the Second World War, the protection of civil society was of much greater interest than the relationship between men and the domestic sphere. Men were less likely to face the choice between their roles as responsible family men and the allure of a bachelor sporting culture.

CHAPTER FOUR

Bingo, Women, and the Critics

'BINGO-PLAYING MOTHER DENOUNCED FOR GAMBLING FAMILY ALLOW-
ANCE,' screamed the *Montreal Gazette* in October 1945. In a Quebec
Superior Court case for separation and alimony, the judge ruled that
this woman had 'a passion for games of chance. She spends every
Saturday evening in parochial halls and not only risks on bingo sums
of money disproportionate to her means, but also engages her young
daughters in this degrading game.' He ruled that she would be required to leave the family home, live with her brother, and endorse the
newly introduced family allowance cheques over to her husband. A
year later, as part of the same anti-vice campaign, the newspaper re-
counted the fictional tale of Mary, a suburban housewife. Mary had
been wasting the household's income and neglecting her family by
playing bingo in the afternoons. Her husband, a factory worker, came
home one night to find 'children were running the streets, the supper
wasn't ready, and when his wife came home she was without funds
and out of sorts.' The *Gazette* pointed out that while most bingo games
were operated by men, the players were wives and mothers. Fiction
foretold reality when two days later, the director of Montreal's morality
squad extended his anti-vice campaign to include bingo.[1]

In 1950, another Montreal-area newspaper reported the story of a
woman in Ville La Salle whose bingo addiction had led her to spend
the housekeeping money, with the result that her children had neither
sufficient food nor clothing. This unhappy situation had led her poor
veteran husband to alcohol. He kept his job only because of a kind-
hearted boss who knew the situation. A reader claimed to be in a
similar position and to be contemplating suicide.[2]

These vignettes echo the tales told in turn-of-the-century temperance campaigns about homes torn asunder by alcohol. But in the 1940s variants, the perceived threat came not from the husband and father but from the wife and mother. Blame for domestic chaos – neglected or endangered children, scorned household duties, misspent household funds, and an obsessed parent – was placed on women and bingo.

Bingo, with its predominantly female, working-class clientele, was an exception to the male environments associated with most forms of gambling. Today, we are more likely to associate it with senior citizens' clubs, charity fundraising, and church basements than with gambling, but until the revisions to the law in 1969, it was technically a lottery under the Canadian Criminal Code. The criticism of women playing bingo paralleled the critique of male gambling, presenting it as undermining family roles and responsibilities and shattering the work ethic. But, while gambling might weaken men's roles as citizens, bingo harmed women's duties as consumers. The criticisms thus bore specific class and gender values and associations. These prescriptive types of behaviour were determined by dominant mores, but bingo's popularity among women and the criticisms of their participation transcended ethnic, sectarian, and linguistic divisions.

This chapter examines the appeal of bingo to its players from its emergence following the First World War to its legalization in 1969 and analyses the threat that it was thought to pose to women's responsibilities as wives and mothers. While the words of gambling opponents were always generally more visible than those of the gamblers, this was particularly true for bingo. Here the class and gender of the critics reinforced the authority of the law. Bingo appealed particularly to working-class women, while most critics were middle-class men. Moreover, the critics' preoccupation with the threat to women's domestic roles led them to concentrate on married women with children, ignoring the single, separated, and older women who played the game.

The chapter begins by examining bingo's popularity and then turns to the abolitionists, who saw bingo as threatening women's traditional roles as housekeeper-mother-consumer. I then direct special attention to movie operators, who were in direct competition for women's leisure spending and among the most active opponents of the game. The chapter next examines the Halifax crackdown of 1938, which was initiated by movie theatres, and then considers the Catholic church's defence of bingo. I explore the difficulty in enforcing a law with low public support and finally look at the critics' focus in the 1960s on welfare mothers and seniors – a replacement for the earlier attack on bingo-playing mothers.

Bingo was never a single-sex activity, but from its rise after the First World War, it attracted a disproportionate number of working-class women. An observer of Toronto bingo in the 1940s characterized the players as 85 per cent women, likely to be between the ages of thirty and fifty-five, and 'strictly a streetcar crowd.' Bingo provided these women with a safe, social, and affordable activity outside the household. Married, working-class women had few leisure options, and playing bingo combined sociability and excitement with the possibility of obtaining money or consumer goods independent of a male breadwinner.[3] Bingo also mixed leisure and consumption, as it held out the potential of acquiring practical economic benefits. It blurred the boundaries between remuneration, consumption, and leisure and, according to its adversaries, challenged appropriate behaviour and assigned social roles. Thus its opponents argued that bingo undermined women's primary duties as mothers, housewives, and consumers, while its players may have regarded it as reinforcing these same identities.

Attitudes towards bingo embodied the general ambivalence about gambling. The game was usually illegal, but courts found it almost impossible to convict participants. Moreover, players generally considered bingo a perfectly respectable form of leisure and differentiated it from other illegal forms of gambling.[4] Supporters recognized the appeal of chance that it offered, but, since players were not seen to be directly betting against each other, they did not consider it gambling.[5] Bingo's respectability came from at least three sources. First, games were usually not commercial but were organized by volunteers for charitable goals. Second, two of the institutions that drew heavily on bingo as a source of revenue – the Catholic church and the Canadian Legion – were paragons of good citizenship. The fact that they supported and hosted the games in their own facilities made it difficult for many to consider bingo deviant. This was particularly true of church games, which did not serve alcohol and offered the opportunity for multi-generational family outings.

Third, there was the law. Under certain conditions bingo, as a lottery, was legal. The Criminal Code of 1892 permitted lotteries in a charity or religious bazaar when the article being given away was not valued at more than $50 and had been first offered for public sale.[6] The law was later amended to restrict activities to an 'occasional practice' – a loose description, open to varying interpretations and appeals. The result was a great deal of local variance in toleration and practice. Some communities regarded weekly games as occasional, while other restricted games to a monthly schedule. Yet others were preoccupied with the eligibility of any group to conduct a game. In this no-win political situation, there was seldom much direction provided by the provinces, which enforced the federal criminal law. They conducted occasional crackdowns, preceded by widely publicized warnings, since their politicians preferred to pass the unwanted task down the line to the municipality, township, or county.

The Bingo Craze

Forms of bingo can be traced back to China, Italy, and New Orleans. Bingo was introduced to Canadian troops serving overseas during the First World War. Veterans carried the game to Canada, and by 1920 it was being played at small-town agricultural fairs throughout the country. Its popularity grew dramatically, but its novelty is suggested by its various aliases, including Beano, Corn and Card, Housie-Housie, Keno, Lotto, Lucky, Radio, Right, and Tombola. Bingo became a major attraction at special events such as agricultural fairs and service-club carnivals and soon was popularly associated with the Roman Catholic church. Unlike most Protestant churches, the Catholic church did not disapprove of moderate gambling and at the parish level had a tradition of raising funds through draws or raffles.

Although bingo announcements rarely appeared in Toronto's *Catholic Register* during the 1930s, advertisements placed there by the Bingo Supply Company suggest that its readership was a targeted market. Local Catholic parishes, however, advertised games in community newspapers, which were willing to accept the announcements. The importance of bingo to parish social life is evident in Roger Lemelin's novel *Au pied de la pente douce* (1944). In this fictional account, respectable, working-class participants in a Quebec City parish's bingo game exhibited a 'show of reluctance' in the light of the game's illegal status. In contrast, the parish's rougher members were 'delighted with the prospect of a wholesale raid by the police' and encouraged their *curé* to defy the law.[7]

But bingo was not restricted to the Catholic parish hall. In 1935 bingo, described as a revamped version of 'the popular old army game,' took Winnipeg 'by storm,' attracting a mainly female crowd to the city's dance halls. Games in those venues were operated perhaps by private entrepreneurs, such as a forty-six-year-old separated woman, who apparently had no idea of bingo's illegality when she made her unsuccessful bid for a Vancouver municipal licence to operate a bingo hall in 1936.[8]

By 1937, bingo had achieved such national prominence that a BC newspaper proclaimed: 'From coast to coast Canada has gone bingo!' The *Victoria Daily Times* wrote: 'The mah-jong mania of 1924 and the euchre craze of several years ago appear easily shaded by the newer indoor pastime.' This report mentioned Charlottetown, Moncton, Montreal, New Waterford, and Quebec City as thriving bingo centres and claimed that only the civic administrations of Halifax and Saint John were keeping the game under control. Cities such as Hamilton were 'threatened with a bingo game on every corner.' Although the article overlooked the popularity of the game on the prairies and in British Columbia, its presence on the front page of a BC paper suggests local interest.[9] Canadian women had found a new leisure activity.

But there was not universal agreement on the consequences of this game. In February 1937, a delegation from Hamilton, headed by Mayor William Morrison, waited on David A. Croll, Ontario's minister of municipal affairs and social welfare, with a plea for some action to curb the bingo craze and stop the 'charity racketeers' in their city. City council reported that it had 150 further applications for bingo permits and, referring to the prizes, claimed that 'women were making a practice of getting most of their groceries that way.' The provincial attorney general's office estimated that 25,000 Hamiltonians were attending weekly games and that approximately 10 per cent of Ontarians were active participants. Bingo grew throughout the 1930s and the Second World War, and by 1946 one observer estimated that fees and prizes worth tens of thousands of dollars were changing hands nightly at bingo games in Montreal alone, although the slow play kept out male 'real gamblers.'

Despite its widespread presence throughout Canada by the early 1930s, the tremendous popularity of the game seemingly went unnoticed by certain members of the elite. As late as 1935, the game had to be explained to Ontario's deputy attorney general.[10] As the popularity of bingo grew, so did the number of its critics, and their preoccupation was its largely female clientele. Critics concentrated on the way in which bingo distracted women from their roles as mothers, housewives, and consumers.

The thrust of criticism did not remain constant over time, however.

During the 1930s, when the rapid expansion of bingo coincided with economic depression, critics zeroed in on the competition that it posed for disposable income. After the Second World War, in a society anxious to contain women within the household, the anti-bingo discourse shifted to the roles of wives and mothers. In the 1960s, during the expansion of the welfare state and the growth of welfare payments, public concerns focused on bingo-playing 'welfare mothers,' who were said to be 'wasting' public funds. This is not to say that these various criticisms did not overlap or coexist, but the arguments against bingo clearly reflected changes in attitudes about women and society.

Critics on Women as Housekeepers, Mothers, and Consumers

Women who participated in games of chance to supplement household earnings were portrayed by critics not as vulnerable or resourceful but rather as selfish or irresponsible. While a poem in a Canadian labour newspaper might romanticize and celebrate a desperate British woman betting her last 'bob' on the horses, no comparative Canadian characterizations were ever made. Critics stated that a betting woman was much worse than a betting man, since her example had more influence on children. Moreover, the money that she used to play the horses or to gamble was seldom money that she herself had earned but had been entrusted to her care for the operation of the household by a male breadwinner. An editorial in a Montreal suburban newspaper in 1950 stated that, although it did not condone the fast-paced and often high-stakes dice game *barbotte*, it was not as harmful as bingo, for 'it [*barbotte*] attracts, as a general rule, men who, in the great majority of cases, have the means to 'take a chance,' and they are not frequented by women who get the money by devious ways.'[11] These women were allegedly stealing from the household to satisfy their own selfish recreational needs, but the critics' underlying anxiety may have had more to do with women's autonomy and the decline of male control.

Another worry was that women and chance were supposedly a dangerous mix. Women who became 'carried away by speculation' were not, according to one parliamentarian of the 1930s, 'mothers or homebuilders.' In a 1957, an anti-bingo pamphlet published by an American religious group listed the first of five dangers posed by bingo as its tendency to develop into an addiction that could become as serious as alcoholism. A U.S. expert witness who testified before a parliamentary committee in 1954 used the words 'female addicts' and claimed that their number was 'not small.' His testimony was reinforced by the chief of police for Hull, Quebec, who claimed that he had witnessed 'night after night ... mothers of large families playing bingo who never thought of anything else for hours when they were playing and you could see it was a real passion with them; it was something horrible to see.' Critics argued that this obsession distracted women from their proper duties and, as with some male gamblers, offered sexual sublimation. Commentators worried that a passion for bingo, like the radio contests that proliferated after the war, overstimulated and excited women, causing them to lose their capacity for rational thought and suffer nervous exhaustion.[12]

Most criticism, however, dealt with women's neglect of duties as mothers, housekeepers, and consumers. As women sought and found a form of leisure and recreation outside the home, they were particularly vulnerable to the label of negligent mothers and were blamed by some child experts for creating delinquents. Before the bingo craze hit Halifax, juvenile court judge J.J. Hunt wrote in his 1920 annual report that 'there are scores of homes in our City where the father of a family is compelled to be away all day earning a livelihood, and where the mother neglecting her family duties is found too often spending her time in some of our many places of amusement.' These venues were probably not what one might assume – dance halls or movie theatres – but rather the church and fraternal organization 'card socials,' which had prizes that attracted female patrons and whose popularity preceded bingo. A 1926 report claimed that there were Halifax mothers 'who either locked their children up at nights or let them roam the streets,' since all they cared about was getting out and playing cards.[13]

While the stereotype of the negligent mother emerged between the wars, it became more pronounced in the 1940s and 1950s. In 1945, Canadians could laugh along with Bert Pearl of radio's 'Happy Gang,' whose hit song, 'Don't Play Bingo Tonight, Mother, Stay Home with Daddy and Me,' adopted the traditional form of temperance ballads to satirize the effects of bingo on family life. Expert witnesses at the hearings of the Joint Committee on Capital Punishment, Corporal Punishment, and Lotteries in 1955 instead linked working-class mothers playing bingo to male juvenile delinquency. While women were criticized for leaving children alone, they were also remiss if they took their children along to the games. One of the charges against the bingo-playing mother from Montreal mentioned at the opening of this chapter was that she was corrupting her daughters by introducing them to this game. In a working-class Montreal suburb, a leader of a Verdun women's organization lamented the fact that while provincial laws kept young children out of movie theatres, there were no restrictions on bingo games, which were 'dens of iniquity and depravity for the young people. They might every bit as well be admitted to taverns and night clubs with their elders.' In a similar vein, she alleged that the public had responded to 'children suffering from polio, but nothing is done for the children suffering from bingo-playing.' In 1963, a concerned but anonymous Vancouverite wrote to the provincial attorney general about the serious effects that bingo had on the city's children and linked bingo to alcohol. The author, probably a working-class neighbour rather than a middle-class reformer, complained that 'some of the kids at night [were] around at all hours when they should be home in a warm bed [and] when some of the people win they go to the beer parlor and spend it. if they stayed home [they] would be better off and [their] kids would be better off.'[14]

Bingo also affected women's responsibilities as housewives, according to critics. In January 1942, complaints from men who could not keep their wives away from a Friday-night bingo game reached Montreal's mayor. Housework was left undone, they said, and meals were not prepared, as wives left early for evening games in order to secure a preferred seat. Women's role as household financial managers was evident in the criticism that bingo diverted funds from the household. Since bingo offered the potential of combining recreation with remuneration, it was said to be particularly attractive to women trying to balance tight household budgets. In families with no money to spare, claimed the chair of the Delinquent and Crime Division of the Canadian Welfare Council in 1955, 'Even a few dollars a night lost in a bingo game can represent a serious strain on the family budget.' Some critics claimed that money spent at bingo was expended to the detriment of young children, who were not being properly fed or clothed. They lacked watertight shoes and rubber boots.[15]

The combination of women, money, and bingo and its effect on women's role as consumers created bingo's most organized and effective opponents. Scholars such as Reuven and Gabrielle Brenner and Gary Dean Best have noted the connection between the growth in the popularity of bingo in the 1930s and the economic depression of the decade.[16] The game was attractive not only for its entertainment value but because, among poor people, winning served a real material need. At the same time as it appealed to players, the general shortage of disposable income made competition for dollars particularly fierce.

Anti-bingo campaigns could attract a range of small business owners who believed that their enterprises were hurt by the game. Among the supporters of a 1949 anti-bingo campaign in the Montreal working-class suburb of Verdun were local merchants who claimed in the newspaper that housewives spent money on bingo instead of paying their store bills. Storekeepers such as grocers, butchers, bakers, and coal and fuel dealers who issued credit claimed that they were particularly vulnerable. Unpaid milk dealers, the paper observed, continued to deliver milk so that young children would not suffer from their mothers' folly. Incredibly, these merchants claimed that consumer debt did not exist before bingo.[17]

In fact, bingo presents a much more complicated image of household economies. Although the prizes varied, bingo in the 1930s generally offered women such practical rewards as irons, toasters, and groceries.[18] The few bingos that offered cash prizes did not disperse large sums until after the Second World War. Although opponents claimed that bingo undermined women's identification with the domestic sphere, the prizes actually reinforced this connection. Small consumer durables such as appliances held out the prospect of new convenience. Vacuum cleaners, steam irons, and electric sewing machines were beyond the reach of many households, and a ten-pound bag of sugar or a ham may have eased the weekly scramble to make ends meet. Although bingo may have temporarily supplemented an inadequate income in some households, few female players pilfered from household accounts but set aside some leisure income for themselves.

The potential prizes at bingo games made it possible for women to imagine themselves engaging in a level of consumption beyond their immediate means. Opponents, however, did not recognize games as fostering consumerist desires but rather saw them as unfair competition for the retail trade. Butchers and meat cutters perhaps lost business when organizations running games bought poultry wholesale from farmers, thereby circumventing their middleman status, and so they complained. Seasonal prizes of turkeys, ducks, geese, or Easter hams dealt a blow to local markets and led meat-trade organizations in a number of cities to petition their provincial government to enforce the law. In 1939, butchers in one southern Ontario city requested assistance because 'with Easter approaching the city would be flooded with hams given as prizes and butchers will lose all this business, as we did at Christmas via the bingo route.' In London, Ontario, for example, during the 1954 Christmas season, an estimated 3,000 turkeys were given away as bingo prizes.[19] For participants, the allure of luxury festival food was significant. Winners shared their luck with their families, reinforcing their domestic stature, but if they did not win, they at least returned home with good stories of how close they had come.

As long as bingo remained on a relatively small scale, the prizes were directed specifically at women. In the 1950s, with the advent of service-club giant bingos in packed local arenas, the large cash jackpots and car prizes benefited the entire household rather than the bingo-playing woman herself. A bingo operated by the Victoria Kinsmen in October 1957 gave away three cars. Two of the winners were housewives in carless families who did not know how to drive themselves.[20] Before the almost-complete move to cash prizes in the 1960s, bingo prizes, even on a large scale, remained gender-specific. At the monster bingos of the 1950s, consolation prizes became major household appliances such as refrigerators and washing machines. Raymond Charlebois, winner of the grand 'mystery' prize at an Ottawa bingo in 1953 may have been disappointed – he came away with a complete lady's Easter outfit and a return ticket to New York, where he could show off his new clothes in the Easter Parade.[21]

Movies versus Bingo

Unlike other forms of gambling, with their loose coalitions of opponents, bingo players from the 1930s through to the 1950s faced organized movie-theatre operators, who competed with bingo for the patronage of working-class women. In the 1930s, cinema operators weathered a depression and falling weeknight attendance, as former patrons now attended bingo games.[22] They responded by offering more value, as in the introduction of double features and prizes. Here, once again, opponents saw games of chance interfering with fair competition. Some theatres began to offer bingo before the show, but nothing equalled the success of 'bank night.' The copyrighted idea of a former Colorado theatre manager appeared in the winter of 1933, and by 1936 one in every three American theatres had adopted it. Members of the audience would write their names in a large ledger in the lobby, and beside every name would be a ticket. On 'bank night' – usually a slow Monday or Tuesday evening – a numbered ticket was drawn from a barrel on the stage, and the name drawn had three minutes to claim the prize. If the prize went unclaimed, it increased the winnings of the following week's contest.[23] Since participants did not buy specific tickets for the draw, it was difficult to prove 'consideration,' but all Canadian provinces prohibited it, as being a lottery, nearly as soon as it appeared. Like bingo, bank nights were illegal but widely operated. In 1938, Hamilton theatre operators threatened to reintroduce them in retaliation for rampant bingo. In the 1950s, as movie theatres faced not just bingo but also television, they again expanded their attractions. A local rivalry between theatres in rural Manitoba led a cinema in Portage la Prairie to report to police a local drive-in that was offering prescreening bingo. Bank nights re-emerged in the form of 'Foto-Nites,' in which a winner, to claim prize money, had to sell a photo of himself or herself to the theatre – a sale of goods to comply with the law. Test cases before juries in Nova Scotia, Quebec, Ontario, Manitoba, and British Columbia all resulted in verdicts of not guilty, which discouraged further prosecution.[24]

Movie theatres not only tried to harness the appeal of bingo but also lobbied government for close enforcement of the law. The Motion Picture Association of Manitoba, which described itself as 'a branch of the amusement industry which has a great deal of money invested in this country,' was active in the campaign against the Criminal Code amendment of 1925 permitting games of chance at agricultural fairs. The association dismissed the argument that gaming devices were already permitted at church bazaars, calling this practice 'comparatively rare' and arguing that the church bazaar had been 'practically monopolized, since the war, by so-called patriotic organizations whose concept of patriotism does not include concern for the preservation of morals.' In a not-so-veiled attack on the Canadian Legion and the Army and Navy Veterans, the association continued that Anglo-Saxon nations, except 'elements of the population whose moral and intellectual status is on a par with that of bootleggers and thieves,' had come to a consensus that gambling harmed the 'economic life of the community.'[25]

Movie theatres initiated official complaints against other bingo operators. Halifax theatre managers influenced local regulation of bingo. In the spring of 1936, after taking bingo to Halifax twice a year since 1924 as part of his travelling exhibition, Bill Lynch of 'Lynch's Greater Shows' and his concession manager were charged with keeping a common gaming house. Prosecution started after a formal complaint from a provincial constable acting on behalf of the Allied Exhibitors, an association of theatre managers throughout Nova Scotia. It was evident from testimony that 'Housie-Housie' was played widely at Halifax fairs and church bazaars. A defence lawyer pointed out that the association had hired an unemployed policeman to gather information – as someone familiar with the rules of evidence, he could set up the police case, and as an employee of theatre operators, he was motivated by private gain rather than by 'public spirit.'[26] The same lawyer also attempted unsuccessfully to introduce evidence to show that at the time bingo was taking place on the fair grounds, local theatres a few blocks away were illegally giving away bags of groceries to lucky patrons. The two accused were found guilty and received a two-year suspended sentence.

The Halifax Crackdown, 1938

Two years later, in May 1938, when Halifax police began an anti-gambling campaign on behalf of movie-theatre operators that targeted bingo, fans of the game organized in opposition. Crackdowns against bingo were attempted in a number of Canadian cities that spring, but only in Halifax did police close down, at least temporarily, all games. Warnings had been issued two months earlier for bingo parties to cease, but it was not until 10 May 1938 that the mayor ordered police to act, after meeting with a delegation of theatre managers. Immediately after suspension of all Halifax games, players organized to reopen the game and resumed play across the harbour in Dartmouth. Petitions in support of bingo circulated, and both amateur and professional bingo operators met to counter the threat. From Catholic pulpits came sermons arguing the harmlessness of the game.[27]

Letters to the editors of Halifax papers revealed a range of opinion. The most vocal support of police and theatre operators came from Protestant leaders, including the Halifax and Dartmouth Social Service Council and Temperance Alliance. Letters of opposition dominated, since many citizens defended the church bingos as a necessary means of raising money in hard times. A Catholic priest affected by the ban criticized 'the selfishness of people who will take away from poor people a little harmless enjoyment.' He also argued about the inconsistency of a law that permitted gambling in private clubs while prohibiting such activities in church halls and concluded that Halifax would become known as 'the most oppressed city in Canada.' Anger was aimed directly to local theatre operators, and there were reports of crank telephone calls. Other bingo proponents seemed to feel that the game's appeal to older women – 'grandmothers,' in the words of one outraged citizen – ensured its respectability. Thomas Deegan, a professional bingo operator, noted that 'it's not the youngster but the elderly people this ban is striking at.' Arguments about the potential moral danger of bingo were dismissed as inappropriate to this mature group. One week into the ban, newspapers reported between 3,800 and 5,000 names on the pro-bingo petition, and they had identified merchants who had sold prizes to games and thus were in the unusual position of losing money with the bingo blackout.[28]

Newspaper coverage and popular agitation culminated in a protest meeting attended by between six hundred and a thousand people and chaired by the past president of the city's Trades and Labour Council. The press explained that practically every family in the working-class North End was represented in the largely female audience. The 'vigor' of the proceedings could be explained by 'the presence of scores of able women workers for both the Liberal and Conservative parties who for the first time in years found themselves for once on the same platform.'[29] Wally Walper, a Saskatoon-born bricklayer turned yodelling cowboy, opened the meeting. Class politics and spectacle blurred in 'a civic political show of song, speech, and story that must be compared favourably to anything their original opponents were putting on down town.'

Speeches that evening emphasized the conflict in class terms. The stock market and parimutuels were cited as legal forms of gambling catering to the middle class, while workers were denied access to fun. Even a local Catholic parish priest suggested that the ban on bingo was class-based legislation, another of the 'pleasure-suppressing laws that stifle the liberties of the working and poorer classes!'[30] The meeting selected a delegation to wait on the mayor. Half of the deputies were female, and members came also from households previously involved in working-class political or union activity. In Halifax in 1938, working-class women who had not attended secular public meetings since the postwar labour revolt now found themselves fighting for their right to leisure activities.

Canadian women organized politically to protect their bingo just as seriously as opponents sought to prohibit the game. When a Winnipeg newspaper criticized the bingo fad in 1937, scores of people wrote, telephoned, or visited its offices to protest. Said one woman: 'It is the

cheapest and sanest form of amusement for people with limited means.'
When a bilingual Montreal suburban weekly launched an anti-bingo
campaign in 1950, it elicited letters of opposition along with testimo-
nies of support. One woman dismissed charges that bingo interfered
with her duties as a housekeeper, by writing that she was 'a respectable
housewife, and run my home carefully and efficiently, and nobody
suffers by my attendance at an occasional game of bingo.' Another
rejected the linking of bingo and psychological addiction, noting that in
her experience women did not devote as much time to bingo as husbands and fathers spent in taverns. Women on the Halifax delegation
used their position as mothers to argue for the harmlessness of the
pastime: 'If we, as mothers of the young men and women attending
these games thought it harmful, do you think we would permit our
children to attend them? ... Of course not. But knowing Bingo to be a
harmless and amusing way of spending an evening we heartily support it. We have attended Bingo games for years. We have never seen
any rowdyism nor are drunks permitted ... which is more than can be
said of many other social gatherings.' According to this spokeswoman,
bingo was a more respectable form of entertainment than other forms
of commercial leisure.[31]

Bingo and the Catholic Church

The respectability of bingo was open to debate. Certainly part of
the complexity of this issue was the game's close association with the
Roman Catholic church. Thus bingo tapped into the Protestant–
Catholic tensions that existed in most Canadian communities and which
I explore further in the next chapter. While anti-bingo campaigns had
the support of the Protestant churches, the most powerful ally of the
Halifax pro-bingo lobby in 1938 turned out to be Catholic Archbishop
John T. McNally. McNally criticized authorities for their failure to distinguish between 'gambling and innocent amusement,' and lambasted
theatre operators whose entertainments were 'not always so innocent.'
He also faulted the unnamed but presumably Protestant 'paid agita-
tors' who were 'nothing more than privateers in the realm of theological grace.' In an address to the Canadian Catholic Students Mission, he
defended bingo as a 'benefit to the individual as well as the community. They gather people together in a spirit of peace and amity. They
do good in building up a community spirit.'[32]

The support that Halifax bingo received from local church hierarchy was not consistent with the general position of the top ranks of Canada's Roman Catholic church. Church authority reinforced Canada's criminal law when the hierarchy in Quebec joined in the attempt to close bingo in the province in 1946. In September 1946, Montreal city prosecutor Pax Plante approached and received the support of Archbishop Joseph Charbonneau and the archdiocese's director of Catholic Action. At the time, forty-eight Catholic churches in the city were running regular bingo games. All churches were warned that their games would be raided the following Thursday, and the two games that none the less opened that night closed when officers arrived.[33]

On 29 January 1951, Charbonneau's successor, Paul-Émile Léger, forbade attendance at, and the organizing of, bingo games: 'L'Eglise n'est pas une organisation financière, encore moins une école du jeu.'[34] The arguments in his pastoral letter echoed positions stated by Mgr Paul Bruchési in 1898 and by Mgr Georges Gauthier in 1922. Two years later, in March 1953, Léger again criticized bingo: 'It is well known that the people who make a practice of attending these games lose their sense of responsibility and neglect their duties. Thus mothers neglect their household duties to attend the bingo games where they think they will find fortune, and children who become habituated to making their living by depending on games of chance will not later accept the responsibility of earning their living by serious work.'[35] Léger embraced contemporary secular rhetoric, drawing on the connection between bingo and degradation of women and the threat that it posed to family life.

Bingo remained contentious within the Catholic church in the 1950s. In 1958, Toronto's Catholic churches closed their bingo games in downtown working-class parishes.[36] The Canadian church's stance on bingo divided the hierarchy from local parishes, and bingo, challenged the upper echelons' ability to control their members.

Bingo and the Law

The greatest obstacle to bingo's reputation was its inclusion in the Canadian Criminal Code. The opponents of bingo, though a minority of the total population, had sufficient clout to dissuade politicians from supporting any liberalization of the law. Massachusetts separated bingo from the legal definition of a lottery in 1931 and decriminalized it, although another forty years passed before lotteries lost their illegal status in the state.[37] The lack of regional flexibility in Canadian criminal law meant that local variations in attitudes could not affect legal practice. Policing bingo proved challenging, since the law often conflicted with community values.

Certainly the strong popularity of bingo inhibited prosecution of players and operators in most communities. Bingo was an indictable offence, and so the accused could (and usually did) select jury trial. In most places a jury would never convict. In April 1953, the Manitoba attorney general's department arranged with the provincial president of the Canadian Legion to cover all costs and take a test case on bingo to the Manitoba Court of Appeal. Their mutual goal was to win a ruling before the Supreme Court of Canada that would force the federal Department of Justice to take a stand or amend the Criminal Code.[38] A giant bingo was staged, charges were laid, and at the end of the ensuing trial the judge made the strongest charge of his career to the jury for conviction. After ten minutes, the jury returned with a verdict of not guilty. This discouraging response led the Crown to drop any plans for further appeal. At this point, though it was never publicly stated, Manitoba made an informal agreement with newspapers, radio stations, and other interested persons that they would not advertise bingo as such, and in return the province would halt prosecutions and stop interfering with charitable bingo.[39]

During the Second World War and afterwards, bingo's popularity continued to expand as it became institutionalized in the very communities that had fought it in the late 1930s. In Toronto, Maple Leaf Gardens opened to bingo in November 1940 with fortnightly games operated by Frenchy Dix and Sonny Higgins, who owned the Toronto Bazaar and Novelty Shop – the largest bingo supplier to the Canadian market.[40] With husbands and sons away, women were free to attend evening games, and the law became overlooked as groups raising money for worthy wartime causes received great latitude.

With the end of the war, the flagrant disregard for the law became difficult to ignore, and bingo was included in an interprovincial agreement to enforce the law that went into effect for lotteries starting 1 January 1946. Ambiguity was still present, however, as bingo games could operate occasionally under the aegis of *bona fide* charities or religious organizations, but private social clubs could admit members only under a very restricted schedule of fees.

However, even this new, clearer policy was difficult to enforce. In Ottawa, the chairman of the local Kinsman Club's bazaar committee in 1946, a well-known businessman, was charged with operating a gaming house after a nightly bingo held during the week of its carnival. Ottawa police maintained that daily games contravened the law. In an attempt to show that the law was equally enforced for prominent citizens as for others, the local businessman was fined $10,000 and costs, only to have the conviction quashed. Reflecting the lack of a consensus or what the law permitted, other Ottawa service clubs such as Kiwanis and Rotary did not participate in any bingos until the mid-1950s.[41]

Vancouver had almost annual crackdowns on bingo between 1948 and 1953. Yet in May 1953, the *Vancouver Sun* reported that bingo was a $500,000 industry in the city. Bingo had 'gone respectable – or at least as respectable as any such game can be under the Canadian criminal law,' and thousands of Vancouverites, mostly middle-aged or older, who would never frequent a racetrack or a 'backroom dice table,' were regular patrons. Two years later the *Sun* estimated that bingo had grown to a $2-million-a-year business. The game's popularity, which observers claimed attracted eight or nine women for every man, continued to grow, so that in the mid-1950s the National Hockey League schedule had to be coordinated with the occasional mammoth bingo game held at Maple Leaf Gardens in Toronto.[42]

Frustrated police and politicians who failed in securing the co-operation of the courts sometimes turned to local by-laws to curb bingo. Vancouver used fire regulations to shut down some of the city's largest bingo games when it introduced by-laws that required operators to keep a distance of eight feet between the tables, forcing them to reduce the number of patrons. Vancouver also resorted to more direct methods. In August 1958, a surprise raid on a private bingo club netted 700 players and instigated a test case. The Cordial Club's charter was cancelled, and two men and the company that they operated were fined a total of $16,000 for keeping a gaming house, because the association was not deemed to be a *bona fide* club. Unable to stop bingo, British Columbia eventually began taxing it. In May 1957, its Social Credit government instituted a 10 per cent amusement tax on the revenue of all bingo games.[43]

Welfare Mothers and Seniors

With the ever-increasing popularity of bingo in the 1950s and 1960s, the opposition concentrated on two categories of players. The modern version of the negligent bingo-playing mother was likely to be a welfare mother or a poor, lonely old woman. A special report written by North Bay's chief of police for the Royal Canadian Mounted Police in 1962 questioned the source of the money spent on bingo. The document estimated that it cost $5 for an evening of bingo in North Bay and that most people who attended belonged to 'the working classes ... to whom $5 is still the $5 that buys good whole milk and nourishing food so necessary for growing healthy children.' The writer then asked, 'How much of it comes out of city welfare? What percentage of family allowance cheques finds its way into the bingo coffers and how much of the unemployment insurance fund flows down the bingo drain?'[44] Reflecting the financial difficulties within Quebec's Roman Catholic church, in May 1970 seventy-eight Montreal parishes held weekly bingo games. Church officials admitted that it was a scandal that some of the players were welfare recipients, in effect using public funds to play bingo, but they argued that the greater scandal was poverty in such a wealthy society. The director of the Quebec Family Planning Centre defended the right of poor women to play bingo, since they were denied access to the drinking and sporting culture that offered an escape for men. The women had 'little time to themselves and little money. The parish bingo is a good way of getting away from their problems for a little while, and of buying a little hope.'[45]

Seniors who chose bingo were also open to criticism. In an older community, Victoria's chief constable reported in 1966 that 90 per cent of bingo patrons in this city were senior citizens. A survey at one of Vancouver's largest bingo halls in 1963 found that among the 500 people who attended each game the average age was sixty-five and that a quarter of patrons lived alone. With attention focused on this group, there came new admonitions. The 5,000 subscribers to Vancouver's *Bingo News* were probably not impressed when their paper reported in January 1970 that British Columbia's attorney general felt 'quite sorry for the few people who are driven to bingo games by a weakness or sheer loneliness.' A British Columbian protested the closure of bingo games, arguing that the elderly were no longer interested in sex but did enjoy a good game of bingo 'and a chat with friends over a cup of coffee.'[46]

It is here that we finally reach the motivation of bingo's devoted participants. Bingo games provided a safe social space removed from the household. Most often, this space was predominantly female. In 1936, female residents of Vancouver's east end objected to a regular bingo 'because of the number of men who frequent the games and the amount of smoking that is done.' These women believed that the solution lay in the establishment of their own game.[47] In Halifax, where, as we saw above, women had become politically active to defend their favourite pastime, the operator of a private bingo hall claimed that the 200 women who attended twice a week liked to get together and talk. The social dimension of bingo was crucial. In advertisements that appeared in Vancouver's *Bingo News* in August 1969, each of three bingo games claimed to be the 'Friendliest Bingo in Town.' The social aspect of the game helps explain its enduring popularity. Ottawa observers noted in the 1950s that bingo was the 'only public social activity ... outside of eating and drinking – that has not only survived the onslaught of television but effectively fights back.'[48]

Conclusion

Bingo served as a leisure opportunity for working-class women. However, critics argued that bingo playing threatened women's primary roles and responsibilities as mothers, housekeepers, and consumers. In the period before cash prizes, bingo circumvented normal consumer purchases. Ironically, the domestic prizes may have reinforced women's traditional roles and ties to the home. The participants valued what they believed was a respectable leisure activity, in a safe female space, which might reap them useful material rewards or at least pay for itself.

Women exhibited the same desire for 'chance' and for same-sex leisure as men. An evening at the parish or legion hall may have taken clients from theatre operators, but it provided a pleasant escape from domestic responsibilities and the chance to go home with groceries, toasters, washing machines, cars, or perhaps sufficient money to pay off household debts. While its middle-class, largely male critics painted clichéd depictions of obsessed women who neglected their responsibilities and wasted household resources, the reality experienced by the largely female working-class patrons focused on social interaction. Gossiping, meeting new people, maintaining old friendships, and celebrating prizes were all part of the game. Despite the ambiguity of the Criminal Code and the criticism of those who opposed bingo on moral or fiscal grounds, the women players themselves displayed extraordinary tenacity and commitment to the pursuit of the pleasures that bingo offered.

CHAPTER FIVE

Gambling 'Others': Race, Ethnicity, and Religion

Current studies estimate that the Australians, followed by the British, spend more on gambling per capita than any other nation in the world, yet for the first half of the twentieth century the opponents of gambling in Canada associated the activity with other ethnic or religious minorities. According to the stereotypes of this largely Euro-American, Protestant group, Chinese gambled; Jews gambled; Catholics gambled. Aboriginal Canadians, while perhaps overpoliced, were invisible in the public discourse about gambling. The association of certain ethnic, racial, or religious groups with gambling, and how this connection evolved, illuminate both the practice of gambling and its meaning. Racial or religious stereotypes and prejudices played a role and defined the very act of gambling. This racialized understanding was often intertwined with and reinforced by parallel associations of problematic gambling with gender and class. Accounts of gamblers in the period after the First World War are replete with examples of aliases for working-class men such as 'Danny the Greek,' 'Jew Jake,' and 'Chinaman John.' These links were so strong in some people's minds that they identified specific ethnic communities with particular gaming operations, such as Chinese lotteries and Jewish bookmaking.[1]

The prejudice of dominant groups shaped what they expected to see. Critics of gambling believed that groups outside their community were the 'problem' gamblers, overlooking the presence of Anglo-Protestant and French Catholic gamblers. For English-speaking Protestant critics in particular, this distorted focus helped them to explain the popularity of gambling – 'others' were the culprits – without having to address the ambivalence within their own culture. This chapter examines both the experience of gambling in minority communities and its meaning for these communities and for the dominant culture. Reflecting available sources and demographics, minorities are usually defined by the Anglo-Protestant majority. But the linking of gambling with 'others' was not unique to this majority. Definitions of problem gambling in Montreal, articulated by the local French Catholic majority, led to fervent policing of Chinese gambling and disproportionate attention to Jewish gamblers. Gamblers from minority communities were visible in part because they were different, and preconceptions about specific cultural traditions could heighten their distinctiveness. For example, moderate gambling played a role in Chinese society, although the commercialized leisure of North America transformed it. Finally, gambling, as part of a complex illicit economy, often had an economic role in marginal ethnic communities, allowing some individuals to make money when racism or anti-Semitism barred other avenues.

There is a problem of historical definitions in discussions of subordinated groups within Canadian society. Ethnicity and sect, or the older words 'colour and creed,' independently and in combination created hierarchies of marginality. Canadian historians have examined ethnic relations, but their insights have sometimes been shaped by present-day racism and a secular society. As a result, they have often ignored the central division for the first part of the twentieth century – Catholic–Protestant. Although post-1945 immigration made Catholics the largest group by 1971, Protestant culture remained the principal force in national institutions and morality legislation. Protestant suspicions of Catholicism permeated political issues such as Quebec's role and future, education, and immigration, as well as every moral question that politicians and the legal system faced. Within this powerful sectarian division, ethnicity and race further increase the number of categories that the Anglo-Celtic Protestant population used to distinguish itself from others. This differentiation did not plot neatly along any single continuum, and only 'others' encompasses all these ethnic, racial, and sectarian communities.

All ethnic groups, of course, were socially and historically constructed, and no group was internally homogeneous. Commonality emerged as outsiders defined and categorized individuals and as marginal communities forged new identities to overcome challenges imposed by the dominant group.[2] In this manner, traditional differences in origins, such as northern and southern Italy, diminished as immigrants to Canada became identified simply as 'Italians.' Although 'Americanness' could and did combine in Canada with other ethnic identities such as

African, Jewish, and Italian, many Canadians ascribed to 'Americans' a collective 'materialist nature' or character. The depiction of communities also overlapped with other attributes such as class, marital status, and gender. In some immigrant communities, for instance, the predominance of single men shaped leisure activities and outsiders' perceptions of the group. The racialized discourses of gambling were concurrent with and reinforced other arguments about gender and class that connected the problem of gambling to men and workers.

Moral questions did not divide society neatly by class, religion, language, gender, ethnicity, or region, but the prominent assumption was that they did. Codes of morality had distinct cultural roots and histories, and the criminalization of gambling reflected dominant Protestant liberal attitudes towards labour, rationality, access to property, and just remuneration. English-speaking Protestants (and less commonly French Catholics) who opposed gambling therefore used this governing moral code as testimony to their own ethical superiority as they elevated themselves above people who contravened their rules. The presence of gambling and betting practices among marginalized groups confirmed dominant prejudices, as it heightened the critics' perception of difference when these 'others' failed to live up to their culturally specific middle-class ideal. While the majority of Anglo-Protestant Canadians held some ambivalence towards this ideal, as evident in their own gambling, other groups rejected it. Many Chinese, Jewish, and African Canadians did not share the same prohibitions against gambling, in part because they had less vested in the value system that kept them on the periphery.

Throughout the first half of the twentieth century, one strain of the anti-gambling argument echoed nineteenth-century climatic determinism. Nations with cool, rational, northern, Protestant temperaments did not condone gambling.[3] Gambling and lotteries were characteristic of 'less civilized' or 'less developed' countries – indirect references to southern and particularly Latin cultures. When a Vancouver newspaper argued against the introduction of a state-run lottery in the 1930s, it dismissed government exploitation of the gambling instinct of its citizens as uncharacteristic of 'civilized' governments. Similarly, Senator George E. Foster argued against government-run lotteries, since they offered no 'advantage ... to the civilized as against the uncivilized man' and rejected 'all judgement, all reason, all experience, all that has accompanied the march of humans from the jungle to the twentieth-century civilization.' Foster concluded that lotteries transgressed the rational and moral evolution of mankind.[4] His notion of the 'moral evolution of mankind' rested on merit and rationality, and his emphasis on civilization reinforced ideas about racial progress. Critics attributed superstition, ignorance, and the general lack of control of some primitive gambling instinct to specific groups that gambled. In 1927 a Manitoba lobbyist, on behalf of local theatre owners, wrote the federal minister of justice (a francophone) to point out that 'Anglo-Saxon countries' such as Canada traditionally prohibited gambling. He stressed 'the cool, reasoning elements of the nation ... to overcome the self-interest of those very considerable elements of the population whose moral and intellectual status is on a par with that of bootleggers and thieves.'[5] The emphasis on reserved, rational, and civilized behaviour could serve as a not-so-subtle attack on French Canadians and on the Roman Catholic church. The English-speaking Protestant opponents of gambling regarded relaxed attitudes among Quebec's political and clerical elites to gambling as evidence of the lack of individual self-regulation and self-control within Catholicism. As we saw above, francophone Quebec's generally more permissive attitude towards moderate gambling was not ubiquitous, and the pronouncements of the upper echelons of the Catholic hierarchy often resembles those of their Protestant counterparts.

In the moral hierarchy created by those with a British Protestant or a French Catholic background, each was respectively at the top of its pyramid, and both linked criminality with other groups. In 1953, American sociologist Daniel Bell argued that this stereotype had a basis in at least the U.S. experience, since a succession of ethnic groups had used crime as a lower rung on the social ladder.[6] The frequency with which ethnic minorities operated gambling establishments related to their general harnessing of available entrepreneurial opportunities. Gambling operations were 'illicit enterprises' that coincided with and occasionally complemented other independent entrepreneurial activities such as keeping shop and operating a café or pool hall. Since racism and anti-Semitism restricted access to the labour market, legal and illegal enterprises offered a strategy for groups shut out of legitimate avenues for upward mobility.[7]

Men who habituated or ran commercial gambling establishments could mix socially with others from different backgrounds, but most small-scale gambling took place among men with a similar background. Sociologists in the 1960s observed that most gambling in Toronto's downtown working-class 'Lower Ward' occurred within specific ethnic and racial groups.[8] This homogeneous expression of leisure was fos-

tered by ethnic neighbourhoods, food, and language and by the likelihood of some community pressure to honour debts or dispense winnings. Conversely, the larger operations such as the organizations that
controlled *barbotte* and betting in Montreal involved men from a wide
variety of backgrounds. Although the largest barrier was always between any group and the Chinese, the potential for profits during the
Second World War led to the creation of temporary syndicates involving lotteries described as 'white, black and chinese.'[9] But even the most
segregated Chinese club was never completely isolated from the larger
community. There were almost constant allegations that operators were
involved in paying protection money to police and local politicians. In
Montreal during the 1940s, both the *Herald* and the *Star* alleged that
Alderman Frank Hanley received money from Chinese lotteries. Vancouver Mayor Lyle Telford in 1939 accused Chinese lottery operators of
joining together with Italian bootleggers and English bookmakers and
attempting to bribe him with a payment of $1,000 to 'lay off and let
things continue as they are.'[10] Given allegations of direct political interference into local policing, the Chinese clubs could not be regarded as
separate worlds unto themselves.

In this chapter I look first at the role of race and ethnicity, next at
three case studies – Americans, Jewish Montreal, and Chinese Canadians – and finally at the role of religion in Catholic and Protestant
attitudes to gambling.

Race and Ethnicity

Racialized Stereotypes

Most contemporaries, however, failed to appreciate this environmental
perspective and adopted a more racial understanding of social behaviour. In this racialist typology, which linked character to ethnicity, no
group was more closely associated with gambling than the Chinese.
Comments from friends and foes of that community linked many forms
of gambling with 'the distinctive traits of the Chinese,' although Kay
Anderson reminds us that Chinese Canadians were also associated
with drug addiction, prostitution, slavery in women, licentiousness,
and more generally 'crime.' Some observers claimed that gamblers
were exhausted after a day's work and resorted to opium and cocaine
to revitalize themselves for their gambling 'mania.'[11] The declaration
that gambling was 'in the blood' was not restricted to Chinese Canadi-

ans. In 1928, a Vancouver lawyer, while defending his Chinese clients, stated that 'black people's natural inclination to gamble was as strong as that of Chinese people.'[12]

Attitudes that connected specific ethnic groups to gambling changed over time, reflecting general preoccupations and prejudices. Racism and nativism could be heightened, for example, by political and security concerns in wartime. During the Second World War, when Vancouver police were instructed to enforce the law on bookmaking, the mayor couched his instructions in the language of wartime xenophobia. Accordingly, he saw 'no reason why offenders of alien enemy extraction should not be made to adhere to the very letter of the law, and a glance at the city's criminal records seem to indicate that many offenders in respect to boot-legging and book-making belong to that class.' He proposed that police padlock their premises after the third conviction, since 'they are mostly enemy aliens anyway.'[13]

'Others' were usually blamed for all serious gambling problems. An undercover policeman sent into a northwestern Ontario town during the First World War claimed that Anglo-Protestants could not participate in any of the town's games, since all the 'gambling is done among the French and foreign population, and unless you are one of these you have no chance of having a game.' Conversely, a retired francophone Montreal bookmaker, Joseph Tremblay, claimed that all of his best clients during the Second World War were Scottish and English. Along similar lines, in the 1940s the problem in Montreal was so serious that gambling was present even in French-Canadian residential districts and was not just an 'industrial' or 'cosmopolitan' issue.[14] 'Industrial' and 'cosmopolitan' were code for class and ethnicity. The tendency for critics to see gambling in relation to 'others' seriously hampered their ability to co-ordinate their actions. The failure in Montreal to create a multi-ethnic anti-gambling coalition is one example from the 1950s. Despite some co-operation immediately after the Second World War, the French Catholic Comité de Moralité publique failed to create alliances with English-language service clubs and to involve the Canadian Jewish Congress in its deliberations.[15] The ethnic lens that shaped opponents' understanding of gambling made cross-ethnic alliances unusual if not impossible.

A lone voice in linking ethnic or racial characteristics with non-dominant groups was J.R. Mutchmor, secretary 1936–62 of the United Church's Board of Evangelism and Social Service and the nation's most prominent critic of gambling. In his memoirs, he described Canadians as essentially a 'pioneer people,' subject to the 'extremes of climate,' who, as a result, 'work hard, play hard, fight hard, drink and gamble hard.'[16] This atypical perspective, which held 'Canadians' as more prone to gambling than other nationalities, reflected Mutchmor's personal, lifelong avocation of addressing 'evils' within the mainstream.

While critics, except Mutchmor, tended to distance their own communities from gambling practices, supporters often embraced gambling as part of their ethnic essence. The magazine *Saturday Night*, a constant supporter of more liberal gaming laws for the elite, noted in 1922 that 'the Anglo-Saxon temperament' would independently perpetuate betting, regardless of its legal status. Ten years later, after British authorities had clamped down on the Irish Sweepstakes, the same magazine's editorial expressed pride in the fact that the British people refused to obey the law against lotteries.[17] When gambling supporters vaunted people's refusal to obey an unjust law, they spoke to the tension between individualism and social regulation in a liberal democracy. Hence the Anglo-Saxon majority's 'independent' stance, as influenced by libertarian beliefs. The conflict between individual autonomy and social order did not pose a similar dilemma vis-à-vis minority groups.

Ethnicity and Policing

An agenda of social order was clear in the policing of ethnic minorities, especially those that were most visible in their differences from majority populations. For example, Asian visibility and anti-Asian sentiments led to careful policing and regulation of Chinese clubs across the country. Official reports in both Toronto and Vancouver showed that most gambling prosecutions were directed at Chinese Canadians, notwithstanding the relatively small numbers. Similarly, almost all raids by the Quebec Provincial Police on Montreal gambling houses in the 1930s and early 1940s took place in Chinatown. Indeed the city was otherwise wide open for gambling. In the first six months of 1945, even before a serious police crackdown on Chinese gambling, 71 per cent of all men charged with keeping a betting or gambling house and 43 per cent of all gambling 'found-ins' were Chinese – and there were fewer than 2,000 Chinese on the Island of Montreal.[18] Moreover, gambling in Montreal's Chinatown almost disappeared completely after police instituted a policy in July 1945 whereby they took any men caught in raids of Chinese clubs to police headquarters, verified their identities, and then held them overnight before being releasing them on bail. In case of all other raids, found-ins – usually hired by operators to be caught in planned raids – received bail on the spot and, after providing false names, would forfeit the bail (provided by the club owner or bookmaker) and evade any conviction. In Winnipeg, the police offered 'foreign' fictitious names to 'members of leading families' who were caught in a poker raid, while those 'without any particular standing in the community' found their surnames published in local newspapers.[19]

Ethnic gamblers' also posed specific challenges to authorities. Racism meant that Canadian police forces did not hire Chinese Canadians – or members of other ethnic minorities such as Jews, or Italians – and therefore police generally lacked language skills of or cultural bonds with the minority groups under surveillance. This was in direct contrast to the male sporting culture that police shared with the 'white' gamblers whom they raided. Police forces occasionally responded to this lacuna by hiring Chinese informers to gain inconspicuous access to Chinese-only establishments. But hiring casual assistance could also bring problems. Quebec Provincial Police in the 1940s found it impossible to procure co-operative witnesses or honest court translators who spoke both Chinese and either English or French because of physical threats and bribes from Chinese gambling operators. Left to their own resources, the police force failed. In 1946, the Montreal force lost cases despite *prima facie* evidence because investigators were unable to speak Chinese, to identify the keepers, or to describe accurately what they claimed to be gambling games.[20] Thereafter, the city's gambling squad took special lessons in Chinese games, with no obvious changes in policing strategies.

Three Case Studies

Americans

In 1950, in a poll by the Canadian Institute of Public Opinion, four out of five people admitted that they gambled in some form – a level of participation that surpassed comparable U.S. surveys.[21] Rampant rates of gambling among Canadians conflicted with public rhetoric that associated gambling with American-style materialism. Some Americans imported organized professional gambling to Canada. Indeed, they played a major role in Canadian racetracks after their own facilities were closed by reformers at the beginning of the twentieth century.

The introduction of anti-gambling legislation in the northern United States after 1895 pushed horsemen, bookmakers, racetrack entrepreneurs, and their money north to Canadian tracks.[22] The Americans, usually in partnerships with established Canadian horsemen, constructed and expanded racetracks in the border cities. By 1911, only six U.S. states permitted horse racing, and a deprived clientele travelled north to patronize Canadian tracks.

Thereafter moral reformers added Americanism to their arsenal of gambling evils. Even E. King Dodds, a veteran of the Canadian track, admitted that there had been an influx 'into Canada of a class of owners of an undesirable kind, many of them owning a few cheap animals and in the game solely for the purpose of making money whether by fair means or foul.' Dodds, however, denied that the problem was Americans in general and found it 'directly traceable to the fact that a low class of Jew gamblers have, during the past few years, invaded the ring and may be said to practically control it.' Thus he isolated U.S. Jews from 'respectable Americans' and lumped them together with prominent Jewish-Canadian gamblers, such as Abram M. Orpen of Toronto, who operated several tracks in southern Ontario. In the 1920s, other Americans, were suspected of interfering with Canadian domestic politics as individuals 'with immense influence.' Americans, not the Canadian-owned associations, lobbied the Ontario government for decreased tax rates. As we saw above, sometimes 'Americanness' could overlap with and reinforce other ethnic categories, such as Jewish American and African American. The 150 to 300 African Americans who arrived in Montreal every summer for the racing season in the 1920s were dismissed by the local Black community as 'the lawless element.'[23]

That perception was consistent with the observation of other Canadian critics that gambling came from 'South of the Border.' Sometimes this was meant quite literally, referring to the patrons of racetracks from Detroit and Buffalo who travelled to Windsor or Fort Erie for a day at the races or to the importation of U.S. manufactured slot machines.[24] Haligonians, however, blamed Montreal for the distribution of slot machines within Canada. More influential and menacing were the U.S. criminal syndicates, which redirected some of their resources into gambling-related enterprises at the end of U.S. prohibition in 1933, when bootlegging lost its enormous profits.

By the end of the Second World War, many Canadians linked American criminals with gambling in their own country. The article 'A Breakdown in Morals' in *Saturday Night* in 1951 noted that Canadians were in danger of importing from the United States more than consumer goods and a commercial culture, but also 'some of the easy cynicism and indifference to corruption of that great neighbour to the south.' The writer continued that Canadians had been shocked by a U.S. Senate committee investigating organized crime, which uncovered the central role of gambling in providing the criminals with cash. He concluded that its findings had 'an impact nearly as great here as in their native country.'[25]

This U.S. inquiry strongly influenced its Canadian counterparts in the early 1950s. In Montreal, the French Catholic prosecutors Pax Plante and Jean Drapeau were determined to make connections between Montreal bookmakers and Americans. According to Plante, the criminal organization was not indigenous but 'streams from the States.' It was not a Canadian or provincial affair, but emerged from 'the underworld in the United States and ... could only live as a brain of the underworld.'[26] Plante saw the same pattern as opponents of racetracks had noted after the First World War. He believed that Canadians were being contaminated by American criminals as they exported their activities in response to domestic investigations. In Montreal Plante concluded (with some reason, as I show in the next chapter), the city was under U.S. criminal influence. In other places, the battle against American corruption was more cultural than directed at specific individuals. While Plante blamed the Americans for Montreal's problems, BC Attorney General Gordon Wismer assured residents of his province that he would remain vigilant in enforcing the law so that Vancouver would never become a 'second Reno.'[27] Thus the United States and Americans served as moral scapegoats for Canadian problems and as a constant warning.

Jewish Montreal

Plante's understanding of the particular ethnic links that connected U.S. organized crime to the local situation in Montreal highlighted the presence of the city's eastern European Jews in gambling, especially in bookmaking. This unsavoury reputation followed from the dramatic murders of Charlie Feigenbaum in 1934 and of Harry Davis in 1946 and from the general connection between gambling and the city's highly visible night life.[28]

The ownership of some of Montreal's most famous nightclubs, theatres, and restaurants, such as the Tic Toc, the Gayety, the Hawaiian

Lounge, and Ruby Foo's, overlapped with the local Jewish gambling establishment. There could be no better example of conspicuous behaviour than Harry Ship, who went beyond the brazen practice of distributing thousands of school-bus yellow pencils embossed with telephone numbers that accepted bets to sponsoring his own junior baseball team, 'the Shipmates.'[29] Ship was further immortalized in Mordecai Richler's novel *The Apprenticeship of Duddy Kravitz* in the fictional character of Jerry Dingleman, the Boy Wonder. The fiction of Mordecai Richler and Ted Allan provides rich anecdotal evidence of bookmaking in Montreal's Jewish community, a perception reinforced by the many bookmakers forced to testify during the four years of hearings for the Caron Inquiry. Jewish witnesses can be clearly identified in transcripts, as they swore oaths on copies of the Old Testament.

As in other communities, gambling was by no means accepted throughout the Jewish community, nor was the ethnic stereotype linking Jews and gambling ubiquitous. In 1939, a member of Parliament challenged that stereotype while reinforcing another, when he claimed that Canadians did not 'find many Hebrews buying sweepstake tickets, because they know what is good and bad business.' Other commentators, however, upheld the stereotypical Jew as gambler 'as indisputable social fact.'[30]

There was no strict prohibition within Jewish tradition on moderate gambling, but this did not ensure its complete acceptability. There was certainly anxiety over criminal activity, but this could conflict with ethnic-based admiration for success in an anti-Semitic environment. This pride expressed by some, usually working-class, Jews resembled the more general celebration of the gangster as a 'folk hero' during the Depression.[31]

In a 1950 article, 'What Is a Jew Like?,' in the *Canadian Jewish Chronicle*, David Schwartz noted the existence of Jewish gangsters, in which he took no pride. Similarly, in the 1940s, men with what appear to be Jewish surnames, such as Rosenzweig, were among those who issued complaints against neighbours and co-workers in the predominantly Jewish Montreal neighbourhood of Mile End for participating in illegal card games. This range of attitudes may have been connected to factors as varied as class, notions of respectability, and place of origin. For example, a tradition of sporting culture that had existed in Odessa in Ukraine may have been perpetuated by individuals such as Montreal professional gambler Eddy Baker.[32] Some Jewish Montreal gamblers achieved upward mobility through their activities. The rigid bounda-

ries between legal and illicit businesses disappeared as gamblers rein-
vested their profits in lawful enterprises, such as theatres, real estate,
and restaurants, thereby gaining local celebrity and legitimate income.[33]

Jewish connections to gambling could provide fodder for French-
Canadian anti-Semitism. *Le Patriote*, the journal of Adrien Arcand's
fascist National Christian Social Party, claimed that every time organized crime was discovered, the kingpin was always a Jew.[34] The
Montreal Yiddish newspaper the *Keneder Adler* responded to the anti-
Semitic insinuations that followed the gangster-style slaying of Charlie
Feigenbaum in 1934. It noted that although the hit took place 'in the
heart of the Jewish quarter' and the victim and suspects were Jewish, 'it
is clear that this has nothing to do with the Jewish community as a
whole.' Despite this attempt to distance the murder, the paper continued, 'For the well being of the Jewish community it would be much
better if the Jews were to be clean of such men and of such damaging
spectacles.'[35] The same paper commented again on another 'spectacle'
at the elaborate funeral of gambler Harry Davis, shot by another Jewish
gangster in 1946. A crowd of almost 5,000 closed down St-Urbain Street
outside the funeral home to pay respects to the deceased man. The
Keneder Adler discounted the crowds, suggesting that Davis had a far
better funeral than he deserved. While distancing itself from the gangster, an editorial described Davis as 'a victim of circumstances' and
blamed his career on a corrupt police force. The problem was not a
Jewish one: 'If the police were not corrupt and had not taken bribes,
gambling houses would not be able to operate and the Harry Davis's of
the world would perhaps be forced to earn their living in the usual
manner.'[36] The *Keneder Adler*, which was bilingual in English and Yiddish by the 1940s, printed the editorial in Yiddish, directing its message
to its Jewish readers.

Conversely, when Louis Rosenberg of the Canadian Jewish Congress
addressed the same connection in his 1939 study, *Canada's Jews: A Social
and Economic Study of the Jews in Canada*, his intended audience was
gentile. Using federal-government criminal statistics for 1923–33, he
concluded that Canadian Jews, compared to the overall population,
had a low level of criminality, given their high level of urbanization,
except in gambling offences.[37] Rosenberg noted that throughout the
world Jews concentrated in recreational services, particularly in billiard
halls, with the largest number in the low-capital businesses of sporting
clubs rather than in the more expensive operations of theatres, motion-
picture houses, and theatrical agencies.[38] Pool halls, bowling alleys,

and sporting clubs of course helped perpetuate male gambling culture. This meant that many Jewish men engaged in 'keeping' a betting or gaming house, as distinct from being actual 'players.'

Chinese Canadians

There was no such distinction made between players and keepers in the Chinese community. Until commercialized gambling and American organized crime emerged as a concern in the 1940s, the gambling 'problem' in Canada had at times been synonymous with the Chinese community. For some critics, Chinatown was nothing more than a front for illicit activities, as it harboured restaurants where one could buy lottery tickets but not a cup of coffee.[39]

The demographic structure of the Chinese community and its cultural predisposition shaped the relationship between gambling, the critics, and Chinese Canadian. Nineteenth-century immigration brought mostly men from China to Canada, and twentieth-century laws prohibited legal Chinese immigration. Thus the settlers could not reproduce themselves and were predominantly male and ageing. In 1951, 79 per cent of Chinese Canadians were male, and more than 36 per cent of the total were men fifty-five or older.[40] (See Table 5.1.) Thus the general anti-gambling discourse, which focused on families, was not applicable in this community.

Most Chinese immigrants were male, landless hired hands, share-croppers, and small landholders from the southeast of China, who regarded themselves as sojourners who had travelled overseas to make money and to return home wealthy.[41] Merchants, who saw opportunities in supplying labour and provisions, also emigrated, but this group was a small minority. The immigrants who arrived before the Exclusion Act of 1923 effectively ended Chinese immigration until it was rescinded in 1947 thus constituted a remarkably homogeneous community. Yet there were major internal divisions, even with regard to gambling. Conforming to ideals of respectability put forward by the dominant middle class offered Chinese Canadians few benefits.[42] None the less, not all Chinese in Canada approved of gambling, and many placed various games such as mah jong, lotteries, and fan tan on a continuum of acceptability. Gambling was more acceptable in some local communities than in others. Denise Chong stated that in Nanaimo, British Columbia, gambling 'carried little of the stigma that it did in other Chinatowns, if only because the profits went back to the company that ran Chinatown.' Her own grandfather, however, an immi-

Table 5.1
Age and sex distribution of Chinese population in Canada,1951 and 1961

Age	1951			1961		
	% males	% females	% total	% males	% females	% total
0–9	5.50	5.09	10.59	11.90	10.91	22.81
10–19	9.39	4.17	13.56	5.97	4.38	10.35
20–34	6.72	5.55	12.27	17.30	10.92	28.22
35–44	7.74	3.10	10.84	3.08	3.23	6.31
45–54	12.86	1.80	14.46	4.43	4.13	8.56
55–64	21.00	.94	21.94	6.20	2.85	9.05
65+	15.67	.43	16.10	13.08	1.59	14.67
Total	78.88	21.08	99.76	61.96	38.01	99.97

Source: Wing Chung Ng, 'Ethnicity, Community: Southern Chinese Immigrants and Descendants in Vancouver, 1945–1980,' PhD thesis, University of British Columbia, 1993, 54.

grant from China, considered gambling a vice.[43] A sociologist at McGill University in the 1920s asked a Chinese student to enter a Chinese gambling club to do research. The student protested that by doing so 'he would fall in status,' since 'it would be indiscreet to mingle with people who frequent the clubs.'[44]

Traditional Chinese entrepreneurship did not always separate hard work and gambling. Some overseas communities used gambling to show a connection between fate and business success. They saw gambling as an opportunity to improve one's status among the entrepreneurial community through the conspicuous display of wealth and the public acceptance of loss. Gambling also had a sanctioned role in Chinese ritual and ceremony but was condemned if it became excessive or took place outside set customs.[45]

But the Canadian and North American context transformed place of gambling within Chinese society. In North America gambling potentially offered a profitable form of recreation for a group of sojourners. The vulnerable economic position increased the allure of 'easy money.' After all, their main objective was to earn enough to return home wealthy. Protestant missionaries inadvertently recognized this connection when they accused Chinese gamblers in British Columbia of being 'seized with a get-rich-quick materialism.'[46] The same economic rationale also motivated owners of gambling establishments. An owner who testified at a Vancouver inquiry in 1928 explained that he wanted to 'get rich.' A traditional taboo against women gambling in public remained, partly because of the small number of women in Canada. Women who did gamble – for example, May-ying in Denise Chong's *The Concubine's Children* – must have been extremely conspicuous. An observer of Montreal's Chinatown in the 1930s remembered the presence of British, French, and Italian women in gambling clubs, but never Chinese women.[47]

Officials could be tolerant of Chinese gambling as long as it was contained within areas known as Chinatowns and confined to a Chinese-only clientele. Chinese establishments sometimes attracted a non-Chinese clientele, which worried critics who favoured segregation. A French Canadian remembered Montreal in the 1930s when 'everyone' went to Chinese gambling houses – 'English, French, Italian, Negroes, especially Italians.' In contrast, the head of the gambling, liquor, and morality branch of the Vancouver police declared that he had 'never yet found or seen a white man' in any of his city's Chinatown gambling houses.[48] Yet Mayor Louis D. Taylor believed that attempts to close down gambling in Chinatown in the 1920s had spread gambling throughout the city. In 1928 an acting chief of police in Vancouver stated that he did not 'consider gambling in Chinatown is so serious because it is among themselves and as long as the whites keep out of it no one suffers. If anyone suffers it is themselves.' A Montreal-area newspaper editor in the 1940s dismissed concerns about gambling among 'harmless little slant-eyed yellow men.' The editor understood that the Chinese community in Montreal did not 'entice white men to their games, and don't invite women.'[49] Vancouver Mayor Taylor's tolerant attitude was shaped not only by the municipal revenue that gambling generated but also by the Chinese community's unique spatial restriction of gambling. In Victoria, Chinese gambling was concentrated around a narrow lane, Fantan Alley. In Vancouver, witnesses to a police inquiry in 1939 stated that 'practically every store in Chinatown' sold tickets for one of the Chinese lotteries and reaped a 12½ per cent commission for their sales.[50]

Mixed clubs undermined the justification by the Chinese and their white supporters for the operation of the clubs. The most common defence for the Chinese clubs was their role as a source of self-help. In 1925 an anonymous petitioner to the Vancouver Board of Police Commissioners observed that the Chinese travelled to Canada 'to earn a respectable livelihood, but there is discrimination against our race and the white people are daily protesting the employment of Chinese.' The clubs provided a place to socialize, off the streets and safe from charges of vagrancy.[51] Elderly Chinese without employment received free tea and rice and slept on the premises during the Depression. In 1930, one of these club's defence lawyers argued that if the organization was forced to close, the elderly men would have to apply for municipal relief. In the 1940s, the clubs provided a place for Chinese men on relief to keep warm.[52] A North Vancouver gaming house even picked up on a Cold War theme during the Korean War – it was 'fighting reds' and served as a 'rallying point for support of General Chiang Kai-shek's Nationalist movement.' In a courtroom plea, the operator claimed that Chinese bachelors, with few recreational opportunities, were 'consequently susceptible to Communist propaganda' and that his club used 'the "gambling blood" of the Chinese to rally them against the Red menace.' He later admitted that he had never actually sent any funds to Chiang Kai-shek.[53]

This caricature of self-help tapped into the common explanation that Chinese men gambled because they had no family and few legitimate recreational opportunities. In 1924, the Chinese Benevolent Association of Vancouver pointed out that Chinese morals were not inferior to those of the 'whites.' While admitting the problems of drugs and gambling in its community, it linked these practices directly to the absence of families, 'and thus this could lead to undisciplined indulgence in bad habits and entertainment.' The association concluded that it was unfair to place sole responsibility for these problems on the Chinese community, since 'westerners' were responsible for lax law enforcement, as well as for the absence of Chinese families and racial discrimination that limited economic opportunities.[54] This claim was made during the first year that the Chinese Exclusion Act of 1923 was in place. This lack of family and its connection to the proliferation of gambling encouraged the United Church in 1949 to urge the federal government to permit the entry of Chinese wives into Canada as a means of destroying what they considered an immoral male culture.[55]

Restricted recreational opportunities compounded the absence of family. In 1921 Protestant clergymen in Vancouver argued that since Chinese men were not admitted to reputable theatres or restaurants, they drifted into gambling establishments 'not because they are inherently evil or wicked and vicious by choice, but because circumstances and environment lead that way.' Similarly, in 1928 Vancouver Mayor Louis Taylor defended his tolerant position by reminding opponents that Chinese men, because of informal segregation, had 'no other form of recreation. They can't go to the picture shows or anything of the kind, and when they gamble amongst themselves, why it is immaterial to me. I wouldn't attempt to stamp it out.' In the 1970s, a Toronto newspaper reporter described the occasional fines against illegal gambling as 'the price of preventing loneliness.'[56]

Fines against Chinese gamblers also provided crucial municipal revenue, especially during the 1930s, when other sources declined at a time of expanding need. A report on fines collected at the Vancouver police court between 1936 and 1939 suggests that gambling fines, generated almost exclusively from the Chinese community, accounted for between 20 and 27 per cent of this revenue – more than twice the amount collected for liquor-related offenses.[57] These so-called fines were more accurately the price of bail for gamblers arrested during raids who subsequently failed to appear in court and therefore forfeited their guarantee and evaded a guilty verdict. Police officers argued that municipalities could not afford the actual cost of imprisonment. Other levels of government also sought to profit from illegal activities. After 1933, Chinese lottery operators were assessed for income tax, notwithstanding the illicit nature of their enterprise.[58]

Despite all these distinctive aspects of Chinese gambling, its opponents tended to use the same arguments as employed elsewhere. Employers opposed Chinese gambling, claiming that it interfered with a productive, reliable workforce. In 1918 authorities complained that while the BC fisheries badly needed workers, the Chinese spent most of their time in the gambling clubs. Employers in the wood shingle industry found it difficult to acquire workers and to keep their attention on the job; it requested a general crackdown against all Chinese gambling clubs.[59] Vancouver police at least temporarily closed down Chinatown.

Anxiety increased when Chinese gambling moved outside the community and to non-Chinese players. Reports alleged that some Chinese lured whites into their establishments. Alarms went up in Victoria after the First World War that Chinese gamblers were allegedly 'living off white men from the Shipyards.' The Vancouver tabloid *Information* in 1927 claimed that white youths were patronizing the Chinese lotteries with 'devastating effect.' At an inquiry into police corruption in 1928, an officer on the Vancouver morality squad testified that as long as Chinese men gambled among themselves and 'did not seduce or tempt Caucasians to gamble, there was no problem.' However, Shi Mei, an important Vancouver gambler, operated several establishments in the 1920s that catered specifically to white men. In the 1930s, the Vancouver gambling squad believed that some Chinese lotteries were run specifically for 'white men' and that these were rigged. Participation in Montreal's Chinese lotteries was probably more diverse, as the lotteries were described as 'the poor man's *barbotte*.'[60] Chinese clubs on Toronto's Elizabeth Street were patronized by 'non-Orientals' at least during the Second World War, and, with the arrival of peace, critics in Winnipeg complained that Chinese lotteries attracted (presumably non-Chinese) women and boys. As public debates accompanied the easing of Chinese immigration laws after 1947, young Canadian-born Chinese were also brought to attention as at risk.[61]

The elaborate system of protection that accompanied Chinese gambling corrupted police departments and implicated municipal politicians. In several cities, a crackdown on Chinatown's gambling was a predictable element of municipal elections. Chinese gambling was a major campaign issue in the 1934 Vancouver mayoralty race, which pitted Gerry McGeer, with his slogan 'Are you for me or the underworld?' against Louis D. Taylor, who in his 1928 campaign had stated that he did not 'believe in running Sunday School City.'[62] Bribes were also at the centre of Vancouver's Lennie Inquiry in 1928, when an alderman on the Police Commission alleged police corruption that reached all the way up to the mayor's office. The three weeks of testimony brought accusations of police payoffs and exposed a proliferation of Chinese gambling dens. The inquiry touched on Italian gamblers who had diversified into prostitution and bootlegging, but Chinese gamblers were at the heart of the investigation. Another inquiry into Vancouver police in 1936 also originated with allegations of bribes by Chinese gamblers.[63] In a third such probe in 1939, Chinese gamblers were portrayed as part of an underworld that had attempted to bribe the mayor, but its report did not accentuate the role of the Chinese. Similar allegations were levelled against Chinese gamblers in Montreal during the Caron Inquiry into commercialized vice of the 1940s, but overall the commission accorded them little attention.[64]

The final concern of critics was the connection between Chinese gambling, 'tong wars,' and violence. Chinese immigrants brought to Canada an organizational culture of secret societies that originated in their homeland's nineteenth-century politics. These associations (or 'tongs') ranged from clan or self-help groups such as the Chinese Benevolent Association, to political parties.[65] Some societies operated gambling establishments to raise funds for their members or causes. Rivalry for monopoly control of gambling in a district or of punishments levied against informers took on the exotic label of 'tong wars,' regardless of the individuals involved. Chinese gambling could lead to violent results such as the 1924 murder of David Lew, a Canadian-educated interpreter, who was shot on Pender Street in Vancouver. Rumours held that he was murdered in connection with his gambling and informant activities.[66]

A tong war broke out in Montreal in December 1933 when twenty-two men fought in Chinatown. The conflict pitted members of the Dat Koon Club against supporters of Kuomintang (the Chinese Nationalist Party), although the English- and French-language press immediately speculated that the dispute was really for control of gambling in Chinatown. Tensions had been running high for over a year, and the intervention of Chief of Police Fernand Dufresne had postponed fighting. According to one observer, the Nationalists had been operating a relief bureau for members of the Chinese community using the revenue from one or two gambling houses as well as private subscriptions. However, the imperial Chinese faction, led by George Hum, a laundry proprietor and so-called Fu Manchu of Chinatown, had attempted to take over local gambling houses and collect a weekly payment from the Nationalists. Prominent criminal lawyer Joseph Cohen was hired by the Nationalists in the subsequent trial and delayed Hum's release on bail. According to Cohen, Hum had flaunted his supposed influence with the Montreal police and municipal officials in order to extract weekly payments for guarantees of protection against raids.[67]

Attitudes towards the Chinese also changed over time. Even in the 1920s, there was the suggestion that Canadian-born Chinese were less likely to gamble and, according to a Vancouver lawyer, to 'swallow abuse from white people the way old and uneducated Chinese people did.' In Vancouver in the late 1930s, the morality squad predicted that 'as the years pass, the volume should gradually grow less, as the Old Country Chinamen will be dying off or becoming unemployed due to old age, and the Canadian born Chinese do not indulge to any great extent in the games so mentioned.'[68] This division between the many old, single men who arrived in Canada before 1923 and the few Canadian-born men with families grew again after 1947, when family reunification generated a new wave of immigrants. The post-1947 arrivals tended to be better educated than the earlier immigrants and served as internal critics to the established Chinese-Canadian community.[69] In 1955, the *Chinese Voice* sponsored a contest on 'My Opinion on How to Improve the Recreational Facilities in [Our] Overseas Chinese

Society.' Historian Wing Chung Ng notes that the two winning essays were almost identical in content. Both were critical of gambling among older Chinese men and upheld the ideal of 'rational recreation.' They put forward sports clubs, libraries, and musical, drama, and literary societies as alternatives to the gambling den.[70]

The demographic impact of an ageing established community and the culturally distinct group of newcomers coincided with slow changes within Canadian society concerning human rights and racism. After the Second World War, police and government officials were much more vulnerable to allegations of racial prejudice in their policing practices, and extreme examples of racism were less acceptable. In 1950, the BC registrar of companies faced formal accusations in provincial court that he was influenced by racial prejudice when he cancelled the charter of a Chinese social club in Vancouver.[71] In 1951, Toronto's chief of police complained that his force was being accused by 'people in all walks of life' of discriminating against the Chinese. Chief John Chisholm defended his force's actions, stating that it was concerned only with the professional gamblers who were exploiting the 'hard-working Chinese dishwasher, cook, market gardener and laundry man.' He was confident that 'the good Chinese' in Toronto supported his force's actions. The clear distinction that he made between the man who operated a business, had a family, and sent his children to school and the 'frequenter of the Chinese "joints"' was based not only on race but also on explicit differentiations by class and marital status.[72]

The change in attitude was also formed by the law. In 1949, amendments to the Criminal Code had permitted a 'new rational approach to Chinese gambling,' and for the first time in Vancouver's history, Chinese Canadians could legally and openly gamble. Reportedly 900 men had paid ten cents to join the High On Club of Vancouver. Not all games were permitted, and the continued prohibition on fan tan created ongoing conflicts between the Chinese clubs, the police, and the provincial attorney general's office.[73]

The charter clubs that permitted gambling were much less threatening to Vancouver's dominant sensibilities than their predecessors. In 1950 Mayor Charles Thompson and Police Chief Walter Mulligan toured the city's legal Chinese gambling clubs. A reporter who accompanied them noted that if they had 'hoped to see anything resembling the dimly-lit, nefarious gambling dens of old, they were disappointed.' These clubs were modern, well-lit, ventilated, and secure. Signs of assimilation were also evident in the presence of both English- and Chinese-language magazines and an expanded menu that placed lemon meringue pie alongside traditional Chinese food. In a patronizing quotation, one older man described his club as 'very good. Chinese no homes, no women, they play gambling. One time all land in jug. Still gamble, never land in jug again.' The mayor pronounced charter clubs a solution to this 'racial problem,' as they kept 'men with no proper homes off the streets and out of trouble.' As long as the clubs remained few, the mayor was 'satisfied.' The chief of police expressed his surprise at the clubs' 'cleanliness and at the large number of old people who seem to be well and happy. Anything is better than the old style of backroom gambling.' By 1963, sixteen charter clubs served the local community.[74]

It was the passing of the generation of single men, more than a shift in policing or general attitudes, that transformed the majority's perception of Chinese gambling. Even traditional games were changing by the late 1960s, as bingo was played three days a week at Victoria's only legal Chinese club that permitted gambling. When the informal 'mayor' of Victoria's Chinatown won $137,500 in a 1953 Irish Sweepstakes, he was fêted for his good fortune in the most acceptable form of 'Canadian' gambling. In 1965, a spokesperson for the Chinese Publicity Bureau of Vancouver lamented that 'Chinatown isn't the same ... they [gamblers] don't congregate down here anymore.'[75]

In 1966, a Vancouver magistrate dismissed charges laid against a Chinese lottery patronized by older Chinese residents that held up to three draws daily, with pots as high as $4,000. The *Vancouver Province*, that once vocal in its accusations of Chinese gambling and general degeneration, applauded the decision and, in a statement that would have no doubt shocked earlier editors, concluded that the practice of lotteries was thousands of years old among the Chinese, and 'there is no noticeable sign that it has corrupted this proud race.'[76]

Change was apparent not only in how the dominant community viewed the Chinese but also in how Chinese Canadians saw themselves. In 1962, the Canadian Chinese Benevolent Association protested vehemently after an article in *Maclean's* compared it with the 'Italian mafia' and a 'Jewish ghetto.'[77] In a strange way, this last example takes us full circle. The association's reaction to public criticism was to assert itself to be on a moral hierarchy above another ethnic community, over which it claimed superiority. Hence we return to the knot of experience and meaning. Discussion of ethnic groups and gambling had less to do with the actual practice of gambling and betting among members than with the myriad ways this behaviour took on significance for those outside the group. The operation of an 'illicit enterprise' was a choice – a response to a society that offered limited economic opportunities and withheld status to groups that it considered marginal. The Chinese Benevolent Association was closer to the mark in its 1924 statement that held whites accountable for creating an environment in which gambling flourished among the Chinese.

Religion: Protestants versus Catholics

Although Chinese Canadians were associated with gambling in the public's imagination, differing attitudes (at least outside the upper echelons) towards gambling was a component in the low-level, ongoing sectarian strife between Roman Catholics and Protestants. This conflict, rooted in religious culture, expressed itself in ongoing political tension between Catholic Quebec and the rest of Canada. In one manifestation of this divide, Quebec relied on religious regulation of moral offences more than on the criminal law. During the anti-gambling campaign that followed the First World War, the anti-gambling *Toronto Mail* noted the specific need for English-speaking Canadian reformers to convince Quebec and the francophone press 'that gambling is a great and growing menace to public morals.'[78]

The Catholic church in Canada was not unanimously in favour of bingo or other games of chance. A 1922 circular from the Montreal diocese reminded parishioners that games of chance such as raffles were always forbidden, even at charity fairs, and that it was humiliating that the numerous complaints about gambling compelled police intervention, as the authority of the bishop 'ne suffise plus … cette tâche.'[79] Likewise, Paul-Émile Léger addressed this issue in 1951 as bishop of Montreal. According to Léger, the growth in fashion of *soirées-bazaars* posed a serious problem for the Christian conscience, as the church was neither a financial organization nor a school for gambling. Therefore he forbade all forms of gambling, even bingo, in all institutions, churches, and religious communities, and he reminded the faithful of everyone's obligation to respect and conform, without exception, to the laws on gambling. A similar stance was taken by the Catholic church in Ottawa.[80] The position of the official church hierarchy, however, often was not shared by local parishes, which had limited resources for heating, needy families, and parochial schools. Catholic involvement in charitable gambling took place at the local level, often despite the disapproval of church officials. This division was not recognized outside the Catholic community and did not affect Protestant prejudices. The United Church of Canada's preoccupation with gambling within the Catholic church continued until the 1960s, when two of the most extreme opponents asserted that 'the time has come when we ought to challenge the Roman Catholic Church' with regard to gambling.[81]

The main thrust of Protestant–Catholic tension about gambling was the perpetual accusation by Protestants that Catholics received preferential treatment before the law. In 1922, members of Ontario's Orange Order who were refused permission to hold raffles or games of chance because they were not a religious or charitable organization cried 'discrimination' because Catholics had the same privilege at their garden parties.[82] The exemption granted to churches offended both opponents of gambling and those who believed that they should be entitled to the same rights.

The prosecution of church-sponsored gambling, primarily bingo, posed a challenge to police and to politicians who required Catholic votes for re-election. After Attorney General William H. Price ordered a crackdown on all gambling in Ontario in 1929, one local crown attorney who was plagued by local bingo games expressed his reluctance 'to write to the Parish Priests along the line in your letter.' Deputy Attorney General Edward Bayly reassured the nervous crown attorney that the attorney general's instruction had not been 'a direction to proceed against anyone, but merely to warn a lot of respectable people against violations of the law.'[83] In 1930, Quebec Premier Alexandre Taschereau, in his capacity as attorney general, directly approached the archbishop of Quebec requesting his cooperation in stamping out church-run lotteries and bingos through his influence and authority, but he apparently had little success.[84]

While many Protestants believed that the Catholic church held a privileged status before the law, some Catholics felt singled out for prosecution. Police intervened in 1933 and 1934 as the attorney general's office in Ontario conducted an annual battle with the De la Salle Auxiliary Lottery operated by the Christian Brothers in Toronto. A Sarnia priest was charged and fined in 1938 after he had conducted a bingo every Monday night for two years and been repeatedly warned to cease. In 1952, after Winnipeg's morality squad recommended prosecution unless a parish stopped its lottery, the priest complained that the head of the division 'had it in for Priests.'[85]

In the years immediately after the Second World War, attacks on bingo became a means to express both anti-Catholic and anti-Quebec sentiments. The conscription crisis had worsened relations between francophone and anglophone Canada, and the postwar years witnessed the influx of a large number of Catholic immigrants to urban centres. For this generally poor but rapidly expanding immigrant population, fundraising through bingo became a vital means to support parochial schools. In the Vancouver suburb of Burnaby in the 1960s, some parishes evaded provincial regulations that sanctioned fortnightly games by registering four social clubs within each congregation, thereby opening the way to twice-weekly games.[86]

During the Second World War, the combination of philanthropy and patriotism encouraged most authorities to turn a blind eye to games of chance linked to fundraising. As long as no individual was seen to profit, the wartime culture fostered a general level of tolerance. With the arrival of peace, however, the provincial attorneys general agreed to return to more rigorous enforcement, which some Protestants did not regard as sufficiently strict and others saw as favouritism for Catholics. The Criminal Code had always permitted a religious exemption from general gambling prohibitions, but with restrictions on intervals and value. Protestant community groups did not see the justice in Catholics' holding bingo games for their schools while they could not do the same for Britain or the Canadian Legion.

One Toronto woman wrote her attorney general in 1945, asking 'Why are the Roman Catholics allowed to carry on their Bingo Games?' She complained that the Catholic church was in no way publicly accountable for the dispersal of bingo revenue and concluded, 'How [can] these Roman Catholics who are admittedly becoming too strong in our City and Country, carry on and use their funds for their own selfish purposes. And why are the Protestants the ones to be stamped underfoot and prevented from doing a most commendable job? Is this the way to prevent Roman Catholicism from spreading?'[87] This letter was by no means the lone voice of anti-Catholic sentiment to arrive in the Ontario attorney general's mail. A United Church minister complimented the provincial government's crackdown on gambling, but protested the exception made for church gambling noting that all the Protestant churches were opposed to the privilege. He wrote, 'Is this just one more favor handed out to the Roman Catholic Church?'[88] Almost twenty years later, another Toronto man reflected concerns about the influx of Catholic immigrants. He protested bingo 'as a lucrative source of revenue for that privileged religious organization' and was particularly concerned that the money was being spent to aid Catholic immigrants. He concluded, 'The Roman priests have assailed the Government on many occasions with the problems created by their interference in immigration, housing, labor and education, to name but a few. The handwriting should have been seen on the wall when bands of immigrant construction workers roamed the suburban country-side during the construction strikes. One had the opportunity to see the Roman army in action at that time.'[89]

While the presence of large numbers of immigrants, especially working-class Italians, was a source of anxiety for some, anti-Catholic attitudes combined with hostile feelings towards Quebec. With the re-election of Union Nationale leader Maurice Duplessis as premier in 1944, Quebec reintroduced its request to amend the Criminal Code so that provinces could conduct their own lotteries. This immediately provoked a reaction from Canada's largest Protestant denomination, the United Church of Canada. The secretary of its Board of Evangelical and Social Service, J.R. Mutchmor, wrote to Louis St Laurent, the federal minister of justice, pointing out that any expansion of gambling would be detrimental, as all 'non–Roman Catholic churches' opposed even the current exemption granted to churches and charities. Mutchmor placed gambling in the midst of the 'national question,' as he believed that 'at a time when the feeling between Protestants and Roman Catholics is far from good, it would appear to be in the national interest to do everything possible to reduce any and all forms of irritation.'[90] The response from the minister's office – that his letter would be 'filed' – enraged the writer, as he regarded this as yet another example of Catholic privilege. In his reply to St Laurent, Mutchmor wrote, 'I do not think you would write to the headquarters of the Roman Catholic church about a serious matter which they referred to you, to the effect that their request would be filed.'[91] Another minister of the same denomination who was an active anti-gambling pamphleteer warned Ontario's attorney general against the provinces', and Quebec in particular, being given jurisdiction over gambling and lotteries. Reflecting his perception of Quebec as a priest-ridden society, the clergyman warned that 'we may expect the Province of Quebec, under the duress of its Hierarchy, to become a North American sweepstake centre ... One is loath to refer to the religious monopoly of Lotteries etc., in South America, but such a reversion of moral practice is unthinkable.' The leadership of the United Church suspected Catholics, through the Quebec electorate, of possessing 'considerable power' in Ottawa and of being an obstruction to any amendments in the Criminal Code that would end the religious exemption.[92]

Even in the more tolerant and ecumenical context of the 1960s, the *United Church Observer*, the official organ of the denomination, expressed concern in a 1964 editorial about the financial dependence of Roman Catholic parishes on gambling. According to the *Observer*, Catholic bingo games 'flout the laws, and encourage laxness in law-enforcement, and undermine dignified methods of raising money for good works.' The United Church admitted 'that there are greater sins in the world than bingo-playing,' that many patrons at Catholic bingo games were Protestants, and that the Catholic church had shown moral leadership to Protestants in other areas such as anti-racism. However, 'in this area of gambling, either the evangelical churches of North America are wrong, or the Catholics are wrong. Gambling has become one of the great social evils of the continent. Catholic and Protestant Christians should co-operate in fighting the evil.'[93]

Although the call for joint action reflected a more tolerant approach, the actual content did not differ over the entire period studied. The Protestant clergy wanted all Canadian society to adhere to its moral standard. This ongoing forum of conflict for many Protestants over Catholic use of charitable gambling was at the core of the political deadlock that prevented any amendment to the Criminal Code until 1969. Gambling reform was a component of the Omnibus Bill that decriminalized contraception, abortion, and homosexuality and created the structures for modern divorce. The delay in bringing the code in line with contemporary morals and practices attests to the enduring political power or at least influence of religious organizations on law-making. The decriminalization of many forms of gambling in 1969 not only symbolized the decline of a dominant Protestant value system, but also reflected the rise of alternative worldviews, influenced by the changing demographic base of the country.

Conclusion

Gamblers and operators of gambling establishments hailed from every community and, except among Chinese Canadians, it often brought together a wide range of men. English-speaking Protestant critics and, less frequently, their francophone Catholic counterparts attempted to accentuate the connections between usually less powerful groups and this so-called deviant behaviour. Part of their construction of gambling

as stigmatized behaviour was its association with 'others.' This definition of 'other' could be rooted in racial, ethnic, religious, or, in the case
of Americans, perceived cultural differences. While critics of gambling
used their critique to create and maintain differences, people who patronized or operated gambling facilities themselves often overcame
ethnic or sectarian boundaries. The critique of gambling through a
focus on minority groups helped to consolidate the way in which
majority groups defined themselves and projected their vision of moral
standards on the rest of society. The classification of those who might
acceptably gamble was based on class and ethnicity and suggests that
many fears about gambling were based not on the activity itself but
rather on the imagined behaviour or consequences of certain people's
gambling.

Finally, it is important to explain meaning and experience concur-
rently, as the practice of gambling by minority communities affected its
significance for the dominant group, and vice versa. The attention
focused on 'others' deflected many critics' attention from gambling's
widespread practice within their own community. Nevertheless, gambling at its core was a 'Canadian' problem, no matter how much critics
tried to associate it with specific groups. Even if one could ignore the
fact that most Canadians who participated in sweepstakes, betting, and
other forms of gambling belonged to majority communities, it was still
the dominant communities, both British and French, who created a
society that made gambling a rational choice for those considered to be
outsiders and an economic opportunity for those excluded from other
avenues of advancement.

PART THREE

Reaction and Reform, 1945–1969

CHAPTER SIX

Professional Gambling and Organized Crime under Scrutiny

Gangsters and organized crime are not themes normally associated with the Canadian experience. In a confident tone, the *Ottawa Journal* in 1943 presumed that it had to explain to its readers that 'racket,' 'a word from American cities,' referred to the connection between criminals and politicians, but was not applicable in Canada. 'We pride ourselves, as a British country, on our honest police forces and our fair courts – and with these aids to collective virtue organized crime cannot long endure.'[1] But these assurances did not ring true about most of the country. During the war, public concern about professional gambling operated by 'the underworld' or crime syndicates became a matter of increasing anxiety, and the postwar years saw stricter enforcement of gambling laws and formal inquiries into gambling operations. Less than two months after the *Ottawa Journal* reassured its readers, the *Vancouver News-Herald* cautioned: 'Don't raise your eyebrows at detective story magazine accounts of big-time gambling in American centres. It may be going on right next door to you.'[2]

Gambling, as a popular but illegal form of commercial leisure, was a major source of revenue for U.S. crime syndicates after the end of prohibition in 1933. This criminal connection influenced the way in which gambling was understood by critics and the general public and made gambling distinct from other 'minor vices' such as alcohol, non-observance of Sundays, and pornography, which were gaining acceptance or tolerance after the war. The link between organized crime and gambling focused attention on *professional* gambling and fostered a differentiation between harmless and dangerous forms of gambling. Organized crime came to embody the menace in gambling, as earlier concerns about thrift and productive labour gave way to images of gangsters and corrupt politicians. The intrinsic moral consequences of gambling mattered less when critics concentrated on who was profiting and on his or her motives. A differentiation also emerged between the players and the professionals. In the decade after the war, the most prominent critique emphasized the threat that organized gambling posed to civil life by weakening the ability of the law to function unfettered and by corrupting local government.[3] The preoccupation with organized crime and the arguments against its gambling operations inadvertently fostered acceptance of forms of gambling that did not accrue profits to individuals but benefited non-profit organizations and eventually the state.

Concern about civil society was firmly grounded in a Cold War context. The policing of gambling caused considerable unease, as most Canadians rejected the arbitrary measures sought in the fight against illegal gambling, such as phone-tapping and surveillance, while fearing the potential damage that illicit gambling could wreak on democratic institutions. In June 1951, an excerpt in *Reader's Digest* argued that 'Stalin could not fine a speedier, surer way to defeat the democracies than by subsidizing gangsters and foul politicians.'[4] The common labelling of a leader of any gambling syndicate as 'tsar,' 'overlord,' 'lord,' or 'king' drew attention to the authoritarian and hierarchical nature of the organization, out of step with a democratic age. The issue of responsible citizenship, both individual and corporate, also became a theme, as inquiries and the press struggled with the ethics of established companies such as Bell Telephone or a telegraph service reaping profits from unlawful clients.

A Diverse Experience

A discussion of gambling and organized crime highlights another aspect of Canadians' diverse experience with gambling. This chapter focuses on Toronto, Vancouver, and Montreal – first, as background, before and during the Second World War, when judicial probes uncovered a growing link between gambling and organized crime. Second, it discusses the postwar transformation of attitudes as Canadians began to question the criminal status of a peaceable activity that funded the dangerous and illegal acts of highly questionable groups of people. Although Halifax and Winnipeg telephone numbers appeared in the 'little black book' of Montreal professional gambler Harry Ship, powerful gambling syndicates were virtually absent from those centres in the late 1940s and early 1950s. In the general postwar crackdown on gambling and in various inquiry reports, there was no indication of widespread organized professional gambling in Halifax. Certainly large card games were part of city life, but these took place in the quasi-legal form of incorporated social clubs. The city's most dramatic police action of the period appears to have been the seizure in 1946 of 1,200 illegal punchboards. A group of professional Montreal gamblers fled to Halifax in 1950 to hide out while gambling in Montreal was under particularly harsh surveillance, but they left within a week. In contrast, professional gambling in Winnipeg was organized and reportedly divided between the control of two local syndicates. Dice games were more popular than cards or horse racing, but all forms of gambling were carefully regulated by strict police enforcement beginning in May 1951. The timing of the crackdown coincided with police inquiries in other cities and may be understood as an effort to avoid a gambling probe in Winnipeg.[5]

Prosperity affected the visibility of gambling: money spent on gambling increased during and after the war. More people had more money to spend, and betting benefited from the increased commercialization of professional sport. The most common professional gambler was the bookmaker, and although betting was a part of all sports, it was most important for horse racing.[6]

Changes in Bookmaking

The continental organization of racetrack betting was the result of modern communication devices such as the telephone and the telegraph and of an organizational structure that duplicated integrated business corporations.[7] A monopoly on gathering race information from tracks and distributing it across North America to bookmakers was maintained through a telegraphic wire service. Distance and location no longer restricted the geography of betting, as up-to-date information on odds and instant race results were available to subscribers. Local daily sports newspapers, or 'scratch sheets,' could now supply even-more-current information than the general press.

In 1939, M.L. (Moe) Annenberg, an American racing publisher who operated Nation-Wide News Service, disbanded his operations after being convicted for income tax evasion. In the aftermath, the Chicago-based service was reorganized as Continental Press Service and, rather than sell its 'news' directly to bookmakers, set up regional distributors that published racing guides and 'scratch sheets' such as the Toronto *Daily Turf and Sporting News*. The distributors sold the information to individual bookmakers across North America, but Continental was not directly involved in this transaction. Control of Continental was finally settled in 1946, when the Chicago-Capone mob began a rival wire service called Trans-American Publishing and News Service and the head of Continental was murdered. Within a year, Trans-American had folded, and the Chicago-Capone gang joined Continental, until its operations were stopped in the early 1950s, when Western Union denied it use of its transmission services after this relationship was exposed by a U.S. Senate committee. Thereafter a telephone 'flash service' replaced the continental telegraph monopoly.[8]

This sophisticated information system was complemented by a complex financing structure, whereby local bookmakers could distribute the risk that they took on a given event or race. The universal adoption of the wire service had led to local bookmakers' offering established track odds and surrendering control over balancing their own 'book.' If bettors in a specific neighbourhood disproportionately supported a particular horse in a given race, the bookmaker would not have the resources to cover payouts if the odds were being determined elsewhere. Therefore bookmakers linked up with colleagues to 'lay off' part of the bets and create a larger pool of bets that would approximate the parimutuel determined odds paid at the racetrack. These informal relationships became formal syndicates, because individual books required access to large reserves to meet daily fluctuations in cash requirements.[9]

Independent bookmakers voluntarily or as a result of pressure joined syndicates that controlled both information and financing. This system of information management and financing formed the backbone of a continental system of what was referred to as 'organized crime.' Before and during the Second World War, these larger structures, however, intersected with the local context, where gambling practice interacted with indigenous attitudes and policing.

Criminal Links: The 1920s to 1945

Toronto

The criminal culture of Toronto was generally less visible than Montreal's or Vancouver's, reinforcing the stereotype of 'Toronto the Good.'

The public imagination did not associate organized crime in Toronto with a single minority ethnic group. In addition, Toronto police may have been better organized, and their enforcement of morality offences appears to have been supported by political will. Indeed, *Saturday Night* could claim naively in 1931 that there was 'no serious gangster menace in Ontario.' A whiff of scandal touched Toronto police in the early 1930s, but this seems to have been buried with the hiring of a new chief with no connection to Toronto's or any other police force.[10] The force's general effectiveness in controlling illicit gambling was evident in professional gamblers' strategy of setting up large operations outside the city limits, beyond its jurisdiction. Bookmakers and relatively discreet gambling clubs, which formed the core of professional gambling in the city, customarily operated from the suburbs. There were many bookmakers downtown, concentrated along Queen Street, including one across from city hall, but even one crime reporter who later referred to Toronto as 'the city of bookies' admitted that Toronto was 'pretty clean.' Toronto's 'magnificent gambling casinos,' all located in the suburbs of Etobicoke, New Toronto, and Long Branch, often catered to an exclusive clientele and were rumoured to be major financial contributors to the Liberal Party of Ontario.[11] Provincial Conservatives took every opportunity to express their political opposition to commercial gambling (at least until they left opposition in 1943).

In April 1942, Conservative leader George Drew, using information supplied by the Toronto presbytery of the United Church, pressed the Liberal government to curb the 'thugs and gunmen who controlled gambling in the Toronto area.' Premier Mitchell Hepburn, always obsessed with the threat of organized labour in the form of the Congress for Industrial Organization (CIO), attempted to deflate the issue by linking the CIO and prominent gangsters in the operation of Toronto's gambling houses. The credibility of this extreme rhetoric is doubtful, but within a month of Drew's attack the Ontario Provincial Police set up a permanent anti-gambling squad. In 1943 this new force undertook 1,400 investigations and raided 311 premises. These were unsubstantiated rumours of a bagman within the Ontario Liberal Party collecting from township gambling clubs, but the local and the provincial police generally were able to avoid suspicions of collusion and payoffs.[12]

The increased interest in policing commercial gambling in Ontario reflected both wartime concerns and prosperity – operators were seen as 'cashing in on wartime payrolls.' By 1942, new or reopened establishments were flourishing in the Toronto suburbs, their success attributed directly to workers fully employed in factories and to a shortage of available goods to purchase. An Ontario government report in the 1960s recalled that 'those who had more money than they had for years were looking for outlets,' which illicit gambling clubs willingly provided. Toronto's gambling clubs – such as the White Castle in Scarborough; Garrity's in Leaside; the Brookwood Club, and the Combine Club, Abram Orpen's National Sporting Club, Max Bluestein's Lakeview Athletic Club; and William Morrissey's, all of Etobicoke – could compete with anything that Vancouver or Montreal had to offer until they were closed in a general crackdown in April 1942.[13]

Bookmaking was also a prominent aspect of wartime Toronto. One Toronto practitioner even claimed in court that he was aiding the Allies' war effort by keeping workers in the factory rather than encouraging them to spend the afternoon at the track.[14] The most notorious bookmaker in Toronto operated just beyond the city limits in an ordinary suburban house at 16 Royal York Road in Mimico. When the newly created provincial Anti-Gambling Squad raided this location in 1942, it discovered fifty-six telephone lines and a telegraph line going into the house. Attempts to have these lines removed were stymied, and when federal officials refused to take action, the provincial police finally got Bell Telephone to remove the lines. Homeowner David Boskin then appealed to the Dominion Board of Transport Commissioners, which ordered the telephones reinstated until guilt was established.[15]

A 1940s study by a Harvard University sociologist noted that in Toronto 'real bookmakers' rarely had any direct contact with the public and operated from a 'back,' a place where his agents, 'stores,' or front ends telephoned bets. This system left little material evidence for police and allowed the bookmaker to remain anonymous. The sociologist estimated that Toronto had ten major betting parlours, all just outside the city limits, and thirty to forty locations in the city tied into the wire service. As well, around 400 'stores,' such as pool halls, barbershops, and tobacco stores, phoned in bets to a back end. In total, bookmaking was the main source of income for approximately a thousand Torontonians.[16]

Vancouver

While gambling in Toronto was popular, it was relatively discreet and invisible compared to Vancouver, where until the Second World War it was almost synonymous with the visible Chinese community. Corruption was a sensitive political issue, as city police were periodically charged with accepting money to protect the operation of Chinese gambling houses.[17] When vice and suspicions of protection by Vancouver politicians and police emerged as an issue in the 1928 mayoralty campaign, the problem did not disappear after election day. Commercial gambling and prostitution were standard municipal election issues in Vancouver, but public discussion was usually restricted to the campaign.

Vancouver's election-time interest in gambling was connected to the perceived political instability associated with seasonally hosting thousands of restless, male resource workers, the city's racial politics, and its self-image as a male frontier town. In 1928, after the election campaign, a member of the Police Commission accused re-elected Mayor Louis D. Taylor of being involved in accepting kickbacks. An inquiry under R.S. Lennie sat forty days in the spring of 1928 and heard from eighteen lawyers and nearly one hundred witnesses. The witnesses reported extensive connections between gambling interests and both police headquarters and city hall. Although they claimed that they paid police $50 a month in 'good fellowship money' for protection against prosecution and that Shi Mei, Vancouver's 'King of Gamblers,' had contributed to the mayor's campaign and met with him regularly, no widespread corruption was proven. Police Chief H.W. Long, who tried to defend his inaction by pointing out that he had been following the directions of his superior, commission chair Mayor Taylor, was not charged with criminal activity but dismissed for tolerating negligence. His successor, Chief W.J. Bingham, issued orders that all members but one of the suspended morality squad were to resign or be dismissed. Police historian Greg Marquis has described the police force during this period as 'caught between interests who tolerated limited vice and those who advocated total war on gambling, illegal liquor and prostitution.'[18]

Certainly the problem would not go away. The 1934 election, which chose as mayor Gerry McGeer, one of the lawyers before the Lennie Inquiry, created a 'shake-up' and the dismissal of yet another police chief. During the mayoral campaign, McGeer argued that conditions in Vancouver were a disgrace, attributed blame 'to the policy of many years standing, commonly referred to as that of "Open House,"' and said that 'persistent interference with the Police Officers in the execution of their duty' had affected both discipline and efficiency. The day after McGeer's inauguration, he suspended seventeen officers, including Deputy Chief John Murdoch, and replaced Chief John Cameron with Colonel W.W. Foster. Ex-chief Cameron later faced charges of conspiracy to corrupt the administration of the force, and the entire department came under scrutiny in 1936, when Wilfred A. Tucker, a fired clerical accountant at police headquarters, accused his former employers of benefiting again from a payoff system. An inquiry headed by W.A. MacDonald found no evidence of graft but reinforced public suspicions of collusion between crooks, police, and politicians.[19]

Occasionally, Vancouver politicians sought to distance themselves from this illicit triad. A 1939 probe into gambling in Chinatown was initiated after Mayor Lyle Telford charged the city police with inefficiency. After an investigation by County Court Judge A.M. Harper, a police magistrate, and two members of the Police Commission, the charges of inefficiency against the chief constable were declared to be 'unfounded.'[20]

There was seldom any middle ground articulated in political debates about the level of morality policing. Mayor Taylor, who supported an 'open city' policy, criticized Police Chief D.E. Edgett in 1932 for too much morality policing. Taylor claimed that 'it is not safe for a man or woman to walk alone on a dark street and that a woman is hardly secure when alone in her home,' but the police were preoccupied by 'blind pigs, chinese gambling, "grocery store coupons," and violations of Sunday observance by small merchants.' Other civic leaders perceived the question in a very different light. In his 1939 inaugural address, Mayor Telford touched on the 'open scandal' of gambling in the city and the perception that Vancouver was 'a wide open town,' claiming that 'the freedom with which games of chance of all sorts for money, are operated can hardly be matched anywhere on this continent outside of Reno and Mexico.'[21]

Montreal

It was striking that Telford involved U.S. and Mexican examples rather than Montreal. Montreal shared with Vancouver the close association between organized gambling and specific ethnic communities. Although some francophones were engaged in professional gambling, they were a minority, but this reality did not interfere with the way many English-speaking Canadians saw Montreal as exotic, exciting, and slightly dangerous. Organized gambling in Montreal was visible and often flamboyant. The 'American style' of violence and the overlapping of organized gambling with other illicit activities such as prostitution heightened the melodrama, but before the end of the Second World War gambling was rarely a local political issue.

The inquiry of Justice Louis Coderre into the administration of the Montreal Police Department in 1924–5 found betting houses in such visible positions as the busy downtown corner of Ste-Catherine and Peel. Coderre classified gambling as an organized commercial vice in the city yet noted that charges or fines were rare and that establishments reopened immediately thereafter. Coderre also suggested the presence of open corruption, as these illegal operations appeared to have been warned about raids. Azarie Choquet, superintendent of clerical staff for the Police Department, recalled that some police raids on private clubs during the 1930s netted as little as thirty-five cents.[22]

Gambling in Montreal suited many tastes and pocketbooks, from three-card monte in the doorways along working-class rue St-Laurent to the glamorous roulette wheel of the White House Inn in Lachine and the 'floating' suburban clubs for *barbotte*.[23] The flight to the suburbs by professional gamblers in Montreal, presumably to evade the municipal police, mirrored the tactic in Toronto and reminds us that professional gamblers in Montreal did not operate in a completely 'open' city. A wire service distribution system was organized around 1920 in Montreal by Cuban José Rodriguez. His successors were gambling kingpins Hector Cadieux, Eddy 'Kid' Baker, Arthur Davidson, and Harry Davis.[24] The owners and operators of gambling clubs and the wire service often complemented their illicit activities with legal enterprises in the leisure sector. Both Baker and Davis were involved in theatre, cabarets, cafés, restaurants, and nightclubs – a milieu also tinged with violence.

Gambling and nightlife occasionally overlapped with other illicit activities. Both Baker and Davis, who immigrated to Montreal from eastern Europe as children, had criminal records dating back to the early 1920s for narcotics, armed robbery, and fencing. In the early 1930s, several of the city's most prominent professional gamblers were charged or suspected of involvement in the international trade in narcotics.[25] In October 1933, Davis, part-owner of the White House Inn, was charged with conspiring with Pincus Brecher of Patterson, New Jersey, and Jack Poliakowitz of Paris to smuggle drugs valued at more than $200,000 into Canada three years earlier. In addition, Davis also faced charges related to smuggling, trafficking, counselling procurers of drugs, and bribing customs officers.[26] Charles Feigenbaum, another partner in the Lachine gambling operation, acted as the main witness for the Crown. Feigenbaum had been serving a sentence for smuggling silk into the United States. However, when he was also implicated in the drug case, he turned 'King's evidence' for the prosecution and exchanged his testimony for amnesty on the drug case and early release from prison on the smuggling conviction. While Davis began his seven-year sentence, a released Feigenbaum opened a new gambling club and was rumoured to be attempting to set up a monopoly on the city's slot machines and *barbotte* games. Then, on 22 August 1934, shortly before he was scheduled to testify against the international co-conspirators connected to Davis, Feigenbaum was murdered in an afternoon drive-by shooting in a quiet working-class, residential neighbourhood. Three thousand spectators attended his funeral.[27]

This large crowd suggests that Feigenbaum possessed celebrity status. By the outbreak of the Second World War, gambling culture was firmly entrenched in the Montreal and the Canadian imagination. Hollywood movies, daily newspaper cartoons, serialized stories and real-life accounts of gangsters such as Al Capone put gambling before the public.[28] North American popular culture had romanticized the professional gambler and glorified the urban underworld. Like the thousands of Montrealers who wanted to catch a glimpse of the murdered Charlie Feigenbaum's coffin, popular culture generated a market for what professional gamblers were selling in terms of entertainment.

The Postwar Years and Public Concern about Organized Crime

An Era of Investigations

The glamour and the pervasive nature of illicit gambling help explain why after the Second World War North Americans were preoccupied not only with the potential internal threat posed by Communism but also with the consequences of organized crime. The postwar crime scare focused on both juvenile delinquency and organized crime syndicates. The almost-limitless potential for profit through illicit gambling attracted crime syndicates in a post-prohibition society, and the resulting epidemic of gambling was not perceived as solely an urban blight.[29] Like radical politics, the operation of this underworld seemed to pose an internal threat to democracy, because its influence infiltrated the police, the local government, and the judicial system. While governments' attempts to ferret out Communists within the media or civil service are documented, we are less familiar with actions against organized crime and gambling. Estes Kefauver, Democratic senator from Tennessee, hoped to launch his bid for the presidential nomination through a Senate committee into gambling and organized crime, which offered the same sort of extensive exposure as Joseph McCarthy's House Committee on Un-American Activities. Although the Kefauver committee was an American investigation, it was watched carefully by Canadians and provided a model for Montreal's Caron Inquiry, which held deliberations between September 1950 and April 1953. In November 1952 the Montreal group behind the Caron probe invited Kefauver to speak in the city. Both the Kefauver committee and the Caron Inquiry popularized the idea that illegal gambling was the principal source of money for organized crime.[30]

The need to examine the relation between commercial gambling and the law was on the political agenda of both North America and the United Kingdom. In Britain, it led in 1949 to the Royal Commission on Betting, Lotteries and Gambling. In Canada, it produced a number of federal, provincial, and local police inquiries. These investigations reflected contemporary attitudes, as they adopted the dominant rhetoric and tendered diverse conclusions.

Many Canadians appeared to share the conclusion of one observer of the Kefauver hearings 'that all gamblers were invariable gangsters.' A Toronto *Globe and Mail* editorialist reasoned that the 'essential evil' in all illegal gambling was its power 'to corrupt police and public officials.' According to this editorialist, 'A police officer who accepts a bribe from a gambler will more than likely accept bribes from a bootlegger – or a brothel keeper – or a dope peddler.' The Christian Council of Canada claimed in 1954 that it did not base its opposition to legalization of lotteries on a 'Puritanical tradition which is now outmoded in the light of present social trends and attitudes'; rather, anti-gambling statutes were based on 'the well-considered action of citizens ... usually after the professional gamblers who controlled the underworld got completely out of hand.' A 1961 report of the Ontario attorney general's Committee on Enforcement of the Law Relating to Gambling claimed that even charity bingo was occasionally a front for organized crime. Another Ontario committee looking into possible sources of tax revenue concluded in 1964 that any move to legalize lotteries was equivalent to inviting 'criminal elements in Canada.' The belief that organized crime had infiltrated all forms of gambling was also held by the executive secretary of the Canadian Corrections Association, who argued in

1963 that his organization opposed loosening restrictions on lotteries, since 'gambling is the lifeblood of organized crime and what might be in itself an innocent project, can be perverted to undesirable ends, not by the people operating it, but by outside organized crime.'[31] This perception of organized crime hiding behind not only every book-maker and gambling club but also every bingo and raffle testified to the extent of the fear and suggested that all forms of gambling placed society in jeopardy.

Furthermore, gambling was understood to diminish the authority of honest policemen, since they found it not only impossible to enforce the law but also to protect from fraud those who gambled. Prizes were not always awarded. In cases where prizes existed, they did not neces-sarily conform with how they had been advertised. One such metamor-phosis occurred in an Alberta lottery in 1965, where a house advertised as worth $7,500 was transformed into a bungalow worth $1,500 when fewer tickets were sold than had been anticipated. In addition, there was always the problem with the circulation of counterfeit lottery tickets. The Irish Sweepstakes were particularly plagued with this prob-lem, and many tickets purchased had no Irish origins.[32]

The federal government addressed the issue of lotteries through a Joint Committee of the Senate and the House of Commons into Capital Punishment, Corporal Punishment and Lotteries, established in 1950. The committee's broad mandate covered areas where criminal law overlapped with public morality. In its final report of 1953, which recommended against any liberalization of the Criminal Code concern-ing lotteries, the main arguments against lotteries drew primarily on the traditional stance that they offered people something for nothing. The conclusions were certainly not surprising, even if they did not reflect current public opinion or practice. The discussion of lotteries was occasionally linked directly to crime and policing through expert witnesses such as American Virgil W. Peterson, who had been associ-ated with the Kefauver committee, and Pax Plante of Montreal.[33]

Toronto

The connection between gambling, crime, and good policing was cen-tral to how the Christian Social Council of Canada described the To-ronto situation in 1949. Despite some suburbs such as New Toronto having been tainted with allegations of police and political corruption, the council concluded that Toronto had 'not been hit as hard by the

Playing dice at Fort York, Toronto, 1924.

Some people made money on Montreal's Laurier Palace fire; police noted that none of the families had been contacted.

Sweepstake ticket (1935) to raise funds for new construction at Université de Montréal. This ticket was apparently for the anglophone, perhaps American, market. The ticket warns purchasers to verify the agent's address and 'trustworthiness' – fraud was not uncommon.

Many Quebec lotteries sought American patronage. This fraudulent ticket bore a U.S. flag.

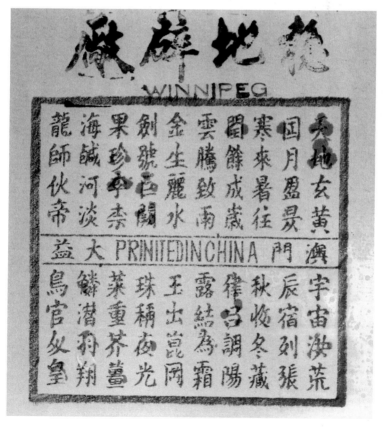

Every city with Chinese Canadians had Chinese lotteries.

Les Callan's cartoon 'It Can't Happen Here?' shows three gangsters, led by a gambling racketeer stepping on Ontario; *Toronto Star*, April 1942.

Gambling during the Canadian special forces' departure for Korea from Fort Lewis, Washington, 19 April 1951.

The Montreal morality squad removes a *barbotte* table during a raid on a Crescent Street gambling establishment, 10 September 1955.

Pax Plante, assistant director of Montreal police, with Mayor Jean Drapeau,
18 August 1955.

The Combine Club, near Toronto, looked remarkably ordinary from outside.

The interior of the Combine Club, after a raid, displayed racing programs
at different tracks on elevated blackboards – here, Rockingham Park in
New Hampshire and Bowie in Maryland. Note the slips of paper
on the floor, the ashcans/spittoons, and the drink counter.

No. 16 Royal York Road in Etobicoke looked like other houses in the suburb.

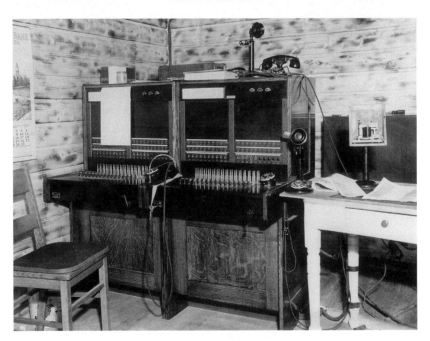

A switchboard in the basement at 16 Royal York served one of Toronto's major 'backends.'

"THIS IS A FAR CRY FROM BINGO, BUT AT LEAST ITS LEGAL."

Duncan Macpherson, in the *Toronto Star*, June 1963, poked fun at a law that permitted legal horse racing but criminalized bingo.

Become a

VOLUNTARY TAXPAYER

OF MONTREAL

Any person may pay a voluntary tax to the City of Montreal

A PAYMENT OF $2 is valid for one month and gives you the opportunity of receiving one of the 151 MONTHLY PRIZES

— ONE GRAND PRIZE —

$100,000

— IN SILVER INGOTS —

PLUS: 30 PRIZES OF $1,000 each in silver ingots
20 PRIZES OF $500 each in silver ingots
100 PRIZES OF $100 each in silver ingots

The selection of the 151 candidates whose names have been chosen for examination will be made publicly. They will be advised immediately of the time, day and place where they will have to answer, in public, questions related to the subjects printed on the reverse side of the official receipt. Having answered correctly, candidates will then be awarded their prize.

You may, if you choose, through a payment to the order of the <u>City of Montreal</u>:

1. Pay $2 for one month: you will receive an official receipt for $2.

2. Pay more than $2 for one same month: you will receive as many official receipts as there are times $2 included in your payment.

3. Pay in advance the total amount that you wish to spread out over the months to come, provided that you advise of the amount you wish to apply to each month. (Example: $2 x 6 months = $12). You will then receive receipts corresponding to your monthly payments.

4. Pay on behalf of other persons. If a child is too young to answer questions, his father, mother or the person who has made a payment on behalf of the child may answer for him.

If a candidate is not available to answer questions, the jury may set another day for such questioning or, upon acceptance of a medical certificate, allow a person duly authorized by the candidate to answer on his behalf.

No distributors, agents or intermediaries.

Fill out the included form, writing clearly the amount to be applied to each <u>particular</u> *month, and mail directly as follows:*

CITY OF MONTREAL
P.O. BOX 9999
MONTREAL 3, QUE.
CANADA

EXPO 67 WAS TOO GREAT TO LAST ONLY SIX MONTHS

VISIT "MAN AND HIS WORLD"
FROM MAY 17 TO OCTOBER 14, 1968

Same islands, same pavilions, 40 new presentations, same minirail, same express, same atmosphere, same admission price and free admission to all pavilions.

(FRANÇAIS AU VERSO)

A Montreal lottery flyer delivered in British Columbia, 1968.

gambling evil as Montreal or Vancouver thanks to the vigilance of the police force.' The Ontario attorney general, Conservative Leslie Blackwell, noted that Toronto benefited from good policing and that many prominent local 'racketeers' had left for Montreal to take advantage of that city's 'wide open' reputation. But plenty of betting and gambling, both legal and illicit, continued in Toronto. In the early 1950s, Canadians were spending more than $77 million a year on legal betting at horse tracks – two-thirds of it in Ontario. A 1944 article in *Maclean's* described Toronto as 'one of the bettingest cities in North America,' despite its 'smugly righteous exterior.' In 1949, the *Financial Post* estimated that between $150,000 and $200,000 was placed illegally in Toronto every day with more than 1,500 bookmakers. The police inspector in charge of the morality squad thought that the city had between 120 and 150 bookmakers.[34]

In 1950, Ontario Premier Leslie Frost, in a sweeping condemnation, cited bookmaking as the 'cause of more trouble in the administration of law in the province than anything else.' While this statement fits nicely with what was happening elsewhere in Ontario, Toronto Police Chief John Chisholm maintained that there had not been a single gambling complaint in his city in the previous nine months.[35] Ignoring Chisholm's assurances, the province, on 30 March 1951, launched a Committee on Administration of Justice to look into professional gambling. It never tabled its report of 28 volumes of evidence and 155 exhibits, as the legislature was dissolved in October of that year.

Bookmaking, however, composed a major theme pursued by the committee. Deputy Attorney General Clifford Magone maintained that bookmaking in the province was not connected to other forms of criminal activity and agreed that bookmakers, apart from their gambling activities, were 'law-abiding citizens.' Likewise, the commissioner of the Ontario Provincial Police maintained that gambling was not a serious problem – the province was 'pretty clean' and not controlled by a single man or a single organization. If the gamblers were clean, so too was the law enforcement, according to the testimony of witnesses.[36]

With gamblers, police, and politicians 'clean,' corporate citizens received the greatest criticism. Bookmaking parlours and gambling clubs had Bell telephone equipment, Canadian National Railways telegraph service, and Coca-Cola coolers, and the commissioners all pointed out that these corporations must have recognized the nature of the businesses that they were servicing. The most contentious example was the installation of forty-six telephone lines in a suburban home at 16 Royal York Road in August 1940, which Bell maintained was before the wartime shortage of telephones. The company repeatedly pointed out that it had cooperated with the police in removing equipment.[37] Bell also noted that it had no legal right to discontinue its service or remove its instruments on the basis of suspicion, only after a conviction.

Prosecutors, however, held that when a client was generating between $100 and $150 in long-distance bills daily between noon and six p.m., it was Bell's 'duty as a citizen' to inform police. In what became an exploration of corporate citizenship, Bell's general counsel maintained that his company was not 'obliged to inform the police.' He explained that his company needed to have access to every home and that if it started to report illicit use of its equipment, installers would be subject to bribery.[38] The other part of Bell's defence at the inquiry fit into the postwar concern about authoritarianism. In a memo circulated in 1947, Bell's president wrote: 'Freedom of communication is as vital a need in a democracy as freedom of the press and is inevitably linked up with it. Any suggestion that the Telephone Company operate an espionage system or censorship over its subscribers' use of the telephone would contain far more danger to the public welfare than would be justified by any incidental help which such a system might be to law enforcement.'[39] Testifying before the Ontario committee, the company's general counsel and executive officer, Norman Munnoch, categorized all its dealing with its subscribers as confidential, and that pact formed 'the whole foundation of decent business.' He continued picking up a Cold War theme – 'the Canadian people do not want a police state established in our country, and you know and have read what happens in places on the other side of the Atlantic where everybody becomes an informer, parents, children and all.' In a final statement, Munnoch concluded with the biblical injunction: 'Thou shalt not bear false witness against thy neighbour.'[40] By mixing fears of Soviet youngsters or German children in the Nazi era informing on their parents with Judaeo-Christian doctrine, Bell claimed a higher moral law in the act of profiting from its criminal customers.

Politicians adopted the same rhetoric to explain why professional gamblers had to be dealt with severely. In the Ontario election of 1951, Leslie Frost used public concern about gambling interests for his own political ends. He drew attention to alleged threats from 'this illegal fraternity,' who 'would use their influence against me whenever an election was held.' Frost committed himself to doing 'everything possible to suppress them' and, unlike Bell Telephone, saw this extreme action as 'fundamental to our democracy.' The Circle-Bar Fourth Column a public affairs column sponsored by the Circle Bar Knitting Company and distributed to various newspapers, pointed out that 'gambling joints cannot be long in operation without people knowing. Foremost among people will be the man on the beat. So if you happen to know of a gambling joint you may be certain that police know, too. They may be paid to close their eyes and their ears; they may be ordered to do so.'[41]

The gambling issue did not disappear in Ontario with the 1951 election. The return of Staff Inspector W.G. Tomlinson as head of the Ontario Provincial Police Anti-Gambling Squad in April 1954 signalled a renewed 'war on gambling.' In the mid-1950s, gambling clubs closed since the crackdown of 1942 reopened in the border cities of Windsor and Niagara Falls and in the Toronto suburb of Cooksville under the same ownership as their earlier incarnations. These clubs held legitimate provincial charters to operate as social clubs, and so police regulated their operations by harassment or other means such as fire regulations. Gambling clubs were of course very lucrative. When self-confessed professional gambler Max Bluestein of Toronto was convicted in December 1960 for his operation of the Lakeview Club on Eglinton Avenue, the presiding magistrate estimated that his club did an annual business of more than $13 million. Allegations of police and political corruption also never completely disappeared. In his response to the throne speech in 1961, John Wintermeyer, leader of the opposition, charged that Attorney General A. Kelso Roberts let his department interfere with and stop a 1960 undercover investigation in Niagara Falls into rumours that members of the provincial Anti-Gambling Squad were accepting protection money.[42] Pressure and rumours mounted, and in 1963 the attorney general's office initiated another probe into police and political conduct.

Justice W.D. Roach found that although the attorney general's office had claimed that there were 'no gambling houses *per se*' in Ontario – only floating crap games – gamblers 'had happy hunting ground with social club charters, aided in the past by slow-moving machinery in the provincial secretary's department.' The commissioner concluded that, although there was a 'Mafia-like' organization in Ontario, it was not a major factor in organized crime. Moreover, the decline of alleged 'gambling kingpins' Joseph McDermott and Vincent Feeley had reduced gaming and bookmaking in the province. The 'unfortunate association' between a former member of cabinet and these professional gamblers (perhaps exaggerated by McDermott and Feeley) did not deter other public officials from doing their duty faithfully. Three provincial policemen were discovered to have been involved in corruption, and the final report recommended the resignation of two senior officers.[43]

Notwithstanding such 'unfortunate associations,' Ontario – Toronto in particular – was considered 'clean,' compared with Vancouver or Montreal. This difference, however, reflected perceptions rather than reality. As we saw above, organized gambling operated in Toronto, but it was probably more discreet and identified less with a visible (or linguistic) minority group. The relative discretion of gambling and its policing was a measure of the greater consensus about its illegal status and consequently of the political will to enforce the law. Although individual officers were accused of corruption and negligence, the force itself remained above suspicion. In Montreal and Vancouver, although not all police officers were 'on the take,' there was systemic corruption. Greg Marquis has argued that the Toronto force many have had a tighter system of discipline and control than other municipal forces. The eventual reform of Montreal's police department stressed decentralization, improved recruitment, and better training.[44]

Vancouver

After the Second World War, violence broke out in Vancouver with the arrival of a new syndicate from the prairies that sought to take control of all the city's dice games. The appearance of a non-Chinese organization and the perceived neglect of duty on the part of city police prompted BC Attorney General Gordon S. Wismer in September 1946 to order the provincial force to close down a 'dice palace' on Howe Street that was operating unchecked. While the province was accused of interfering in municipal affairs, Vancouver police believed that they were being used – once again – as pawns in the run-up to a municipal election. The department's claim of political interference was probably correct, since Wismer, who was so quick to act on the Howe Street raid, would later at least twice refuse requests from the Vancouver Police Commission to order an inquiry into the same department's activities. But neither did the Howe Street raid involve merely local politics. One local editorialist demanded an 'immediate reorganization of the city's police force,' since professional gamblers were operating openly and growing rich despite the occasional attention of police and the police commission.[45]

The outcome of the 1946 provincial intervention and of a major probe by Mayor Gerry McGeer was the appointment of a new chief of police, Walter Mulligan – a relatively junior internal candidate and close friend of the mayor. Mulligan acted as a new broom to sweep out the Vancouver force, immediately discontinuing the permanent vice-squad system and putting all its members on a two-year rotation.[46] Yet another scandal broke in April 1947 about police accepting protection money from gamblers. When 'self-confessed gambler' Louis Tisman accused the former chief and former deputy chief, along with the gambling squad, of having accepted graft, he and his brother were in turn charged with offering bribes.[47]

None the less, Mulligan appeared to take the enforcement of gambling offences seriously, and he eliminated local graft. In May 1947, a raid on the Western Sport Club resulted in 142 arrests – the largest non-Chinese crackdown in Vancouver since the 1920s. Intense policing of gambling offences continued to follow the electoral calendar, with annual crackdowns coinciding with campaigns, but gambling appeared to be under control. Occasionally newspaper reports claimed that illegal gambling was only more discreet: 'The boys who know will tell you that it has never been easier to wager in the downtown district than it is right now. That goes right back to the big purge in the late 20s.' In September 1948, an undercover report by the *Vancouver Sun*'s Jack Webster maintained that Vancouver was still 'wide open' and that 'hundreds of professional gamblers' operated illegal games – mostly poker – 'in city clubs, in phoney sports clubs, and really illegal joints.' As the visibility of enforcement against bookmakers heightened across Canada, Mulligan issued a warning to Vancouver bookmakers in July 1949 that they must close or expect police intervention.[48] This warning indicates the virtual immunity that these operations enjoyed.

Several municipalities employed padlock legislation to close down repeat offenders. Commercial gambling was understood to be spatially defined. The very word 'underworld' and the common description of a 'wide-open city' or '*une ville ouverte*' reinforced this connection. Gambling was simultaneously hidden from view (or underground) and operating in an open manner, with little fear of police intervention. The role of space and the feeble attempts to regulate it were evident in the paddock – the primary strategy that police in cities such as Montreal used to control gambling and brothels during the 1940s. While the padlock now has infamous associations with Quebec Premier Maurice Duplessis and his attempts to quiet political dissent and Jehovah's Witnesses, the padlock law in Canada was used more often to regulate offenders against public morality. Under Montreal's municipal by-laws, gaming and betting houses, on their third charge, were to be physically closed by padlock for a specified number of days. In order to circumvent this legal measure, operators in Montreal, for example, responded to potential closures by providing police with fictional addresses or placing apartment numbers on fake doors, broom closets, and even toilets. The front door was always left open for customers. This police strategy resulted in 'la comédie des cadenas.' The law was a dismal failure in Montreal at controlling gambling but had somewhat more success in Toronto and Vancouver.[49]

In the spring of 1951, Vancouver, after a great deal of debate in city council, began employing padlocks to close bookmakers' establishments after a third conviction. City council also considered cancelling the municipally issued trade licences of those bookmakers who hid behind legitimate businesses such as tobacco or barber shops following a first conviction, but this, according to one alderman, would create a police state and 'deny men the right to work.' Prompted by the continent-wide crackdown that coincided with the Kefauver committee and the Caron Inquiry, the Vancouver force's thoroughness momentarily impressed local critics.[50]

But a mention of the Vancouver publisher of the Sporting News during the Kefauver hearings, and the suggestion by one of its counsel in an interview with the Vancouver Sun that the city could be a link in a continental syndicate, ended this calm. The publicity forced extension of tight policing to 'big time gamblers' with rumoured American connections. Assistant City Prosecutor A. Stewart McMorran, inspired by the Kefauver committee, argued that in Canada too big operators made protection payments to undermine the law. When BC Attorney General Gordon Wismer asked for evidence to collaborate this assertion, McMorran admitted that he had nothing specific in mind.[51]

Then, in October 1951, Vancouver joined other North American centres in holding a major local probe. As part of a police crackdown on bookmaking, police identified 234 individuals and arrested twenty-three men and one woman on conspiracy offences allegedly between January 1944 and the arrest date. The Vancouver Province described the decision as 'a crippling blow to the city's rich bookmaking "industry" that could be compared only 'to the celebrated investigations of the late

Gerry McGeer in the 1930s.'[52] The ensuing trial proved dramatic. Book-making was described as a major Vancouver business, with estimates of $6 million to $15 million in bets being transacted each year. Federal tax records were subpoenaed; the Crown's eyewitness, onetime gambling 'kingpin' Abe Forshaw, spoke freely; and the owner of the local wire service and his wife were assaulted one evening outside their home. In March 1952, after twenty-two days in court, all accused were acquitted, although fifteen had admitted to being professional bookmakers to shorten the trial.[53] The complete failure of the largest prosecution in Vancouver's history dampened enthusiasm for further crusades. Gambling-related stories vanished from the front pages of city newspapers. Two reporters writing in 1997 recalled that local reporters, especially at the *Vancouver Province*, continued to hear rumours and gossip about 'graft, corruption and bookmaking,' but their publishers 'hesitated and blanched at the prospect of a libel suit.'[54]

The silence came to a sudden end in June 1955. Roy Munro, a local, rather melodramatic crime reporter, acted on rumours circulating in the city for some time and began a series of articles in the Toronto-based tabloid *Flash*. Munro, with 'purple prose and searing sensationalism,' alleged that Chief Mulligan himself had accepted money from underworld figures in exchange for lenient policing of their gambling operations. Mulligan, former chief of the Canadian Association of Police, had allegedly kept most of the money himself but had divided the rest between Detective Sergeant Len Cuthbert of the gambling squad and his men. Within days of the first article in *Flash*, Cuthbert attempted to kill himself, adding credence to the accusations. The following day a full inquiry was announced, with Reginald H. Tupper, dean of the University of British Columbia's law faculty, as sole commissioner, while Mulligan embarked on an indefinite paid leave of absence. Rumours abounded that the entire affair was the result of a smear campaign led by the police union, but testimony soon unnerved Mulligan's strongest supporters.[55]

Cuthbert had recovered sufficiently that by 21 July he was able to testify. In April 1948, he said, he had given Mulligan a paper bag that he had received from a local bookmaker, which contained $500. According to his statement, Mulligan kept half and returned $250 to Cuthbert. Cuthbert's memories were corroborated. In 1949, another detective sergeant had discreetly approached the Police Commission after he claimed that the chief had suggested splitting graft with him. At that time, the commission decided to conduct an undercover investigation into Mulligan and, on the recommendation of the province's attorney general, hired Terry G. Parsloe, a former Royal Canadian Mounted Police officer, for the task. In retrospect, police commissioners explained, the mayor insisted on such secrecy that a thorough inquiry was not possible by the hired investigator.[56] The city prosecutor recalled that 'a lot of information but not facts' emerged.

The rules of evidence made inquiries very different from criminal proceedings. In inquiries, hearsay was admissible, and prosecutors and witnesses had considerable leeway. Inquiries often revealed information that could not be employed in legal actions, and during the inquiries there was little to deter witnesses from taking revenge by smearing others' private lives.

Testimony at the Tupper Inquiry, notwithstanding 'the epidemic of memory loss,' undermined the credibility of the Vancouver police and their chief. One bookmaker testified that he had been operating in Vancouver for thirty years and had never been convicted. The city prosecutor revealed that on one occasion the Police Commission had taken action when officers from one large part of the city gathered to play poker, leaving their beats unprotected. Intimate details of Mulligan's private life, including a mistress and a private apartment that he maintained while still living with his wife, added to the general picture of immoral behaviour and lax discipline. A former deputy chief, Harry Whelan, had refused to become involved in the protection racket and claimed that he had been demoted to superintendent of traffic as a result. After his first day of testimony, he killed himself with his own service revolver. Before Mulligan could be called to testify, he fled to the United States, where he took up permanent residence in Los Angeles. Later, the attorney general decided that Mulligan would face no charges and would not be extradited, as there was insufficient admissible evidence.[57]

Beyond the personal tragedies and destroyed reputations, the eight-month probe cost $57,000 and created a 161-page final report, released in January 1956. Tupper concluded that Mulligan was guilty of corruption and of accepting money from bookmakers and that the Police Commission had handled the scandal negligently. Ironically, the probe and Mulligan's departure may have destroyed organized gambling in the city. In the 1960s, the Royal Canadian Mounted Police would warn Vancouverites about organized crime from San Francisco or eastern U.S. syndicates moving into the city but claimed that there had been no syndicate in the city since 1955: 'Vancouver is considered by police to be the only major city in Canada in which legal – and illegal – gambling activities have so far been free of overall control.'[58]

Greg Marquis, examining the Tupper Inquiry in another context, concluded that the testimony revolved around the world of 'petty criminals, vengeful subordinates, and a jilted lover ... The results read like the script for a 1950s movie on police graft.'[59] The widespread belief that the Vancouver police, even at the highest level, were 'on the take' from professional gambling seriously threatened law enforcement and civil society. If the events in Vancouver had the potential to be a movie plot, with organized gambling, widespread police corruption, and incompetent or dishonest politicians, Montreal's Caron Inquiry provided material for the popular Quebec *télé-roman* 'Ville Ouverte' in 1991. When the Mulligan scandal broke in 1955, the types of allegations were very familiar to most Canadians. Not only had the Kefauver committee been prominent in 1950–1, but between September 1950 and its final report in October 1954, the 'inquiry of the century' had been busy uncovering police and political corruption in Montreal.

Montreal

The deliberations of the Caron Inquiry between September 1950 and April 1953 coincided almost exactly with the Korean War, but agitation for the probe began much earlier and was connected to the city's own Second World War experience. Although Montreal's economy was focused on war production, the city showed greater ambivalence towards and more public dissent directed at Canada's involvement in the Second World War than other Canadian cities. Full employment, the influx of a transient male military population looking for pleasure, and a political culture that took the need for wartime austerity less seriously allowed the licit and illicit branches of the local entertainment industry to prosper. One historian of jazz wrote that 'the sheer frivolity and extravagance of Montreal nightlife mocked the exhortations of Canadian leaders to sacrifice and sobriety.'[60] In 1944, the Canadian army threatened to make Montreal completely out of bounds for its personnel unless an immediate crackdown on prostitution was undertaken to curb the threat of venereal disease.[61]

In this vibrant wartime environment, commercial gambling emerged, in the words of a reporter, as 'one of Montreal's major industries.'[62] Some observers even considered it the city's biggest industry, allegedly grossing more than $100 million per year in the mid-1940s. There were an estimated 200 gaming establishments, with the most money riding on *barbotte*. But like Vancouver, and to a much lesser extent Toronto, there was a lack of political and judicial will to enforce the law. One reporter in 1945 claimed that 'no other city in Canada would tolerate what goes on there.'[63]

The North American postwar crackdown and the death of Eddy Baker signalled the end of this period of tolerance. Eddy 'Kid' Baker, a former featherweight boxer and part owner of the Gayety Theatre, controlled commercial gambling in Montreal when he died of natural causes in July 1945 at the age of forty-two.[64] His death led to a struggle for control of gambling in the city, which fostered instability and eventually violence. In the spring of 1946, for example, all local bookmakers closed 'voluntarily' for two weeks during discussions over who would control the city's 'wire service.'[65] It was not clear who emerged as the 'king' of Montreal gambling, but Harry Davis, out of jail from his narcotics charge, reputedly emerged as edgeman – the individual responsible for collecting protection money for police and municipal politicians and regulating the number of establishments that could coexist.[66] Davis's term would not last long.

While the gambling underworld was undergoing a transfer of power, in December 1945 a rare coalition of anglophone and francophone reformers came together in the ecumenical Ligue de vigilance sociale headed by Catholic Archbishop Joseph Charbonneau and John Dixon, his Anglican counterpart. The Ligue formally requested an inquiry into vice and police in Montreal; its petition included 152 allegations of wrong-doing, but its request was rejected before the courts in January 1946.[67] But the reformers' defeat was temporary.

On 20 July 1946, a pineapple bomb was tossed into the most important *balbo* (a card variation of *barbotte*) club on Mansfield Street, south of Ste-Catherine and mere blocks away from several of the city's largest department stores. Rumours circulated that reform pressure had been successful in limiting the number of gambling houses downtown to three, but a fourth had opened on nearby Phillips Square without syndicate approval.[68] The violence of the explosion foreshadowed Harry Davis's murder less than a week later. On a sunny summer afternoon, Davis was killed outside his operations at 1244 Stanley, barely a block from the Mansfield Street club.

The murder temporarily galvanized Montreal public opinion towards enforcement. Here, on one of the busy downtown streets, less than a block from the popular shopping district of Ste-Catherine, a man was shot in broad daylight. Reporters noted the ordinariness of the street, with the exception – alluding to Davis's colleagues – of 'the sharp clothes and diamond rings' sported by bystanders. As many as 5,000 curious spectators closed down St-Urbain to catch a glimpse of the city's underworld decked out for the funeral 'with sunglasses and fat cigars.'[69]

There was never any question about who shot Davis, but there were many questions about why. The answers lay in the complex world of Montreal's Jewish gambling community. When Louis Bercovitch killed Davis, he was already well known to police. Louis was a cousin of Leo Bercovitch, who was a partner with Max Shapiro in the restaurant Ruby Foo's. Leo's brother Morris was an employee of Davis's, who was an associate of Eddy Baker's, and had killed himself after an unsuccessful New York robbery. Louis himself also had a criminal record, having served time in an American prison for armed robbery. After his release, he married in 1937 and returned home to Montreal, where he justified his entry into commercial gambling as a means to support his wife. Bercovitch enlisted in the Canadian army in 1940 and was back home two years later from overseas. In the 1944 provincial election, he served as a campaign manager for an independent veterans' candidate, and he was a member of the executive of the Victory Branch of the Canadian Legion. After Davis's murder, Bercovitch fled to the Montreal Herald building in search of Ted McCormick, the paper's managing editor. McCormick and a fellow newspaper employee then hid the fugitive while the Herald collected his side of the story and ensured Bercovitch's security, so that he could safely turn himself into police. Bercovitch always maintained that he had killed Davis in self-defence when the two had argued over Bercovitch's attempt to open up his own gambling operations downtown.[70] None the less, he was convicted of first-degree murder.

Davis's murder temporarily created enthusiasm for enforcement of laws against gambling. Captain Arthur Taché was removed as head of the police morality squad and replaced by 'special lawyer' Pax Plante. Plante became the central figure in the anti-gambling campaign over the next decade. He was often described as 'dapper' and in a 1948 report appeared as a 'dashing 40-year old French Canadian ... Slight frame and thick horn-rimmed glasses gave him the look of a third violinist or prosperous beauty salon proprietor. In action, he was pure radio-serial gangbuster stuff – "Mr District Attorney" plus a dash of Tom Dewey with a Gallic accent.'[71] Plante had served as a lawyer in the city's recorder's court. His personal life was flamboyant, with interests in yachts, beautiful women, and theatre, where he helped promote the annual Fridolin Revue for his friend actor and writer Gratien Gélinas. He had not lived with his wife since 1943, and in 1948 she received a formal separation from the same judge who would preside over the Montreal probe into vice.[72] Plante's unconventional private life probably limited his public career to non-elected offices.

As new director of the morality squad, Plante sought publicity for his raids on both brothels and gambling clubs. He invited journalists along and was accused of staging special events for their cameras.[73] He also began arresting the genuine managers, not the employees who were paid to 'take the pinch.' In his first month as director, he went after Harry Ship, who was arrested on 17 September 1946.

Harry Ship was nothing if not conspicuous. He lived in a beautiful yellow brick mansion in one of Montreal's most prestigious and respectable streets – Côte-Ste-Catherine in Outremont. Ship was not only a business success but a 'great man for publicity' and was alleged even to employ his own public relations team, which called him the 'Boy Plunger' or the 'Boy Wonder.' The business cards and embossed pencils with his name and telephone numbers appear almost discreet compared to his self-promotion through sponsorship in 1946 of a junior baseball team in the Dufferin League – the Shipmates.[74]

Ship admitted to having made book since his early twenties, when he left Queen's University before completing his degree. Pax Plante would later note that this 'Queen's man' worked for a bookmaking establishment on St-Urbain before 1940 but with the war was able to expand his own operations dramatically, hiring one brother as a manager and having another employed by another bookmaker. Ship's establishments took bets on everything from horse races to elections results. Ship was also associated with the 'largest and "swankiest"'of Montreal's gambling clubs in the suburb of Côte-St-Luc, which provided filet mignon and whisky to guests free of charge. As with many of his colleagues, illegal commercial operations coincided with legal businesses; Ship was involved in the Chez Paree Cabaret, which had a variety of incarnations, such as the Tic Toc Club and the Hawaiian Lounge.[75]

His visibility among Montreal professional gamblers made Harry Ship a conspicuous and symbolic target for Plante, whose style could also be described as ostentatious. The evidence that Plante was able to gather against Ship was compelling. First, there was the appearance of police cooperation with the gambler, since Ship's bookmaking outfit at 906 Ste-Catherine est (across from the famous department store Dupuis Frères) had forty-three apartment numbers recorded for the same address in the police raids that took place between 1940 and 1946. Second, during this period, Ship had also paid nearly $24,000 in long-distance bills for the eighteen telephones maintained at this location. Third, bank records showed that in 1945 alone he had deposited $1 million. Ship's original trial took six months in 1947, and he appealed his conviction. Finally, on 13 January 1949, Ship was convicted on a charge of keeping a common betting house and sentenced to a good-behaviour bond of $20,000 for two years after his sentence and three six-month terms in jail.[76]

During this lengthy prosecution, Plante faced his own trials. In 1948, he was dismissed as assistant police director for 'insubordination' when he refused to take part in censuring of another officer on what he claimed to be false charges. Plante argued that this charge was manufactured and that the real reason for his dismissal ran 'much deeper' and could be explained by the corrupt career officials who ran the force and their counterparts in city hall. Although Plante attempted to fight his termination, his efforts to bury the city's executive council in mounds of paper came to no avail. At this point, Plante appears to have considered politics and claimed to have been approached by the federal Liberals, but their provincial counterparts were linked closely to a bitter municipal government.[77]

Plante was more successful in keeping his case alive in the press. Municipal politicians were enraged in August 1949 when the U.S. edition of *Time* reported that Montreal had returned to its 'Old Look' after suffering through 'a spell of unaccustomed purity in 1947–8 under the racket-busting rule of the deputy police director.' In the late autumn of 1949 Plante, together with journalist Gérard Pelletier, began publishing a series of articles in *Le Devoir* that ran until February 1950. *Le Devoir* and the group of relatively young anti-Duplessis Catholic *néo-nationalistes* who comprised its editorial board embraced the reform cause, targeting especially the tolerance of commercial prostitution and gambling by former Chief of Police Fernand Dufresne (1931–47) and the current chief, Albert Langlois. The newspaper regarded commercial vice and the corruption that it bred as an example of the threat that modern urban society posed to Catholic cultural values. The series made exciting reading for Montrealers as Plante revealed the names of members of the city's gambling underworld.[78]

By the first week of December, readership of *Le Devoir* had increased by 25 per cent. There was some concern about potential civil libel suits, so the paper engaged a young lawyer named Jean Drapeau, also a *néo-nationaliste*. None of the people named in the articles took legal action, and when the series was complete, the Ligue d'action nationale, closely associated with *Le Devoir*, republished the articles in book form as *Montréal sous le règne de la pègre* (Montreal under the Reign of the Gangster). The book sold 15,000 copies in two weeks.[79]

The publication of *Montréal sous le règne de la pègre* coincided with the creation in March 1950 of the Comité de moralité publique (CMP), aimed at addressing the problems raised by Plante. The CMP has been described by historian Danielle Lacasse, who has examined its work against prostitution, as 'clérico-nationaliste' in orientation, and its membership overlapped with that of the editorial board of *Le Devoir* and the Ligue d'Action nationale.[80] Affiliated with international organizations such as the Fédération abolitionniste internationale and the Union internationale pour la protection de la moralité publique, the CMP adopted a variety of causes, from temperance to ridding society of obscene literature and burlesque. But the focus of the organization in Montreal was prostitution and commercial gambling, and the CMP was able to attract approximately 7,000 individual memberships and got 275 religious and nationalist associations to affiliate with it, including the influential fraternal organization the Order of Jacques Cartier.[81]

The explicit links between religion and the public demands for a police probe made the Montreal situation unique. Postwar anti-gambling agitation outside Montreal was mostly secular. The grass-roots origins of the Caron Inquiry lay firmly within the tradition of Catholic reform and support from Catholic associations. The CMP's primary achievement was its presentation in May 1950 of a 1,095-page petition prepared by Plante and Jean Drapeau containing 15,000 specific charges and requesting a public inquiry into commercial gambling, prostitution, policing, and municipal politicians in Montreal. Its mandate would ideally cover all aspects of commercial gambling in Montreal in the 1940s. The inquiry was granted, and in September 1950 the *Montreal Gazette* predicted that there was so much material to be presented that investigations were 'expected to last three months, and possibly six months.'[82]

In fact, the Caron Inquiry lasted nearly four years, and before it issued its final report in October 1954 it would call 373 witnesses, present 1,000 exhibits, and create over 4,000 dossiers. The cost would be estimated at half a million dollars, with *Le Devoir* and the CMP providing major financial resources during the initial year.[83] From publication of the Plante–Pelletier series through formation of the CMP, *Le Devoir* was at the centre of the campaign to rid Montreal of vice. While the probe was still in its first year, an editorial in the paper pointed out that the Caron Inquiry was different from other similar investigations taking place in the United States and Ontario, since it did not originate with officials or politicians. The editorial claimed that if the commission found and punished the guilty, it would amount to a '*Victoire des citoyens contre leur gouvernement, victoire de l'homme dans la rue contre les politiciens, victoire de l'honnêteté contre le vice.*'[84]

The inquiry revealed an overwhelming degree of complicity involving both politicians and police in commercial gambling. The city levied business taxes on obviously illegal businesses, issued food service licences to them, and inspected canteens and snackbars in bookmakers' operations and illicit card clubs. Personal connections between municipal politicians and professional gamblers were also revealed. One city councillor's brother-in-law was a well-known gambler, while a member of the municipal executive committee had links with Eddy Baker dating back to the early 1920s. The *Montreal Star* reported that this alderman, along with two of his colleagues, was even present at Baker's funeral in 1945. The telephone number of Mayor Camillien Houde and his personal secretary appeared in Harry Ship's 'little black book,' along with a 'who's who' of Canadian and eastern U.S. gamblers. Even the lawyer representing the city in the proceedings was involved, as his wife owned a building that housed a gambling outfit on Bleury Street.[85]

The portrait painted of the Montreal police was no better. Examples of police complicity, corruption, and negligence abounded. Repeat offenders, such as Barney Shulkin, a bookmaker's slip writer, was treated like a first-time offender on each of his 103 arrests. After a year as head of the vice squad, Captain Arthur Taché, on an annual salary of $3,000, was able to purchase two fur coats, a diamond solitaire, bonds, a $3,000 car, and property outside Montreal. When Taché's sister-in-law was required to explain the $14,500 that she deposited into her own bank account in $100 bills, she claimed that she had won the money at an illicit roulette club on Peel Street. If the source of Taché's personal wealth was incredible (he explained the extra revenue by his moonlighting as a handyman), so was the testimony of the professional gamblers. Harry Ship explained his ability to operate under the noses of the Montreal police as the result not of protection money being paid but rather of the force's financial dependence on revenue from fines.[86]

Police and municipal politicians tried many tactics to stop the inquiry. In May 1951, a group of police officers obtained a temporary injunction, and in 1952 the Supreme Court of Canada rejected an attempt by Chief Langlois to stop the probe. In the spring of 1952, the cost of financing the inquiry became a matter of dispute. The CMP dissolved in 1952, and its new incarnation, the Ligue d'action civique, was continually trying to raise funds to support the prosecution, often with little success. A campaign of telephone solicitation in October 1952 netted only $63, and $57 had to be paid out in expenses. The sorry state of the Ligue's finances was further evident in January 1953, when the executive decided to suspend publication of its monthly newsletter, *Action civique*.[87]

The inquiry heard its last testimony in April 1953, and on 8 October 1954 Justice François Caron issued his judgment. Eighteen police officers were found guilty and fined between $200 and $2,000. Chief of Police Albert Langlois was fined $500, and former Chief of Police Fernand Dufresne, $7,000. None of the charges against the five members of Montreal's executive committee was upheld.

Two weeks after Caron announced his findings, Jean Drapeau was elected mayor on a reform platform as the candidate of the Ligue d'action civique, with support from religious organizations and indirectly from Archbishop Paul-Émile Léger. Drapeau's visibility as co-prosecutor provided a springboard for a mayoralty that would last, except for 1957–60, through the 1980s. Mayor Drapeau, with the assistance of Plante as acting chief of police, immediately instituted 'un grand nettoyage,' which curbed the most obvious examples of unofficial tolerance of gambling and prostitution and claimed to drive out five big U.S. gambling syndicates, including one organized by the infamous racketeer Frank Costello. During Drapeau's initial term he was rigid on all forms of gambling and would not permit even lotteries. Claude Ryan, who belonged to many of the same religious organizations as Drapeau in the 1930s and 1940s, later claimed that Drapeau owed his electoral success in 1954 to support from the Catholic church and Léger in particular. Ryan contrasted Drapeau's rigid public opposition to lotteries in the wake of the Caron Inquiry to his previous and his later actions. During the 1940s, Drapeau had organized a highly successful lottery to raise money for L'Action Nationale, and in 1968 he established a lottery to assist municipal coffers.[88]

But the success of the Montreal reformers was relatively short-lived. Although Plante claimed in 1961 that prostitution, bookmaking, and gambling never really recovered from his vigilant leadership in the 1946 and 1955 crackdowns, it is difficult to substantiate this direct link. In March 1957, former police chief Langlois was reinstated by the appeal court and absolved of tolerating vice, and Plante was banished to the basement of city hall to codify municipal by-laws. Langlois's 'jubilant welcome' consisted of a motorcade escort of 1,200 police cars to city hall, where he was welcomed by one of the accused but acquitted aldermen. Indeed, Langlois was greeted as a 'cop's cop,' compared to Plante as 'outsider.' His reinstatement coincided with the return to '*une ville ouverte.*' The *Herald* observed that with his return the 'general spirit of exuberance gained momentum throughout the day,' and nightclubs roared that evening. An unnamed veteran observer remarked that, despite the Lenten season, Montreal had not 'seen anything like this in years.' Plante's departure as acting chief of police foreshadowed Drapeau's defeat at the polls that autumn. The successful mayoralty candidate, Sarto Fournier, promised Montrealers a less puritanical city that would be 'wide open but honest.'[89]

Founier's assessment of popular opinion was accurate. Montrealers' concern was not with commercial gambling (or organized prostitution), but rather with the way it could contaminate the police force and municipal government and support organized crime. Not surprising, tolerance towards gambling had been evident in testimony before the Caron probe. Sidney Shorr, who had worked as a bookmaker until 1945, explained that he did not consider his occupation a real criminal offence. According to Shorr, he 'was not committing robbery or anything like that ... It was not a serious affair, this question of bets ... I did not think I was committing a serious crime against society.'[90] This claim by a professional bookmaker was supported by an increasing number of Montrealers and Canadians.

A Sea Change

If the consequences of professional gambling were not regarded as serious, but the potential harm was perceived in terms of gambling's support of organized crime or its corruption of police and politicians, other issues could also factor into the equation. One was the balance between diligent law enforcement and creation of a police state. The covert structural organization of gambling offered special challenges to police in gathering evidence within the law. For example, a spokesman for the Ontario Provincial Police in 1951 claimed that that body was impotent in fighting organized gambling unless the law was changed so that the force could have 'an even-money chance to combat that evil.'[91]

While some anti-gambling activists, such as United Church Secretary J.R. Mutchmor, claimed that the police were not 'using the full force of present legal machinery,' other leaders of church, politics, and trade unions vocally opposed the proposal by Ontario's attorney general that the Criminal Code be amended to permit wiretapping to secure gambling convictions. The proposal would permit police to install a device to record the numbers being called, not conversations, but even this seemed an egregious breach of individual liberty. Agnes Macphail, deputy leader of Ontario's Co-operative Commonwealth Federation, argued that although she did not condone illegal gambling, 'wiretapping would be a cure just about as evil as the disease.' She was joined by C.H. Millard, Canadian director of the United Steelworkers of American, and Irving Himel, secretary of the Association for Civil Liberties, when John Diefenbaker led the opposition to expanded police powers in Ottawa, since such an amendment was a threat to individual rights and was the 'sort of thing one expects in a police state and must be guarded against.' An editorial in the *Toronto Star* argued that 'the whole business of organized overhearing of private communications is repulsive to the people of a free democracy.' Although it was 'easy to do wrong with a good cause,' it would also be 'fatal.' Wartime images of the Gestapo were invoked and combined with contemporary fears about totalitarian regimes such as the Soviet Union. To the chagrin of the Ontario Provincial Police, the amendment was dropped.[92] Clearly, public opinion did not regard illegal gambling as a threat to civil society, but any abrogation of individual liberty was.

With the rejection of increased police powers, there started a gradual shift towards the idea that legalization of commercial gambling might reduce crime. In 1951, a British royal commission into gambling reported in favour of a more tolerant legal attitude towards gambling. It noted that establishment of legal betting offices in Ireland had eliminated the practice from streets and factories and hoped that legalization in Britain would achieve the same results. The commission presented a series of recommendations that would prohibit betting by minors under the age of eighteen, ban slot machines and gambling in public places, reject state-promoted gambling but tax commercial gambling like other amusements, compel publication of football-pool accounts, and set up betting shops.[93] These recommendations generated much discussion in Canada.

Former Ontario Premier Gordon Conant, a Liberal, proposed legalization of commercial gambling 'to curb crime.' He supported strict governmental supervision, as in the suggested British system, and drew parallels with government regulation of the sale of alcohol. Despite evidence of increasing tolerance of regulated gambling – as in the 1951 recommendation by Ontario's attorney general that religious and charitable groups be permitted to operate raffles and lotteries under government supervision – no definitive public consensus emerged. The *Toronto Star*, which had been so adamant against expanding police powers to curb commercialized gambling, rejected government supervision, noting that 'everyone knows that liquor drinking has vastly increased under it and the revenue obtained by the province has become a barrier to genuine control ... What is needed is not legalization, but a more strict enforcement of the anti-gambling laws.'[94]

The *Vancouver Province* came to other conclusions in 1952. According to it, the laws concerning commercial gambling were 'largely unenforceable because they have no weight of public opinion behind them.' Police made occasional attempts to execute the law, but this was usually time wasted. The problem was therefore not one of civil liberties or the threat of a police state, but rather the profound ambiguity about what was being policed in the first place. The Vancouver editorialist concluded: 'The public, generally, are largely indifferent or even passively hostile to the enforcement of anti-gambling laws. The average man, who doesn't do very much gambling, doesn't see, if he wishes to buy a sweepstake ticket or take a flyer on a horse or that, that it is anyone's business but his own.' This position marked a shift in attitude at the *Province* that would continue along the path to liberalization. By 1954, the same newspaper would identify the lack of 'common sense' in the criminal code as driving gambling 'underground.'[95]

This theme was adopted in the 1960s by J.D. Morton, who was commissioned to report to the Ontario government on commercial gambling. Morton emphasized the harm caused by professional gamblers. 'Being birds of prey, [they] tend to flock together and as an assembly of the least industrious and most unscrupulous members of society are collectively a danger to society.' By drawing a comparison between gambling and adultery (which was declared to be immoral but not illegal), Morton advocated a system of government licensing that would share the same premise as liquor regulation. The strict criminalization of gambling did not have sufficient public support, policing violated individual rights, and, most important, a great many Canadians wanted to gamble.[96]

In the decade after the Second World War, the definition of the problem of commercial gambling underwent a sea change. Although Protestant reformers and their traditional arguments, which associated gambling with destruction of the work ethic and profligate spending, did not disappear, new kinds of reformers offered new grounds for opposition. Critics, often linked to legal reform, based their opposition to commercial gambling on its links to organized crime. Gambling was a vital source of revenue to crime and responsible for corruption of the police, the politicians, and the judiciary. In this reorientation, critics were less likely to worry about the moral consequences of gambling, but focused instead on its impact on civic culture and civil society. The very notion that commercial gambling could be discussed without consideration of its moral consequences was significant.

By affixing the gambling problem to professional criminals, critics recast the public debate. Motivation and objectives took on increased importance. A world of difference lay between gambling that profited an individual and that which raised funds for religious, recreational, cultural, and charitable organizations. The distinction between charitable gambling and proceeds accruing to individuals was not new. The tolerant attitude towards philanthropic and patriotic fund-raising during the wars and the lenient position of the lower echelons of the Roman Catholic church had reflected this tradition. But the preoccupation with criminals in the gambling probes of the 1950s allowed charitable and criminal gambling to emerge as completely distinct. This complete differentiation set the contours of public debate in the late 1950s and early 1960s and put Canadians one step closer to legalization.

CHAPTER SEVEN

Redefining the Public Interest: Gambling, Charity, and the Welfare State

After the Second World War, increased tolerance towards non-commercial gambling coincided with new perspectives on moral issues as diverse as alcohol, extramarital sex, and Sunday observance. A permissive climate reflected the general secularization of a pluralistic society and, in particular, the decline in the ability of the traditional Protestant churches of 'old Canada' to establish and maintain the dominant moral standards. But their power did not disappear overnight. By mid-century, the vast majority of Canadians supported legal access to some form of gambling, but an effective anti-gambling lobby staved off change until the revision of the Criminal Code in 1969.

Debate about non-commercial gambling centred on its persistence, notwithstanding its illegality and the motivation behind its purveyors. Professional gamblers and those who used gambling methods for charitable fundraising were now less frequently perceived as taking part in the same kind of activity. Just as gambling operators were classified according to their motivation of personal gain or charitable projects, the 'problem' gambler emerged as distinct from the majority of players, who could control their degree of participation. As in other activities considered deviant, problem gambling became medicalized, with a focus on specific individuals rather than on the entire society or even subgroups within it. As a result, ambivalence about gambling weakened as moral issues gave way to a dominant rhetoric of pragmatism and utilitarianism. Since gambling could not be stopped, it might prove to be of some use. By 1969, public discussions of gambling revolved around its 'painless' potential to raise money for worthy causes or to provide a new source of revenue for an expanding and expensive state.

The emergence of a wider consensus of toleration towards non-commercial forms of gambling reflected attitudes about both charity and the process of state formation. Greater expectations and expanded definitions of the state's jurisdiction and responsibilities resulted in the eventual transfer to the government of the exclusive privileges to license or conduct raffles and lotteries once held only by religious and charitable organizations. Government-sponsored lotteries were by no means new, and of early modern and colonial states had used them to raise revenue for major construction or for the military. Moreover, Canadian governments already profited from gambling, since provincial and local governments taxed parimutuel machines and entrance fees at racetracks. But the postwar discussion of state lotteries in Canada concentrated on them as a means of meeting expenses generated by the welfare state, formerly assumed by private charity or religious organizations. Between 1945 and 1969, the lobbies for non-commercial gambling put forward new arguments, as a new paradigm began to emerge, and finally, in the 1960s, governments began to get involved. Meanwhile, the older arguments of opponents, both moral and social, lost their effectiveness.

Tenacious Puritanism

Traditional Protestant opposition persisted into the 1960s but was increasingly marginalized, despite the lack of political will to amend the Criminal Code to reflect the wishes of the majority. Proponents of reform regularly attacked the tenacity of puritanism in English-Canadian culture. In 1962, a New Democrat MP from British Columbia, J.F. Browne, observed that in laws about liquor, divorce, and gambling, 'the effects of puritanism are lasting much longer in Canada, at least on the surface, than elsewhere.'[1] His fellow MP Doug Fisher noted that puritanism 'still has a great deal of vitality in this country,' especially among Protestant ministers and the newspaper editors who followed their lead. Ontario Attorney General Arthur Wishart, in 1967, even explained his own ongoing personal opposition to government lotteries by calling on his 'old puritan upbringing.' This puritan tyranny obviously enraged one hotelkeeper from a resort town on Lake Huron who demanded in 1963, 'What petty, self-righteous Methodist minister in Toronto has more influence than intelligence? And what right has this individual to dictate to the rest of the Province?'[2]

Proponents of liberalization were correct about the continuity of puritan influences, since many opponents of legalization of gambling used arguments employed since the First World War. The rhetoric of puritanism continued to assert that it was wrong to encourage 'something for nothing' at the expense of thrift and savings. Lotteries, in this perspective, encouraged reliance on luck rather than on work and in particular sent the wrong message to children.[3] With general opinion swinging towards legalizing lotteries, the Protestant churches unsuccessfully tried to convince both Canadian society at large and their own adherents to abstain. In one example, the United Church in 1962 took out an advertisement in Maclean's for its pamphlet 'Gambling in Canada,' which attacked the idea of using lottery revenue to fund health care. It launched articles in the United Church Observer, where it referred to government lotteries as 'the most perniciously anti-social' form of gambling. The Presbyterians' 1963 pamphlet 'Gambling and the Gospel' also emphasized traditional arguments against gambling, such as its conflict with domestic responsibility and the particular allure that lotteries offered to 'those least able to afford it.'[4]

Within Protestant opposition, there continued a strand preoccupied with the issue of productive labour. A 1963 statement from the Canadian Council of Churches maintained that lotteries, like all forms of gambling, were 'always non-productive' and went against 'a just distribution of goods.' In a letter to BC Attorney General Robert Bonner, the ever-persistent J.R. Mutchmor, leading spokesman of the Protestant anti-gambling cause, suggested that periods of general prosperity required particular vigilance against 'something for nothing.'[5]

But the Protestant churches clearly did not have the support of even their own member. Adherents expressed criticism of the churches' rigid positions against bingo and lotteries, and, according to one, 'the rot we read sometimes is no doubt the reason young people don't attend church.' Another United Church member who was also involved in a service club noted that, while he commended the church's opposition to organized gambling, its antagonism to raffles and lotteries 'makes the whole stand against gambling look ridiculous.' Ottawa municipal politician Charlotte Whitton noted during her campaign against bingo in that city in 1960 that she had not received the full support of local churches, since their ministers believed that opposition 'would be "murder" for them with the service club men in their congregations.'[6] Increasingly, opponents such as Mutchmor and Whitton appeared shrill and anachronistic and seemed like burlesque performers rather than participants in serious public debate. When the Women's Missionary Society of the United Church of Canada in 1954 made a presentation on lotteries to a parliamentary committee, ignoring the committee's other two subjects, capital and corporal punishment, an MP mocked the group for what he saw as its warped priorities.[7]

Admittedly the pace of change in public attitudes was dramatic. When Ontario saw its first day of Sunday racing in July 1968, one Hamilton newspaperman declared it 'a historical date in the white, Anglo-Saxon Protestant culture of the colony of Upper Canada.' Sunday racing was anathema to Mutchmor, who was quoted in the *Toronto Star*: 'One could expect this in Moscow or some other Communist centre, but in a community that calls itself Christian – it's wide of the mark.' Nor was he finding support among his counterparts in other denominations. Ecumenical solidarity faltered after the Anglican dean of Montreal declined his support and rejected Puritanism as something apart from 'the mainstream of Christian thinking.'[8] Mutchmor also went on the attack against Toronto municipal politician Allan Lamport, whom he accused of changing his position on Sunday racing. Lamport responded that his views of 1948 could not be applied to 1968. He went on to suggest that when public leaders were not successful in changing public opinion 'then we must assume that the public must be listened to as far as their demands are concerned.'[9]

Towards a New Paradigm

Charity Fundraising and Political Deadlock

The close connection between gambling and charitable fundraising had legitimized and encouraged more tolerant attitudes.[10] As we saw in the previous chapter, the public's postwar preoccupation with commercialized gambling and organized crime had emphasized the motivation for gambling rather than the act itself. A member of the Ontario legislature wrote to the attorney general in 1945 that most people did not consider charitable gambling a form of gambling 'in the true sense ... where no private gain is made,' while a federal politician claimed that community lotteries and sweepstakes were not viewed 'as gambling in the ordinary sense of the word.'[11] E. Davie Fulton, a Conservative MP, emphasized the distinction between lotteries and other forms of commercial gambling in 1954. While he condemned commercial gambling as 'undesirable in our civilization,' he urged his fellow parliamentarians to consider 'whether rather the crime does not lie in the conducting of a dishonest lottery or the raising of money, whatever be the motive, by dishonest means.'[12] For the growing majority of Canadians, community fundraising through sweepstakes, raffles, or bingo seemed worlds apart from professional gambling in clubs or with bookmakers.

The Protestant churches meanwhile opposed any distinction between commercial gambling and charitable lotteries. Some church members dismissed lotteries as an inefficient method for raising money for charity and as having the potential to undermine private charitable giving. A 'Statement on Lotteries in Canada' issued in 1963 by the Canadian Council of Churches placed the relationship between lotteries and charity at the forefront. This group held that lotteries would 'strangle voluntary giving by discouraging people from contributing to a worthy cause unless there is a chance of winning a prize.' The paper argued that the self-interest of 'unearned wealth' would replace 'the generous impulses which so ennoble men when gifts are voluntary.' This perspective was not unique to religious organizations. A BC newspaper maintained that charitable lotteries were particularly insidious, since they exploited 'kind-hearted' people who were 'least prone to gambling,' and the Canadian Hospital Association worried that lotteries might deter voluntary giving. In 1963, as public opinion lined up behind lotteries to finance hospitals and health care, the public relations director of the Ontario Hospital Association explained his organization's opposition in terms of its fear that sweepstakes would discourage future private donations. [13]

Part of the explanation for Montreal Archbishop Léger's 1950 condemnation of gambling within the Catholic church related to his interest in more rational, scientific, and bureaucratic methods of raising funds, such as annual campaigns based on the co-operative community-chest model. Léger opposed raffles and bingo in local parishes, believing that they 'destroyed' real charity and were 'economically unsound.' But his move against raffles and bingo coincided with the general and widespread impression that traditional sources of charitable giving were disappearing as a result of increased taxation and the proliferation of charitable appeals.[14] The apparent success of the Irish Sweepstakes in supporting hospitals appealed in Canada to local parish, private, and state interests.

Léger's type of concern for a rational and stable funding base for Catholic charities also appeared in general discussions about using lottery revenues to pay for the welfare state. In 1953, the Trades and Labour Congress of Canada divided on the question of support for government-operated lotteries. A resolution sponsored by the Quebec Federation of Labour in favour of lotteries was opposed by those who felt that a state lottery would interfere with the prospects of a stable national health insurance plan.[15] Here opposition to government lotteries was based on the political program of constructing a welfare state. Throughout the years between 1945 and 1969, there was a constant thread of argument that lottery revenue should not replace taxation, because it was a levy unrelated to income and provided an uncertain source of revenue.[16]

Another position maintained by opponents concluded that all forms of gambling, including lotteries and seemingly harmless bingo, were vulnerable to racketeering and political corruption. Robert Bonner, BC attorney general 1952–68, remained unwavering in his opposition to any liberalization of the law, because he believed that any gambling, except 'a gentlemanly game of poker in company where you know who's involved, and bingo with a specific charity in mind,' involved the 'corruption of public officialdom.' Bonner was successful at influencing his good friend Premier W.A.C Bennett, and when a BC legislator suggested that the province operate a sweepstake, Bennett responded that this would call for a sign outside the legislature reading 'Gambling Casino.'[17]

As we saw above, proponents of legal government lotteries in the 1930s had argued that sweepstakes could be a way to raise necessary and scarce funds for hospitals and universities. The powerful mixture of wartime patriotism and philanthropy had encouraged lotteries and raffles to operate unabated in some jurisdictions, but the end of the Second World War moved the issue of regulation – at least temporarily – to the forefront. In August 1945, federal Minister of Justice Louis St Laurent stated his intention to amend the Criminal Code to create a 'proper discretion between those things which could not be considered harmful and those definitely harmful.' The proposed initiative appears to have been modelled on the federal Lord's Day Act, which permitted some latitude in local enforcement, but Prime Minister W.L. Mackenzie King's continued rigid stance against any liberalization of the law doomed the proposal. The lack of federal action led the premiers to agree to act jointly, and a period of vigilant enforcement of the law began on 1 January 1946. With this and every subsequent crackdown came comments to the effect that this period of intense enforcement was merely a prelude to substantive changes in the law.[18] Opponents of gambling, however, would be successful for another twenty years, since the political deadlock was much deeper than what most bureau-crats and social commentators understood.

The Case for Legal Reform

In the twenty-five years following the Second World War, most Cana-dian laws governing public morality came under increasing pressure to change. Liberalization of laws governing the conditions under which alcohol could be legally consumed, the censorship of books, movies, and magazines, Sunday observance, and the legality of birth control, abortion, and homosexuality were all matters of public debate. This increased tolerance in Canada was part of an international trend in western Europe and the United States. In 1953, British Columbia be-came the first province outside Quebec to legalize cocktail lounges and to license alcohol sales in restaurants. Toronto permitted professional Sunday sports in 1950. The local and provincial piecemeal dismantling of 'blue laws' was buttressed by the federal Omnibus Bill of 1969, which addressed many of the morality offences in the Criminal Code, easing access to divorce, permitting therapeutic abortions, and decriminalizing birth control and homosexuality.[19] Among these controversial issues, the 1969 bill also set the framework for regulated gambling.

It is important to see the discussion of gambling in the postwar period in the context of evolving definitions of morality. In 1964, a Vancouver columnist noted with a large measure of irony, 'It was no longer "immoral" for women to publicly display their ankles. It is no longer "immoral" to enter a movie house. Nor is it irreligious to doubt the existence of a man-god or to whisper the free thought that many Biblical stories were but myth and allegory.' Criminalization of lotter-ies, based on a 'pagan taboo ... upheld in the name of righteousness also belongs in the ashcan of antiquity.'[20] Imbued with the language of modernity, opposition to morals laws held that customary ambivalence towards gambling, and lotteries in particular, would have to go if Canada were to escape the Protestant parochialism of its past. When the Ontario Advisory Committee on the Enforcement of Law Relating to Gambling tabled its report in November 1961, it emphasized that it had 'not considered the moral or social evils of gambling, if any.' The very fact that gambling could be examined by a public body without such reflection was striking. Moreover, the report referred to a British royal commission that had concluded that it was impossible, without resorting to unresolvable definitions of 'the nature of good and evil,' to judge 'all gambling is inherently immoral.'[21] Again, no reference to 'traditional' Christian morality – the framework of ethics applied to the question was decidedly secular. Given such a report, perhaps the most surprising element of debates about non-commercial gambling between 1945 and 1969 was the tenacity and residual power of traditional arguments to block efforts by bureaucrats, interest groups, and politicians to effect change.

The language exalting new standards of community behaviour emphasized individualism and individual freedom over what was considered to be antiquated community standards. Rather than defending a church or a dominant class, populist moves to liberalize the law promoted the right of the individual to determine his or her own standard of moral behaviour and actions.[22] It is therefore necessary to acknowledge the connection between an increasingly permissive society and a coinciding current of strongly libertarian, populist thought. Irate letters, often unsigned, reached government officials, such as that from a Manitoban who wrote to the province's attorney general in 1952 that it was 'entirely a mans own business if he wishes to gamble and it would be appreciated if you would look after your own affairs instead of meddling with other peoples and it is too bad that a person of your age has not acquired a little human knowledge and education.'[23] Such populist articulation of individual freedom, unhindered by the state – the 'right' to gamble – dovetailed with impulses towards more permissive moral standards, making it difficult to disentangle these two streams of pressure for change.

The Compulsive Gambler

Populist libertarianism and new moral standards led to a new language in the discussion of concerns associated with gambling. British historian Dave Dixon has outlined the abandonment of a 'moralistic condemnation of gambling' over the course of the twentieth century and its replacement with 'compulsive gambling as a serious social problem.'[24] The Victorian morality that was held by anti-gambling reformers at the beginning of the century was steeped in the language of self-control, rationality, and self-discipline. The gambler contravened ideals in a way that critics regarded as constituting a personal moral failure, which affected his or her family, work, and community. Moreover, British historian Carl Chinn has noted that earlier middle-class opponents did not differentiate between gamblers who were 'compulsive' and those whose behaviour was moderate.[25] After the Second World War, widespread relative affluence meant that it was less likely that moderate gambling would topple a household into poverty, and the prevailing acceptance of gambling as a natural human characteristic led to a more benign general attitude, except when the behaviour was classified as either compulsive or pathological. The issue of 'problem' gambling migrated from a focus on the social and familial consequences to the mind. With the advent of a psychological explanation, American historian John Rosecrance has argued, problem gambling was no longer labelled 'derelict, immoral, and criminal.'[26]

Gambling had attracted the attention of psychoanalysts since Sigmund Freud, who regarded the behaviour as substitution for masturbation. Through the 1920s and 1930s, Freud's followers viewed gambling as compulsive behaviour.[27] But gambling did not attract serious study until the American Edmund Bergler's work in the 1940s and 1950s. In *The Psychology of Gambling* (1957), Bergler termed a distinctive type of gambler 'neurotic' and linked this neurosis to a self-destructive mechanism.[28] A 1948 article in *Maclean's* on 'neurotic gambling' introduced Bergler's ideas to Canadians, who were told that 'neurotic gambling' led to crime, suicide, or the poorhouse. Problem gambling had entered public discourse, and in the 1960s the more specific notion of compulsive gambling gained currency.[29]

The medicalization of deviant behaviour led to many parallels being drawn between excessive gambling and alcohol abuse.[30] In 1957, two former gamblers in Los Angeles founded Gamblers Anonymous and based it on the successful program and philosophy of Alcoholics Anonymous. Gamblers Anonymous was able in 1969 to convince the psychiatric staff at a Veterans Administration hospital in Ohio to develop a treatment program, and in 1980 the American Psychiatry Association formally defined pathological gambling as a disease.[31] A popular understanding of the disease-like quality of excessive gambling was evident long before this formal recognition. In 1968 debates in the Canadian House of Commons, Réal Caouette, leader of the conservative Le Ralliement des créditistes, referred to bingo-playing as a 'disease.'[32]

Even traditional opponents of gambling adopted the powerful rhetoric of gambling as a medical problem. In a 1954 presentation to a parliamentary committee on the legalization of lotteries, J.R Mutchmor, secretary to the United Church's Board of Evangelical and Social Service, drew on what he defined as his own 'extensive experience' in social work. He concluded: 'Persons whom I have known who have fallen victims to the gambling evil are far more pathetic and far more difficult to help than those who have become alcoholics, and they are as difficult to help as those who have become drug addicts ... It looks like a simple thing to play a game of bingo or buy a $2 ticket or put some money on a horse's nose, but the results – the net results – are serious.'[33] Such language, which emphasized the individual consequences of gambling, may have helped keep gambling illegal, but it further dissipated the underlying moral and social arguments. Historian Peter Stearns has noted that the language of addiction permitted condemnation without a direct attack and could be used as a tactic to regulate gambling without complete repression. The problem was that, unlike with drugs or alcohol, the addiction to gambling could not be connected to a chemical property, and as a result it was seen not as a social problem but only at the level of individual self-control.[34] Gambling became not a vice or a moral weakness, but a potentially addictive activity for certain vulnerable individuals. Overall regulation would be achieved through the self-governing of individuals continually self-assessing their behaviour to evaluate their degree of impulse control.[35] This reorientation towards the individual promoted by the medical–psychiatric model partially overcame older prejudices, which had directed anti-gambling forces against the working class or specific ethnic groups.

Celebrated Winners

If the rhetoric of gambling opponents maintained its extreme qualities, one of the ways to gauge public attitudes towards minor, non-commercial forms of gambling, such as sweepstakes and lotteries, is to examine how newspapers reported the stories of winners. Notwithstanding the activities' illegal status, lucky winners were front-page news, with photos of smiling faces and tales of good fortune. Most stories were told in positive terms and remind us of the major role that fantasy played in the popularity of this type of gambling. A Vancouver editorial of 1958 favouring legalization of lotteries observed: 'It gives most of us a warm feeling to know that a man who has been struggling to make a go of it is suddenly on easy street.'[36] Reports of winners tended to emphasize the less fortunate, their hard work before the winning, and the domestic comforts that their new good fortune would bring. The forty-three-year-old Vancouver immigrant widow with children who worked as a dishwasher and won $140,000 in 1956 was portrayed as deserving, as was the New Westminster pensioner living on social assistance who won the same amount in 1959.[37] The hard-luck story of a Vancouver widow who in 1966 spent her last $3.50 on her first Irish Sweepstakes ticket and won $150,000 was another example of this kind of story. Rather than admonishing her for spending what little she had foolishly, the story celebrated this fifty-eight-year-old woman, who had been living on insurance for the two years since her husband's death. Her good luck was acceptable, since she had been unfortunate and her win coincided with her return to the paid labour force.[38] The emphasis on the deservedness of these often-unfortunate, hard-working winners may have been a means to accommodate the enduring value placed on work.

Winners often listed their intended future purchases, and the modest aspirations remind us of the era's uneven prosperity. The $40,000 won in a 1948 Irish Sweepstakes by the operator of a Vancouver shoeshine stand led to a story that he was 'back at work' and that his wife had the modest intention of buying a chesterfield, for they had no such luxury before their win.[39] A union man from the Vancouver Hospital Employees' Federal Union who won in the Army and Navy Sweepstake in 1951 was delighted that the two Vancouver winners were 'working-class people who can really use the money.' According to this man, 'Most working people have to look to the sweepstakes for that one grand chance for a major boost.'[40]

The same perspective emerged in a 1959 survey: one man explained high working-class support for legal lotteries this way – 'Many workingmen know they are unlikely to go very far in life by themselves. When they take a ticket they are not gambling, they are buying a little piece of hope.' A victorious garage mechanic in Vernon, British Columbia, with three young children, planned to leave a veteran's housing development, build a new house 'with a great kitchen,' and place the remainder of his $20,000 in the bank. Another young husband who won $18,700 quickly spent it on a first home, furnishings, and a car. The success of a married Vancouver woman employed by Eaton's meant that she could quit her job and comfortably achieve the postwar ideal of being a full-time housewife. Similarly, a 1962 winner of $150,000 was quoted as saying, 'Boy, now my wife can quit her job.'[41]

In the 1960s, sweepstake winners were less frequently front-page news, but their stories still could appear in the local-news section. Accounts continued to emphasize the widowed, disabled, unemployed, and retired, and their prominence no doubt corresponded to the vulnerable population that bought sweepstake tickets.[42] Stories of winners who were well off were less frequent, unless there was a 'hook' to capture the reader's attention. One striking example was the 1969 report of the $26,000 winnings of an attractive twenty-three-year-old married woman who was photographed in her bikini holding the winning ticket, suggesting some magical combination of money and sex. Simple good fortune and cash were not sufficient to attract readers.[43] Sweepstake winners were good-news stories that sold newspapers and permitted readers to daydream about the changes that such a windfall could make in their own lives. Their prominence and the publicity showered on the fortunate ticket holders, particularly before 1960, testified to widespread approval of sweepstakes – or at least of winning prizes. These less fortunates were legitimate participants in the enjoyment of consumption.

Public Opinion

Another measure of public support for non-commercial gambling was the public opinion poll, taken regularly after the Second World War. The way these surveys framed questions indicated a separation in Canadians' minds between gambling for public fundraising and that for private gain. In 1944, a poll by the Canadian Institute of Public Opinion found that six out of ten Canadians favoured a lottery to help pay for the war effort. Those least favourable were farmers, 'who are traditionally used to earning their livelihood the hard way, [and] are not very enthusiastic about paying for the war "the easy way."' Quebec was the most enthusiastic province, men supported the idea more than women, and workers more than the upper classes.[44] When peace came, support for lotteries fell, but in 1949 65 per cent of Canadians in a Gallup poll continued to see government lotteries as 'a painless way of raising money for laudable ends, and, at the same time, keeping the tax rate down.'[45] A poll conducted by the Canadian Television (CTV) network in December 1963 found that three-quarters of Canadians favoured sweepstakes, raffles, and bingo. In particular, 65 per cent answered that sweepstakes were 'not immoral,' and more than 17 per cent thought that they were 'inevitable.'[46]

A series of Gallup polls between 1955 and 1969 (see Table 7.1) plotted the gradual increase in support for legalized lotteries and sweepstakes, and the pollsters concluded: 'As in the past, public opinion is ahead of law makers.'[47] These polls not only charted the dramatic shift in public

Table 7.1
Public support for legalized lotteries and sweepstakes, 1955–1969*

	1955	1959	1967	1969
Approve	69	75	73	79
Disapprove	23	21	17	14
Qualified	–	–	–	1
No opinion	8	4	10	7

*Questions asked:
1955: Whether or not the public approved of legal lotteries.
1959: Whether or not the public approved of legal lotteries to raise money for education and public health.
1967: Whether or not the public approved of legal lotteries to raise money for health and welfare.
1969: Would you approve or disapprove if sweepstakes and lotteries were legalized in Canada?

Source: Gallup Report, May 1969, Canadian Institute of Public Opinion, Archives of Ontario, RG 4, AG, series 4-02, Minister's Office Files, 1926–78, f. 458.7.

opinion but explicitly tied it to funding of health, education, welfare, and culture.[48] The public seemed to believe that since lotteries and sweepstakes were inevitable and could not be effectively prohibited, society should reap the profit from their existence.

The ascendancy of the belief that gambling was an instinctive aspect of human nature represented a sea change from the premise of progressive reformers of the early twentieth century who believed in the perfectibility of humans and society and the prohibition of vice. Post-1945 Canadians were more likely to believe that the law should reflect 'realistic' objectives and that society had to accept that – as with commercialized sex and liquor – gambling would always exist. The failure of the 'prohibition experiment' was regularly cited as an example of the futility of attempting to suppress all forms of gambling. In a democracy, the law could be enforced only when it had the support of its citizens, and so, according to one government report of 1961 on gambling, 'to be enforceable criminal law must be realistic.' If gambling, like alcohol, could not be prohibited, it could at least be regulated.[49] Vancouver reporter Jack Webster earned the audience's applause when he stated in a 1959 public forum: 'The law, in this respect, is an ass. It's an imperfect sinful world we live in, and the best we can do is to do away with the hypocritical, stupid laws we now have on gambling.' A letter to the editor supporting a sweepstake to fund hospitals was signed with the nom de plume 'Realist.'[50]

The gradual change in editorial policy of the *Daily Province*, which billed itself 'Vancouver's Family Newspaper,' embodies the move towards more permissive legislation. At the end of the Second World War, the newspaper argued that the status quo dealt adequately with the difficult dilemma of gambling. A 1946 editorial described the existing Criminal Code in 'practical effect' as a 'working compromise between absolute repression and absolute license,' since it permitted betting between individuals and at government-taxed parimutuel machines.[51] The paper's position had changed slightly by 1949, when it noted that the present law did not prevent gambling and that public opinion, except for some Protestant churches, supported charitable lotteries and sweepstakes as 'legitimate means of raising funds for worthy objectives.' It demanded that Parliament address the issue and put 'an end to these senseless skirmishes that neither the public, the police nor well-meaning community workers can appreciate.'[52] Almost ten years later, in 1958, the *Province* finally reversed its longtime opposition to government lotteries and 'after a great deal of thought and soul searching' accepted their merit.[53]

As public opinion shifted, older arguments were inverted. A long-standing axiom was that gambling corrupted youth. In 1950, however, the Vancouver crackdown on lotteries was blamed for the closure of a popular youth centre, since the Lions Club had depended on lottery revenue to fund its operation. The report in the *Vancouver Sun* claimed that the crackdown and closure were turning boys to smoking, dice, and pool. The following year, a Liberal MP from the Vancouver area claimed that he was campaigning to legalize charitable lotteries' in order to combat juvenile delinquency in the city.[54]

Older arguments of lotteries' being associated with 'less civilized' and primitive nations were also inverted as attention focused on the sweepstakes, football pools, and lottery bonds in western Europe and the Commonwealth. In 1963, New Hampshire became the first jurisdiction in North America in the twentieth century to operate a legal lottery, and this successful benchmark encouraged Canadian proponents. As justice minister in the Diefenbaker government in 1961, E. Davie Fulton undertook a review of the law and began informal and unofficial discussions with provinces towards reform, but with no immediate results.[55] That same year, the Ontario Advisory Committee on the Enforcement of Law Relating to Gambling, in anticipation of Fulton's success, recommended that once the federal law was altered Ontario should establish a Provincial Gambling Board to oversee government-operated off-track betting and a licensing system for lotteries and bingo.[56]

Ottawa was stymied by the divergent positions of various provincial governments. At a federal–provincial meeting in November 1963, the prospect of a government-operated lottery met intense opposition in principle from British Columbia, Alberta, and Prince Edward Island. Nova Scotia opposed a government lottery but asked that the law be amended to permit small charitable raffles.[57] At another joint conference in 1966, Quebec reintroduced the subject of government lotteries conducted by the provinces. This time Manitoba and Saskatchewan lined up with the opponents but, like Nova Scotia, favoured relaxation of the law for charitable and benevolent organizations to permit them to expand their fund-raising options. Ontario was less enthusiastic around government lotteries than it had been three years earlier. The compromise of permitting any province to determine its own policy, or 'local option,' was rejected by Nova Scotia, which argued that operation of a lottery by another province would place it in a 'very difficult political position.'[58]

General opposition to the criminal status of lotteries often centred on the lack of consistency – often dismissed or understood as hypocrisy – that the law seemed to inspire. Cars could be given away as door prizes at agricultural fairs but not at 'peach festivals.'[59] Various provincial governments maintained what amounted to distinct policies of toleration. New Brunswick, for example, did not interfere with bingo games held for charitable purposes but enforced an informal arrangement that did not permit games to be advertised in newspapers or by radio. Constancy was a matter not only of enforcement but also of principle, argued opponents, some of whom again noted that governments themselves sanctioned and profited from gambling at racetracks. This lack of consistency and the contradictions in enforcement were often identified as 'Protestant hypocrisy' – particularly by French Canadians frustrated by a law that did not reflect their values. But rather than constituting some false pretence of morality, the inconsistency and contradictions reflected the enduring ambivalence among some non-Catholics towards gambling and lotteries.[60]

The Forces of Liberalization

The forces putting pressure on the federal government for legal lotteries were concentrated in three groups – service clubs, municipal and provincial governments, and taxpayers. Service clubs, patriotic societies, and community centres were often mostly Protestant, yet opposed their own churches on charitable gambling. These lay organizations typically drew on a 'respectable,' middle-class membership or one marked by its pride in citizenship through service during war. An editorial in *Lion News* in January 1945 called for an amendment to the Criminal Code to permit charitable lotteries and referred to service clubs' commitment to 'moral standards and good government' as evidence of why the law needed to be changed.[61] Service clubs' illegal use of lotteries placed politicians in a delicate situation, forced to choose between upholding the law and condoning illegal behaviour by 'community leaders.' When the Manitoba government moved against the Flin Flon Legion lottery in 1947, the Legion had 'the unqualified hearty support of this whole district,' including the 'best citizens,' such as the local Anglican clergyman, the Catholic priest, the mayor, the postmaster, and the head of the Good Roads Department.[62]

The crackdown on charitable lotteries in 1946 cost local organizations a major source of revenue. A Vancouver newspaper adopted an analogy from the fishery: 'Raffles were the seine nets which brought money in quantities. Dances, donation campaigns, concerts represent the substitution of a dip net.'[63] In 1945, the National Advisory Council of Service Clubs in Canada, representing Gyro, Kinsmen, Kiwanis, Lions, Optimists, Progress, Rotary, Soroptimist, and Zonta Clubs, actually repudiated gambling methods of raising funds for charitable purposes, but local adherence and enforcement of this policy created difficulties, since the official national policy did not have widespread local support. Only the Kiwanis Club seems to have had support for the measure at the local level and was able to maintain this position into the 1960s.[64]

Charitable gambling by service clubs was a matter of public debate following the war. The Canadian Baptist Convention Ontario and Quebec, at its annual conference in 1946, alluded to this conflict when it included in its usual resolution against gambling that it 'deprecated' gambling by local organizations, even if the causes were worthy. While Baptist churches condemned any kind of gambling, service clubs sought to change the law. The Jaycees and Lions clubs lobbied alone or alongside traditional advocates of reform such as the Elks. A special edition of the *Lion Echo*, newsletter of the Toronto North Lions Club, protested bitterly after a United Church layman labelled its fundraising raffles 'kindergartens of gambling.'[65]

While a war of words between churches and service clubs was occasionally apparent, the full force of the law was brought to bear on delinquent service clubs in Vancouver. In 1948, the executive of a Vancouver Kinsman club was charged with operating an illegal raffle for a fully furnished bungalow and cash prizes. The club had hoped to raise $100,000 for its 'Food for Britain' campaign.[66] Public support generally favoured the well-meaning service club, and a jury acquitted its executive. In its closing statement, the defence had emphasized the respectability of the Kinsman's actions by comparing it with other 'local technically illegal practices' such as the Sunday concerts given by the Vancouver Symphony.[67]

The following year, charges were laid against the Point Grey Community Association for a car raffle that it was conducting. The decision to prosecute this group in an upper-middle-class neighbourhood was no doubt an attempt to apply the law evenly, although charges were subsequently dropped when a magistrate declared that no reasonable jury would convict it. Police action against the association was followed by charges against the nine-year-old annual sweepstake of the New Westminster Rotary Club, which required predicting the amount of time it took for a barrel to travel a section of the Fraser River.[68] Efforts to apply the law uniformly were not so evident in other cities. In 1950, when the Winnipeg Trades and Labor Council was prosecuted for operating a car raffle, a spokesman noted that the organization had 'no complaint if others are being treated in the same manner.' But in Vancouver, at least, in the late 1940s and early 1950s, few organizations appeared to escape police notice, regardless of their members' standing in the community. One enduring battle that began in 1950 and lasted twenty years was the conflict between Vancouver law officials and local Legion branches conducting bingo games. But despite such examples of tenacity, public reaction measured in newspaper letters and editorials generally opposed this rigid enforcement of the law.[69]

Notwithstanding publicity and strict enforcement, Vancouver service clubs were not willing to surrender this means of raising money. In January 1950, police seized a barrel containing 36,604 tickets at the drawing of a raffle for a new house and car sponsored by the Optimist Club.[70] Readers of the *Sun* woke up to a front-page photo of the barrel being hauled into the back of a 'Black Maria' van. A jury of three women and nine men actually found the club guilty of illegal activities. The court acknowledged that the raffle was being conducted by 'respectable people with best intentions' but observed that the law had been breached. Subsequently, the conviction was quashed by an appeal court, since there was 'no criminal intent.'[71]

Juries usually shared this perspective. In 1953, the Manitoba attorney general's office 'arranged' with a local Legion branch to conduct a test case in the Manitoba Court of Appeal with the intention to proceed to the Supreme Court of Canada. The mutual objective was to prompt the federal government to address the lottery section of the Criminal Code. The attorney general's office had arranged to pay for the Legion's appeal, and the Legion cooperated fully. The branch operated a weekly bingo and after deducting expenses donated the proceeds to the Department of Veteran Affairs hospital and other charities. Charges were brought forward against the Legion, and this case went to trial. The presiding judge charged the jury strongly to convict, but ten minutes later the ten men and two women returned with a finding of not guilty, or what one newspaper described as a 'commonsense view.'[72] The judge, defence counsel, and Crown attorney were 'thunderstruck,' and plans for an appeal to any higher court to change the law ended. After the case, the deputy attorney general spoke with a member of the jury and asked why the jury had found the Legion not guilty in the light of the law and of the evidence presented. The jury member reported that 'everybody played Bingo, including the twelve jurymen.'

The reluctance of juries generally to convict charitable organizations for contravening the law posed an insurmountable obstacle to police and bureaucrats and again reflected public opinion. In one of the rare instances where cases were not tried by jury, a Vancouver magistrate apologized before levelling a twelve months' suspended sentence on officials from an Elks club.[73]

Government Acts: The 1960s

Government Lotteries

Government lotteries and the regulation of gambling were very much in the public eye by the early 1960s. While no political party would promise revisions to the law on lotteries, amendments received regular attention in the House of Commons as doomed private member's bills.[74] The public's conflation of charitable lotteries and government-operated lotteries made any political compromise even more elusive. Elements within parties across the political spectrum supported and opposed lotteries. This tension was most obvious within the federal Liberal Party; its complex composition created the challenge of balancing the pro-lottery support of Quebec and vocal opposition within the same caucus. The frustration that parties experienced may have reflected their political power. Recent emphasis on institutions and bureaucratic power in the decision-making process of postwar states may not be applicable to issues touching on morality. In debates on issues such as lotteries, elected officials and parties retained the power to shape (or not reshape) laws.

Other claims for more permissive legislation focused on utilitarian aspects. Governments' increasing need for revenue, especially for health care, made government-operated lotteries attractive to them. The existing situation saw this potential wealth exported to countries that ran sweepstakes and lotteries. Lobbyists recognized that Canadians enthusiastically participated in foreign lotteries and were sending millions of dollars out of the country without any effective interference from the government.[75]

Support for a state lottery was most consistently put forward by the government of Quebec, where Premiers Alexandre Taschereau and Maurice Duplessis had drafted legislation in the 1930s and 1940s that could not be enacted until the Criminal Code was amended. Duplessis picked up his campaign for a legal provincial lottery in 1949 under the 'battle cry of provincial autonomy.' In September 1949, he even announced plans for a provincial lottery to assist with education and health costs.[76]

Pressure to establish a lottery increased with the Quiet Revolution of the 1960s and its expanding state structure. The 1960 provincial campaign, which saw the election of Jean Lesage's Liberals, raised a lottery as a way to finance large projects and achieve rapprochement with the rest of Canada. Opinion polls on government lotteries got the highest ratings in Quebec, and politicians and editorials assured Ottawa that this was a non-partisan issue.[77] In 1962, Lesage became the third Quebec premier in the twentieth century to announce a provincial lottery to be set up after amendment of the criminal code. He asked the federal minister of justice to give 'serious and official consideration' to this request but received no immediate response.[78] Editorialist André Laurendeau in *Le Devoir* wrote that such a lottery would probably reduce taxes: 'Heaven knows how heavily we are being taxed in the province since the Liberal government came into power.' Debates and private members' bills in Ottawa proposing a state lottery were dominated by Quebec MPs and frequently invoked provincial autonomy.[79] Ironically, Quebec's Royal Commission on Taxation (Bélanger Commission) estimated that lottery revenues would make little difference to taxpayers, net only about $10 million a year, and contribute 0.55 per cent to provincial revenues.[80]

Support for lotteries was not restricted to Quebec and was strong among ordinary English-speaking Canadians. A growing coalition had begun attracting an ever-increasing collection of interest groups from across the country and the political spectrum as early as 1954. Organizations such as the Vancouver Local Council of Women, at the forefront of opposition to lotteries in the 1930s, now added their support.[81] In 1962, Mary English, a 'spunky' Calgary grandmother, began her campaign for 'Operation Sweepstakes' to establish a Canadian lottery and stop money from leaving the country. She and nineteen other Calgary women organized a national petition and collected more than 500,000 signatures. 'Operation Sweepstakes' noted that a government lottery had the strong support of Canadians and would provide revenue for worthy causes at a time when taxes were 'at an all time high' and requests for charitable donations 'epidemic.' Its 'Canadian Sweepstake Song' was unabashedly populist:

> Canada needs a sweepstake, which is plain to see,
> Under Government control the way it ought to be.
> There's an unpopular law that we all know about,
> that is long overdue for the heave-ho and out.
>
> Buying a sweepstake ticket, or perhaps a jug,
> Doesn't mean you're a gambler or an alcoholic bug.
> Sweepstakes are practical and good business to boot,
> They're here anyway – why give others the loot.[82]

English complained that it was 'just the higher-ups in the church and Parliament who are against it. They should get out and talk with the common people a bit more and find out what the country really thinks.' Her proposal called for one national lottery sponsored by the federal government, the proceeds of which would be split among the provinces.[83]

The proposal for government lotteries was also popular among municipal governments. In 1951, Vancouver city council restated its support for lotteries as a source of revenue to help fund local hospitals – a position that it put forward in a resolution at the meeting of the Canadian Federation of Mayors and Municipalities. As Reuven and Gabrielle Brenner noted, government interest in state lotteries corresponded with government deficits. Municipal lotteries and hospital funding were annual topics at the mayors' meetings and had wide support across the country.[84]

The most famous example of municipal promotion of lotteries was a Montreal lottery launched by Mayor Jean Drapeau in May 1968. Forty years earlier, another Montreal mayor, Camillien Houde, had attempted to establish a lottery to eliminate his municipal debt.[85] The late 1960s, however, proved a more amenable time, with the federal government exploring permissive legislation. In an attempt to assert a pre-emptive claim for municipal lotteries and in the face of a budget that would bring tax increases of 20 per cent, Drapeau announced his own lottery, which he optimistically forecast would generate an additional $32 million a year for the city. The Montreal lottery sought to get around the law by offering a $100,000 monthly grand prize to the fortunate 'voluntary taxpayer' who had made a $2 donation to municipal coffers. Each month, 151 names were drawn, and winners outside the city received free accommodation (and originally free travel) so that they could attend the grand-prize draw. If we assume that winners reflected the distribution of 'voluntary taxpayers,' the lottery attracted participants from all across Canada and the United States, with BC residents leading those outside Quebec.[86]

The contest was almost immediately declared illegal by Quebec, and Drapeau challenged the province to move against him. When the Quebec Court of Appeal ruled the draw an illegal 'lottery,' Montreal appealed the decision to the Supreme Court of Canada and continued to conduct the contest while the case was being heard. One of Montreal's tactics was to distribute prizes in silver, not cash; another was use of skill-testing questions, although the answer to most was 'Montreal.'[87]

Funding the Welfare State

The Montreal lottery saw one local government tapping into a new source of revenue. The debate about lotteries as a source of government revenue emerged as the dominant theme of the 1960s, as the focus and debates shifted away from private charity through service clubs to the expanding welfare state. It is here that we can identify the relationship between lotteries and state formation. The debates about using lottery revenues to fund the welfare state raised fundamental questions that reflected conceptions of citizenship and jurisdictions. Certainly there was no general agreement that this would be an easy and relatively painless way to collect more revenue. In a House of Commons debate in 1963 one MP employed the old argument about the work ethic by drawing attention to the postwar reconstruction of West Germany and Japan and contrasting this with a philosophy by which Canadians would 'have a higher standard of living in this land by some easy and painless method, that we can have more social benefits for our people without paying the price for those social benefits.'[88]

The public's increased expectations of government services and rising taxation made new lottery revenue attractive. Lottery proponents noted that levels of taxation were believed to be at 'the breaking point' and that there were no obvious sources of new income. In fact, supporters noted that much of revenue tax already went to 'good works' and that the state was replacing traditional sources of charity. In addition, money currently being exported might stay in Canada, and Canadians would benefit from foreign sales.[89]

The prospect of government-operated lotteries divided those who had favoured charitable organizations' being permitted to operate lotteries. Among the proponents of legalized lotteries, one camp favoured private charitable lotteries but not lotteries operated by government. An editorial in the *Toronto Telegram* argued that public funds should be raised only 'by a levy, on a proper, and fair basis.'[90] In a private letter to the district governor of Lions International, Ontario Attorney General Arthur Wishart said that he opposed state-operated lotteries to 'raise revenues for a public purpose' but had no 'reasonable objection' to extending lottery provisions to charitable organizations. An editorial in *Maclean's* by an anti-gambling United Church minister questioned how people could pay for lottery tickets if they could not afford taxes and concluded that any government that did not have 'the guts' to raise sufficient taxes was 'unfit for office.' A Victoria newspaper editorial in 1953 claimed that nations that turned to gambling revenue had general difficulty in collecting taxes.[91]

It is possible to understand the growing acceptance of state lotteries as a middle-class strategy to shift the tax burden elsewhere. Like those who saw government control of alcohol as a means to raise funds and expand old age pensions during the 1920s and 1930s, supporters in the 1960s had a long list of programs that government lotteries could support. Like government alcohol regulation, government lotteries offered a means to 'control' this phenomenon and keep profits out of the hands of the underworld. The appeal to the middle-class taxpayer was thus individual and social – a positive combination of lowering taxes and reducing social danger.[92]

Supporters of state lotteries articulated a wide variety of benefits. One Quebec MP, campaigning in 1955 for a national lottery to reduce interest rates at the Canadian Housing and Mortgage Corporation, believed that the resulting homeownership would counteract the Cold War threat from Communism. More commonly, hospitals and universities, formerly private institutions now financed by the state, were to be the recipients. Some optimists believed that revenue from lotteries would generate sufficient funds 'to operate all our Provincial hospitals.' In the 1960s, people suggested lottery support for old age pensions and family allowances. Municipalities were frequent supporters of government lotteries, since local property owners believed that expenses in health and education were falling unevenly on them.[93]

The credibility and respectability of the government sweepstake campaign gained from the federal Royal Commission on Health Services. In June 1964, the Hall Commission tabled its final report, which would provide the basis for universal medical insurance. One of the central issues was the financing of such a program, and the report settled on a system whereby the federal government would contribute 50 per cent of the costs to provinces that conformed to its minimum standards (i.e., universal coverage, with no user fees). The provinces would be responsible for raising the rest.[94] The commission, while maintaining that it did not support lotteries, suggested that if a province wished to establish a lottery for the sole purpose of financing health care, Ottawa should amend the Criminal Code to permit such a development. Lotteries received relatively little attention in the report's recommendations. This may have reflected the report's ambivalence about lotteries or its realization that they probably would not cover projected costs.

At least some Canadians recognized that lotteries alone would not generate sufficient cash to pay the excepted bills. A 1963 article in the *Financial Post* estimated that a Canadian sweepstake equal in size to the Irish Sweepstakes would keep hospitals going for only four days and not raise a cent for new construction.[95] In response to the Hall Commission, BC Attorney General Robert Bonner claimed that Canadians would have to become a 'nation of professional gamblers' in order to raise the money required by the health system; moreover, 'a medical program should not have to depend on the vagaries of the bettor's whim.' A 1966 report by the Tax Institute of America referred to government lotteries as 'only one manifestation of the pervasive current search for Santa Claus in financing public services.'[96]

This depiction of lotteries as an irrational means of financing the welfare state was reinforced by those who argued that tax relief was not even the real motivation behind the call for state lotteries. An editorial in the *Brantford Expositor* in 1967 expressed suspicion that motivation for the current push for government lotteries lay not so much in tax relief as in the dream of winning the cash.[97]

Some politicians got around their unease about supporting public services through lottery revenues by allocating potential profits to new areas of government spending. A member of the BC legislature did not believe that 'care of the sick' should be left to gambling but thought that such revenues could be raised for government support of the arts and culture; symphonies, theatre, and art galleries were necessary for 'the development and growth of a *civilized* nation.'[98] Whereby previously prohibition of lotteries had marked Canada as civilized, now their legalization could do so.

The Omnibus Bill

In November 1967, Minister of Justice Pierre Elliott Trudeau announced that he would introduce to Parliament an omnibus bill to provide an extensive revision of the Criminal Code. The legislation touched on a wide range of matters, from therapeutic abortion, gun control, divorce, and breathalyser analysis to homosexuality and birth control. In discussing the bill in 1967, Trudeau stated that he 'didn't intend in any way to say there will be lotteries,' but rather that it should be 'easier to hold them.'[99] The Omnibus Bill died on the order paper when Parliament dissolved for an election and was reintroduced as C-150 in January 1969 under the new minister of justice, John Turner. With regard to gambling, the proposed law extended parimutuel betting at racetracks, established a maximum prize ceiling of no more than $10,000 a year for non-government lotteries held by charitable and religious organizations under provincial licence, and eliminated the right of social clubs to collect fees from members gambling in their facilities.[100] The law permitted both federal and provincial governments to operate lotteries of any size.

As Turner introduced his bill in January 1969, he acknowledged that lottery clauses had provoked some of 'the most public response and comment,' as opinion varied greatly according to region.[101] Turner held that the bill recognized geographical differences and, using the language of alcohol regulation, claimed that it allowed for 'local option.' The lack of public resolution on how best to deal with lotteries was recognized in the placing of lotteries, along with abortion and homosexuality, as the most contentious areas that the bill addressed.

Opposition to the lottery provisions divided between those who rejected all forms of gambling and those who criticized the amendment that allowed governments to raise funds by this means. David Lewis, leader of the New Democratic Party, opposed government lotteries as being a means by which those who had money could avoid contributing their fair share to social programs through taxation.[102] Lewis also argued that depending on lotteries as a revenue source made social planning impossible, since income could not be predetermined. Fellow New Democrat Stanley Knowles described state lotteries as 'the most regressive form of taxation the mind of man can conceive,' because Canada's poor would contribute disproportionately. Another parliamentarian went so far as to label government lotteries 'an evasion of the principle of responsible government,' avoiding the process of taxation legislated by elected officials.[103]

Opponents of state lotteries used traditional arguments, drawing Parliament's attention to the weak economies of most countries that held lotteries and their inefficiency in raising general funds. The initial failure of the Montreal, New York state, and New Hampshire lotteries to live up to financial forecasts provided ammunition for this attack.[104] While occasionally the dichotomy of civilized–uncivilized was presented, lotteries were also condemned as 'unscientific.' But despite the abundance of arguments at their disposal, opponents recognized that they were fighting against the tide of public opinion. One MP acknowledged that anyone who opposed lotteries was portrayed as 'antediluvian, a sort of social jingoist ... suffering from what might be called a residual puritanism.' In vain, he tried to reclaim the language of reform and progress for the opposition, but there was no popular resonance. The language of 'modern' attitudes was clearly aligned with those who favoured more permissive legislation.[105]

Most francophone MPs supported the lottery provisions, but not all. Conservative member Henri Latulippe noted that if the budget was balanced, national '*barbottes*' would not be necessary. The conservative Ralliement des créditistes upheld the right of parishes and religious organizations to hold lotteries but would not recognize either the federal or the provincial governments as a charitable organization. One Quebec MP even drew the attention of his Ottawa colleagues to what he saw as an absurd proposal made in Quebec's National Assembly to transform the site of Expo 67 into a gambling casino.[106]

The passage of C-150 into law in May 1969 marked the end of Victorian Canada. Legalization of lotteries opened the flood gates, perhaps not as quickly as, but certainly with greater momentum than, anyone had predicted. Quebec was the first province to set up its own lottery, in 1970. The same year, Manitoba organized a Centennial Sweepstakes, paying $70,000 to the winner, while Alberta held two smaller sweepstakes. In 1971, Manitoba followed Quebec's lead and established its own lottery, with Alberta and Saskatchewan getting on board in 1974. Throughout 1970, the BC government vetoed large sweepstakes and rejected an application to fund projects for its centennial in 1971 through this means. British Columbia licensed only charitable groups and agricultural affairs until 1974, when it passed its own Lottery Act and joined the prairie provinces in the Western Canada Lottery Corporation.[107]

Like British Columbia, Ontario also succumbed to the pressure of neighbouring provincial lotteries. There a political compromise assigned the revenues (at least originally) to new areas of spending, such as sports and culture, not to support existing programs and expenses. The creation of the Ontario Lottery Corporation in February 1975, however, coincided with economic recession, pressures on tax revenues, and cuts to spending. By 1976, public approval by Ontarians for their new provincial lottery had risen to 82 per cent, after lottery revenue exceeded expectations in its first full year of operation.[108] Every other Thursday, 1.3 million Ontario residents tuned into the Global TV network's live half-hour televised draw. In 1979–80, the 'Wintario TV Show' was Global's highest-rated program. The Ontario Lottery Corporation, in an effort to keep its success in an acceptable perspective, noted that Ontarians continued to spend much less per capita on lottery tickets than on tobacco or alcohol and emphasized the benefits that sales of lottery tickets had for the 20,000 small businesses that sold them.[109]

The eastern provinces created the Atlantic Canada Lottery Corporation in 1976. The same year, Canada's four regional organizations cooperatively introduced a national lottery, called 'The Provincial,' adding Superloto in 1980 and 6/49 in 1982.

The federal government coordinated the Olympic Lottery in 1973, hoping to pay for the 1976 games in Montreal. Lotto-Canada's competition with the provincially based corporations led to federal–provincial jurisdictional disputes, and in August 1979, under Joe Clark's Conservative government, Ottawa withdrew from lotteries in return for receiving an annual inflation-adjusted cash payment from the provinces. This role of the provinces in gaming was formalized under Brian Mulroney's Conservative government, which in 1985 amended the Criminal Code to place lotteries solely under provincial jurisdiction. In 1990, the first year-round, government-operated casino opened in Winnipeg, and the following year New Brunswick introduced the first legal video lottery terminals (VLTs) in Canada.[110]

The evolution of liberal thought from a preoccupation with private property to an increased emphasis on moral autonomy and individual freedom had ironic repercussions for the law on gambling. The unscientific, intuitive characteristics of gambling – once regarded as a repudiation of modern, rational liberal tenets – no longer carried the same weight. Contemporary liberal capitalism no longer required the moral ideology of restraint, as its precursors had. As the engine of the economy shifted from production to consumption, the links between labour, merit, and remuneration became less relevant. Individuals' willingness to embrace new, tolerant attitudes towards gambling reflected the economic role of the citizen as consumer, particularly once thrift was no longer thought to carry merit in itself (except among the poorest). With this transition, many traditional preoccupations also disappeared. Gambling was not seen as a threat to the family, and many concerns about gender, race, and age disappeared. Critics, however, continued to see class as a continuing factor, with working-class Canadians regarded as particularly vulnerable to the appeal of easy money and to disposal of their meagre income. This widely expressed concern through the 1960s' debates was occasionally countered with the accusation that such an understanding reflected the paternalism of middle-class reformers.[111]

But the liberalism expressed in these debates was not idealist. This worldview was strikingly pragmatic and utilitarian – if gambling could not be stopped, then at least some public good should be derived from it. Programs could be funded without the unpopular and politically dangerous method of increasing taxes. In fact, government expenses, debt, and taxes continued to rise even after governments initiated lotteries. Revenue from gambling simply comprised one more source of income.

The appeal to the taxpayer explains the timing of the federal government's finally introducing legislation that reflected long-held public opinion. There was no new consensus, nor had the stalemate of the late 1950s really been resolved. Rather Lester Pearson's Liberals needed to hold out the possibility of state lotteries as a strategy to counter political opponents who could and did make effective use of anti-tax arguments against the expanding welfare state. The Liberal Party had staked its political fortunes to a particular rate and kind of expansion in social services. It did not matter that lotteries would not, according to the best tax expertise, reduce individual tax burdens. Rather, the tantalizing fantasy that such relief was possible was sufficient to make liberalizing gambling law politically attractive.[112]

The adoption of government-operated gambling, however, reminds us of the continuing links between the development of the welfare state and private charity.[113] The right of governments to enter into this arena of fundraising reflected its shouldering of responsibilities once held by private charity and religious organizations, and it could hardly be surprising that the areas of overlapping jurisdiction would lead to conflict. The move of the state into this form of revenue was hardly unique to Canada – governments all over the world were looking to new means of balancing budgets – and thus Canada's adoption of government lotteries must be understood as part of an international trend. The particular way the changes transpired in Canada reflected the loss of power to determine and maintain moral standards by those who held moral authority in 'old Canada,' the lessening of regional differences, and the emergence of a more homogeneous, global standard of behaviour.

Conclusion

In remembering the moral climate of his Victorian, Methodist child-hood in Ontario, historian Arthur Lower recalled that the taboos about cards, dances, Sunday reading, and even alcohol were 'intermittent.'[1] This admission of the lack of consistency within one household offers an entrance into Canada's erratic approach towards gambling between 1919 and 1969. It is a story as much about continuity as about change. From the First World War to the revision of the Criminal Code in 1969, an overlapping of moral and economic concerns led to maintenance of unenforceable laws and the absence of a political consensus to bring these troublesome laws into line with behaviour. Gambling, together with other morality offences involving alcohol, commercial sex, narcot-ics, and Sabbath non-observance, was a focus of Protestant moral re-form and of the social purity movements in the period from 1885 to 1920. The prominence of the temperance movement and its dramatic rise and fall around the First World War has shaped our historical understanding of all these campaigns, and it is easy to imagine that these issues were resolved in the roar of the 1920s. Indeed, it is easy (and perhaps convenient) to forget that prohibition remained in effect in Prince Edward Island until 1948.

Moral discourse should never be confused with behaviour. Nor was there ever one universal moral standard in Canada. Nevertheless, it was the perspective of the largely English-speaking, Protestant, middle-class critics of gambling that was encased in Canadian crim-inal law. By 1969, values that had given gambling its illegal status no longer seemed either persuasive or relevant. Opponents of gambling persisted in thinking that it preyed on the lazy and the poor, encour-aged the wrong sort of charity, or victimized those now classified as addicts, but their moralizing tone had largely disappeared. The transformation of the ideology surrounding capitalism, religion, and gender roles in Canada after the Second World War offers a partial explanation. The growth of consumerism and the public acceptance of a value system that celebrated material success no matter what the price necessitated general renunciation of older values that revered thrift and production. The shift in attitudes towards the economy was accompanied by a general secularization of society and, most important, the secularization of the Protestant and Catholic political elites.With changes in the form of capitalism and the role of religion came widespread political utilitarian pragmatism, which antedated the rise of neo-liberalism in the 1970s. Today most gambling in Canada has moved from the jurisdiction of federal criminal law to provincial 'commercial' regulation under the new, preferred name 'gaming industry.' Indeed the 'gaming sector' is now just another element within the 'leisure service industry.' The somewhat creative linguistic efforts by contemporaries to avoid the word gambling reminds us that at least some ambivalence remains.

Concern about lotteries and poor citizenship dissipated as the provincial governments eventually gained a monopoly over lotteries and sweepstakes after 1969, and, in a complete reversal of an earlier position, the good citizen now purchased lottery tickets to finance public health care facilities and community centres. During the 1950s and 1960s conventional thinking upheld progress – a belief that politicians, businessmen, and science and technology would secure full employment and rising living standards. The timing of the eventual legalization of lotteries and bingo corresponded not only to an economy driven by consumption but also to the shattering of economic expectations by inflation, recession, rising unemployment, and increasing income disparity. Equality of opportunity in the realm of chance was more consistent with day-to-day leisure and consumer experience than equality of opportunity in the world of work.[2] Uncertain economic conditions coupled with a culture that equated success with material wealth elevated consumption in unprecedented ways. Slogans created to advertise lotteries, such as the Ontario Lottery Corporation's 'Imagine the Freedom,' linked spiritual and material well-being through prize-winning in a way that nineteenth-century moralists may have thought about labour. One historian of U.S. lotteries has written: 'The twentieth-century celebration of consumption has increased the occasions to gamble. State lotteries hire advertisers to overcome the middle-class resistance to games of chance. We have largely abandoned the nine-teenth-century belief in the deep morality of production, but we have not constructed a vital substitute.'[3]

Between 1919 and 1969, moral ambivalence towards gambling provided a means of accommodating the tensions and contradictions associated with gambling and its participants. Rather than hypocrisy, ambivalence was a conscious but unintentional strategy to achieve balance and moderation. The forces and pressures that it attempted to reconcile were as varied as Protestant and Catholic constituencies, frequently expressed in the different stance of Quebec and the rest of Canada. Although there were examples of similarity, such as popular support for legalized gambling in both (Catholic) Quebec and (surprisingly secular) British Columbia, the federal legal system had to accommodate diverse moral cultures. The illegal status of gambling also had to balance class and racial assumptions and gender and family identities. Those in power associated 'problem' gambling with certain groups demarcated by their ethnicity, religion, or class and were prepared to support laws, such as those allowing parimutuel betting at racetracks, that circumvented these groups. Concerns about the preservation of peace, order, and good government were poised against the threat of corruption associated with organized gambling. Distinctions made between private profit and public good explained the bifurcation between professional gambling, in which benefits accrued to an individual or individuals, and acceptable gambling, whose purpose was to raise funds for patriotic or philanthropic causes and, later, the state. Gambling itself in the twentieth century was probably a cognitive contradiction: the act of buying a lottery ticket was a testimony to the persistence of a belief in luck in what was supposed to be a rational, technocratic society. Finally, gambling, like other moral issues, exposed the tensions between individual liberty and the coercive actions of liberal democratic governments to enforce moral values.[4]

The ambivalence towards gambling can also be explained by the failure of binary pairs, such as work and play, or labour and speculation, to reflect experience. There was too much work in the business of gambling for it to be regarded only as a leisure activity. Gambling and speculation shared too many similarities for distinct categorization. When investments turned sour, they were dismissed as gambling, but when they succeeded, similar forms of speculation could be praised as examples of intelligent foresight.

This study suggests several insights beyond the particular topic. First, it warns us against underestimating the ongoing influence of social purity and moral reform well into the twentieth century. Change in dominant moral codes began in the 1920s, but it took at least another thirty years for a consensus to emerge. The puritan supporters of this older value system could not control what people did but were remarkably tenacious in preventing legal reform. Second, this study also indicates that recent attention to political institutions and state bureaucracies offers few insights into policy development in moral issues. Third, and finally, it also tells us something about the ongoing nature of power in Canadian society. Although I provided a materialist interpretation to explain the timing of attitudinal change in the move from a production-driven to a consumption-based economy, economics alone could not explain the kind of power being contested. The struggle for moral authority could (and often did) coincide with economic power. But as we saw most clearly in the 1950s and 1960s, those who blocked legislative change and appeared to be almost shrill voices screaming against the wind of change had no material motive behind their passion.

Gambling threatened the world of the Mutchmors that was trying to hold onto its disappearing political privilege despite the decline of 'old Canada.' The excitement and passion of gambling evoked images of people out of control – and this was particularly threatening when these frenzied people were different on the basis of race, class, or religion. While there was much that was both racist and classist about opposition to gambling, this critique was mixed with the ideal of charity, the recognition of vulnerable women and children, and the rejection of materialism. At the other extreme were those who saw gambling as an opportunity to celebrate qualities such as masculine honour and test the limits of keeping one's word. Most Canadians probably found themselves somewhere in the middle. They understood gambling as an inevitable aspect (for good or bad) of human nature and accepted the existence of gambling as one of those many compromises with ordinary life. Buying a sweepstake or lottery ticket did no real harm and in fact often did some good when profits went to some worthy cause. If gambling was legal at the racetrack, what difference did it make if one placed a bet with a local bookmaker or agent? Governments also found themselves in the middle. Colin S. Campbell and Garry J. Smith have recently made the crucial observation that provincial and federal governments do not promote gambling 'for its own sake, that is, as a harmless and worthwhile recreational activity.' Instead, governments have since 1969 linked liberalization of the law to such pragmatic and practical concerns as enforcing the law, keeping money in Canada, generating income for government and charity, and creating employment.[5]

In contemporary debates about on government-licenced VLTs or regulated casinos – which take place everywhere from local referendums in Alberta, through provincial referendums in New Brunswick, to the back seats of taxis in major cities – gambling continues to evoke feelings of ambivalence. This is not new but suggests an important lesson. Moral ambivalence had kept most forms of gambling – except in the cases of individual and family tragedies – at a relatively moderate level. Today, this balance is at risk of disappearing, as researchers identify high levels of problem gambling among children and teenagers who have come of age in a society increasingly different and distant from that of 1969. The advertisements and commercials that assault us constantly rarely express any ambivalence, and it is a cliché that among those most addicted to gambling are the provincial governments. The recent public service campaign by the Régies des lotteries vidéo du Québec to address compulsive gambling – 'It's only a game' – is benign compared with similar campaigns against drinking and driving or speed on the highways. This campaign acknowledges the enjoyment of VLTs and suggests that gambling is a problem only for the few individuals who lack self-control.

It is obvious that morality is difficult to inject into political debates in a pluralistic, secular country, and the examination of gambling shows how its use in the past reinforced race, class, and religious prejudices. The problem is that there may be some moral consequences of gambling that the current philosophy of common-sense pragmatic utilitarianism denies. Rather than remaining silent on moral and ethical principles, we need to find a means to insert them, where they are relevant, into a vigorous and open public debate. Pragmatic utilitarianism's attempt to discount moral stances is no more ideologically neutral than past versions of uncompromising Protestant morality. Issues such as gambling that touch public morality need to be discussed, even if the result is ambivalence.

Notes

Abbreviations

AG	Attorney General
ANQ-Q	Archives nationale du Québec à Québec
AO	Ontario Archives, Toronto
AVM	Archives de Ville Montréal
BCARS	British Columbia Archives and Records Service, Victoria
CA	crown attorney
CBA	Canadian Baptist Archives, McMaster University, Hamilton
CDH	Catholic Diocese of Halifax Archives
CRLG	Centre de recherche de Lionel Groulx, Outremont
CTA	City of Toronto Archives, Toronto
CUL	Concordia University Library, Montreal
HC	House of Commons
JCSHC	joint committee of Senate and House of Commons
MLA	member of legislative assembly
MP	member of Parliament (federal)
MPP	member of provincial assembly
NAC	National Archives of Canada, Ottawa
NSARM	Nova Scotia Archives and Records Management, Halifax
OBU	One Big Union
PAM	Provincial Archives of Manitoba, Winnipeg
TPA	Toronto Police Archives
UBC	University of British Columbia, Vancouver
UCA	United Church Archives, Toronto
VCA	Vancouver City Archives, Vancouver

Introduction

1 *La Presse* (Montreal), 20 Jan. 1968
2 Donna Laframboise, 'Governments and Gambling: Long-Armed Bandits,' *Globe and Mail*, 21 Feb. 1998
3 Nova Scotia Gaming Corporation, *Annual Report, 1999–2000* (Halifax, 2000), 26
4 *Globe and Mail*, 26 Nov. 1997; Clare Sambrook, 'Camelot's Casino Kids,' *Manchester Guardian*, 23 Feb. 1998
5 Devereux, *Gambling*, 200; Lears, 'Playing with Money'
6 *Victoria Colonist*, 6 April 1933
7 Wamsley, 'State Formation,' 80
8 Eadington and Frey, Preface, 9
9 *Montreal Gazette*, 17 Sept. 1946
10 PAM, GR 950, AG, K/4/6/4, 'Horse Racing, Horse Track Gambling, Ice Racing, 1946,' clipping, letter to the editor, *Winnipeg Tribune*, 10 July 1926
11 I am indebted to Tina Loo for this term.
12 Burnham, *Bad Habits*, 150–1
13 *Montreal Herald*, 2, 4 June 1927
14 *Vancouver Daily Province*, 31 May 1932. It is possible that women were less likely to use an alias.
15 Paula Fass, review of Burnham, *Bad Habits*, in *Journal of Social History* 28, no. 2 (winter 1994), 410
16 For example, see Metcalfe, 'Organized Sport'; Itzkowitz, 'Victorian Bookmakers'; Ponte, 'Religious Opposition'; Fabian, *Card Sharps*; and Burnham, *Bad Habits*
17 Lears, 'Playing with Money,' 8
18 Brenner with Brenner, *Gambling*, 1
19 Ibid., 15
20 Ibid., 14–15
21 Ezell, *Fortune's Merry Wheel*, 271
22 Brenner with Brenner, *Gambling*, 16
23 Leonoff, 'Harry L. Salmon of Victoria'; *Daily Province*, 8 May, 29 Oct. 1931
24 Anthony B. Chan, *Gold Mountain*; 'Yee Ah Chong Remembers,' 249; Anderson, *Vancouver's Chinatown*, 101–3
25 PAM, GR 542, AG, J/13/2/5, 'Slot Machines,' 12 Oct. 1928, Manitoba Provincial Police Report; correspondence to W.J. Major, AG, from J.K. May, Sales Manager, Scott-Bathgate Co., 9 Oct. 1928
26 McKibbon, 'Working-Class Gambling'; Dixon, *From Prohibition to Regulation*

27 Clotfeller and Cook, *Selling Hope*, 46–7
28 JCSHC, *Minutes*, No. 7, 30 March 1954, 296. The Women's Missionary Society of the United Church of Canada was initially ridiculed by committee members for preparing a presentation on lotteries and bingo while neglecting what the committee felt to be the more important moral–ethical mandates of the committee – capital punishment and corporal punishment.
29 Lears, *No Place of Grace*, 220
30 JCSHC, *Reports*, 63; Criminal Code, 1892, part XIV, sections 196–205
31 *The Criminal Code and Other Selected Statutes of Canada* (Ottawa 1951), chap. 36, secs. 225–36
32 *Statutes of Canada 1922*, 12–13 Geo. V, vol. I–II, chap. 16, sec. 1038, 72; amendment to sec. 236 proclaimed 28 June 1922
33 Waters, 'Operating,' 23
34 Ibid., 29–30
35 Ibid., 22; Wise, 'Sport'; Bouchier, 'Strictly Honorable Races.' For a discussion of the parallel situation in Australia, see O'Hara, *A Mug's Game*, 88–9, 120.
36 There were few francophones in leadership roles at the Montreal Jockey Club, but J.P.B. Casgrain and Rudolphe Forget were among the prestigious founders. NAC, RG 33, series 55, vol. 1, Canada, Royal Commission on Horse Racing (Rutherford Commission), 65
37 NAC, RG 33, series 55, vol. 2, Canada, Royal Commission on Horse Racing (Rutherford Commission), 207, 237–9
38 *Halifax Citizen*, 25 Sept. 1936
39 Raney, 'Scandal.' Raney was also a vigorous prohibitionist. See Hallowell, *Prohibition*.
40 AO, RG 49-63, Press Clippings, Office of the Minister, 1902–1934, ms. 755, reel 589, *Toronto Mail*, 2 June 1922
41 Norman Baker, 'Going to the Dogs,' 105–7
42 HC, *Debates*, 22 May 1934, 3277 (J.A. Fraser, Cariboo); Brenner with Brenner, *Gambling*, 18; Labrosse, *The Lottery*, 108
43 Vance, *Analysis*, 55–7; Alexandre Taschereau, *The Lottery Issue*, text of speeches to Quebec Legislative Assembly on 14 March 1934; *Vancouver Sun*, 13 Jan. 1934; *Toronto Globe and Mail*, 14 May, 10 June 1938
44 Josie, 'Social Effects,' 29; Brenner with Brenner, *Gambling*, 18
45 ANQ-Q, E-17, Correspondance du Procureur-General, 1930, f. 558
46 *Victoria Colonist*, 28 May 1920
47 Osborne and Campbell, 'Recent Amendments,' 129

48 *Vancouver Daily Province*, 8 May 1931; *Vancouver Sun*, 28 Nov. 1936, 29 March 1938

49 *La Patrie* (Montreal), 20 Feb. 1935. Thanks to Andrée Lévesque for this reference.

50 JCSHC, *Minutes*, No. 9, 28 April 1954, 370; Stein, 'Why,' 48; Davies, 'Police,' 88. See also Petrow, *Policing Morals*. Two Canadian examples that suggest similar circumstances are Weaver, *Crime*, and Rogers, 'Serving Toronto.'

51 ANQ-Q, E-17, Correspondance du Procureur-Général, 1931, f. 6400, 18 Nov. 1931; 1932, f. 1784, 21 March 1932

52 NAC, RG 13, Department of Justice, vol. 2192, 1522/1927, 'Criminal Code S 236 Games of Chance at Agricultural Fairs,' 10 March 1924

53 Stearns, *American Cool*

54 AO, RG 4-32, AG, Central Registry, 1920, f. 3067, n.d.

55 For the Canadian context, see Little, *No Car*; Valverde, *Age of Light*; Adams, 'In Sickness'; Sangster, *Regulating Girls*. Hunt's *Governing Morals* offers a useful international context.

56 McKibbon, 'Working-Class Gambling,' 118

1: The Critics' Views, 1919–1969

1 Fox, 'In Search,' 85–6

2 Dunkely, *Gambling*, 13

3 Fabian, *Card Sharps*, 5. For a discussion of luck and working-class culture, see Suzanne Morton, 'Men and Women,' 287–90.

4 McMillen, 'Understanding Gambling,' 13

5 AO, RG 4-32, AG, Central Registry, 1935, f. 2761

6 Rodgers, *The Work Ethic*, 8; Baker, *Moral Framework*, 14

7 Brenner with Brenner, *Gambling*, 70; Fabian, *Card Sharps*, 1; Dixon, *From Prohibition*, 49–51

8 Howell, *Northern Sandlots*; Riess, *City Games*; David Grant, *On a Roll*, 17, 79; Fox, 'In Search,' 85

9 PAM, GR 542, AG, Central Registry, J/13/2/5, 'Slot Machines,' Memo for W.J. Major, AG, citing *Rex v. Canada Mint Co.*, 1928, Supreme Court of Alberta; *Arhambault v. Marconty*, 1928, Montreal Recorder's Court; *Rex v. Larsen Mills*, 1928, County of Carleton (Ottawa)

10 AO, RG 49-126, Committee on the Administration of Justice, Exhibit 154, Statement of Christian Social Council of Canada, 25 May 1951, 3; Clapson, *A Bit*, 39; Kavanagh, *Enlightenment*, 5

11 Lears, 'Playing with Money,' 20; *Senate Debates*, 17 June 1931, 279 (George E. Foster)

12 Brenner with Brenner, *Gambling*, viii–ix
13 JCSHC, *Minutes*, No. 8, Testimony of Director Canadian National Police, 27 April 1954, 354; Zelizer, *Morals*, 73. There continued to be variations in the use of insurance among ethnic groups. For example, in the United States members of the Dutch Reform community did not buy insurance, as they regarded it as an attempt to circumvent the will of God. Whaples and Buffum, 'Fraternalism,' 106. According to Zelizer, life insurance today is still 'not legally recognized in Islamic countries as religious law prohibits speculation on human life'; *Morals*, 33
14 Robert Borden and Charles Tupper were both presidents of Crown; Mackenzie Bowell was president of the Imperial Life Assurance Co. of Canada; Wilfrid Laurier was a director of Mutual Life; John A. Macdonald was president of Manufacturers; and Alexander Mackenzie was president of North American Life Assurance Co. McQueen, *Risky Business*, 8; John Ashton, *The History of Gambling in England* (London 1898); cited in Brenner with Brenner, *Gambling*, 101. In 1833, the British enterprise Standard Life established the first firm to offer life insurance in Canada, and in 1847, Canada Life, the first Canadian-owned insurance company, opened its doors. Zelizer, *Morals*, 33; Fleming, *Merchants*, 15.
15 W.L. Morton, *The Progressive Party*, 45. The link between land speculation and gambling was present in other agricultural frontier societies such as New Zealand. David Grant, *On a Roll*, 125. Land speculation could also create an environment that fostered the appeal of gambling. Paul Voisey, in his study of the area around Vulcan, Alberta, noted early settlers' preoccupation with gambling and baseball and attributed their popularity 'to the speculative character of frontier society.' Howell, *Northern Sandlots*, 137; Voisey, *Vulcan*, 27, 60, 162–4; Cook, 'Henry George,' 143. See also Homel, 'Fading Beams.'
16 Heron, 'Labourism,' 59. See also Naylor, *The New Democracy*; Canada, Department of Labour, *Labour Organization in Canada* (Ottawa 1917), 38–9. See also Ankli, 'North American.'
17 'Need for Reasonable Gaming Code,' *Saturday Night*, 4 March 1922, 10; *Victoria Colonist*, 10 May 1931
18 *OBU Bulletin*, Winnipeg, 6 Nov. 1930, 28 April 1932; *Vancouver Daily Province*, 25 March 1935
19 *Victoria Colonist*, 17 Nov. 1926; *Vancouver News-Herald*, 22 Feb. 1939
20 Letter to the editor, *Halifax Star*, 16 May 1938. See also AO, RG 23, Ontario Provincial Police, Series 4-02, f. 22.2, letter to AG from Stratford, Ont., 2 Jan. 1946; BCARS, GR 1323, AG 47, c. 95-8 2966, vol 5, f. 47, Vancouver Bingo

21 Attributed Osler quote made in House of Commons and quoted in 'The Front Page,' *Saturday Night*, 11 Dec. 1909; *Senate Debates*, 8 May 1931, 85 (George Lynch Stauton); HC, *Debates*, 18 April 1933, 4040 (A.L. Beaubien)

22 HC, *Debates*, 18 April 1933, 4042 (J.S. Woodsworth); 22 May 1934, 3278 (John Fraser, Cariboo)

23 JCSHC, *Minutes*, No. 7, 30 March 1954, 301

24 Armstrong, *Blue Skies*, 41; Ontario, *Report of the Attorney General's Committee on Enforcement of the Law Relating to Gambling*, appointed 5 July 1961, reported 6 Nov. 1961, J.D. Morton, chair, Rolf Eng, M.L. Friedland (counsel), 3

25 *Halifax Herald*, 18 May 193; 20 April 1934. Thanks to Shirley Tillotson for this reference. For Neil Herman's reform activities, see Suzanne Morton, 'Labourism and Labor Politics.'

26 Israel, 'Montreal,' 192–3; UCA, fonds 197, United Church of Canada Board of Evangelical and Social Service Office of Secretary, 27 April 1945, J.R. Mutchmor to C.M. Nicholson, Sydney, N.S. Mutchmor expressed similar expectations in *Victoria Daily Times*, 24 July 1945.

27 Waters, 'Operating'; Campbell and Smith, 'Canadian Gambling Legislation,' and Brown, 'Thoroughbred Horse-Racing'; 'The Front Page,' *Saturday Night*, 11 Dec. 1909

28 Price, 'Investment,' 49–50. For Raney on gambling, see Raney, 'Scandal.'

29 Price, 'Investment,' 50; *Victoria Colonist*, 22 Feb. 1962. Nearly the exact sentiment was expressed in 'All That Glisters [*sic*] ...,' editorial from the *Economist* reprinted in *Globe and Mail*, 12 May 1997.

30 Allingham, 'Is Speculation Destructive?'; Cody, *Why?'* 15

31 Paton, 'Gambling,' 166; Zelizer, *Morals*, 88

32 AO, RG 4-32, AG, Central Registry, 1925, f. 1103, 2 April 1925

33 Ibid., 1927, f. 3347; 1928, f. 1028, 18 April 1928; ANQ-Q, E-17, Correspondance du Procureur-Général, 1928, f. 7174, 19 Oct. 1928; HC, *Debates*, 22 May 1934, 3317 (Samuel Gobeil, Compton); J.A. Mercier (Laurier-Outremont), 22 May 1934, 3289

34 JCSHC, *Minutes*, No. 7, 30 March 1954, 279–80; No. 15, 28 April 1955, 469

35 *Victoria Colonist*, 17 Aug. 1935

36 UCA, fonds 197, United Church of Canada, Board of Evangelical and Social Service, Office of Secretary, J.R. Mutchmor to Rev. F.E. Barrett, 10 April 1945 See also Porter, *Vertical Mosaic*, 518.

37 NAC, RG 13, Department of Justice, vol. 2192, 1522/1927, 'Games of Chance at Agricultural Fairs,' to Ernest Lapointe, Minister of Justice, from

W.G. Wallace, Clerk Presbyterian Church in Canada, 9 July 1925. This was
the only time a religious body made this specific argument – male lay
leaders dominated this meeting after the exodus of ministers to the newly
formed United Church of Canada. Fraser, *Social Uplifters*; HC, *Debates*, 11
April 1933, 3933, 3937 (G.D. Stanley). Also A.M. Carmichael (Kindersley), 'I
do not think I am exaggerating when I say that the speculation and gambling carried on in this and other countries during recent years have played
a very large part in bringing about the depression now existing,' 3936

38 JCSHC, *Minutes*, No. 8, 15 March 1955, 218–9

39 NAC, RG 13, Department of Justice, vol. 2226, 126/1934, Guessing Games,
to Lomer Gouin, Minister of Justice, from Charles F. Roland of Employers'
Association of Manitoba, 10 June 1922; to Lomer Gouin, Minister of Justice,
from F.R. Hyde, Acme Amusement Associates Limited, Winnipeg. 1 June
1922. Also vol. 2192, 1522/1927, 'Games of Chance at Agricultural Fairs,'
to Ernest Lapointe, Minister of Justice, from G.C. Lindsay, Motion Picture
Association of Manitoba, 27 Nov. 1924

40 PAM, GR 950, AG, Central Registry, K/4/6/4, 'Horse Racing, Race Track
Gambling, Ice Racing, 1946,' *Winnipeg Tribune*, 17 Sept. 1925; Resolution of
the Winnipeg Board of Trade Protesting against Increase in Period Devoted to Horse Racing each Year in Greater Winnipeg, passed by Council 9
Sept. 1925; *Tribune*, 3 July 1930, letter to editor; *Tribune*, 30 June 1925; memo
for file, 7 July 1932, re: dog racing; JCSHC, *Minutes*, no. 8, 15 March 1955,
217; JCSHC, *Reports*, 67

41 PAM, GR 950, AG, Central Registry, K/4/6/4, 'Horse Racing, Horse Track
Gambling, Ice Racing, 1946,' *Programme of Studies for Manitoba Schools*
(1924), 27

42 Suzanne Morton, *Ideal Surroundings*

43 HC, *Debates*, 22 May, 2211 (J.L. Brown, Lisgar); McIlroy, 'Is Gambling
Ethical?'; *Vancouver Sun*, 27 May 1950. A similar argument of gambling's
draining of household resources was made against alcohol. See Harrison,
Drink; Brenner with Brenner, *Gambling*, 9–12.

44 ANQ-Q, E 17, Correspondance du Procureur-Général, 1927, f. 5744; 1932,
f. 1784. See also 1932, f. 1343, f. 3254

2: For Richer, for Poorer: Gambling, 1919–1945

1 See Collier, *Rise*, especially 162–7.

2 Cohen, *Rebellion*; Gordon, *Pitied*, 46

3 Brenner with Brenner, *Gambling*, 87, and Devereux, *Gambling*, 134. A similar

growth in gambling was noted in England, especially among the unemployed. See Stephen G. Jones, *Workers*, 119.

4 Desmond Morton, *When*, 239; Frayne, 'Biggest,' 16

5 Canada, *King's Regulations*, 34, 400; Desmond Morton, 'Kicking,' 357

6 Desmond Morton, *When*, 268; AO, MU 8470.9, WCTU Papers, pamphlet,
   Deet Pickett, 'Fool's Gold: The Truth about Gambling' (New York 1936), 7,
   19; *Senate Debates*, 13 March 1933, 325

7 'State Lotteries in England – History,' *Saturday Night*, 13 Dec. 1919; *Social
   Welfare*, for the years 1919–25, especially Oct. 1924, editorial

8 Formed in 1908 as the Moral and Social Reform Council of Canada, this
   organization changed its name to the Social Service Council of Canada.
   Christie and Gauvreau, *Full-Orbed*, 208; *Canadian Annual Review 1910*
   (Toronto 1911), 239

9 Colin S. Campbell, 'Canadian Gambling Legislation,' 170–1; Brown,
   'Thoroughbred Horse-Racing,' 264; *Canadian Annual Review, 1909* (Toronto
   1910), 199–200; *Canadian Annual Review, 1910* (Toronto 1911), 224. See
   Keller, *Regulating*, 112–15.

10 Waters, 'Operating,' 55, 89

11 *Montreal Herald*, 24 June 1925, 2 June 1926, 4 June 1927

12 'The Front Page,' *Saturday Night*, 11 Dec. 1909, 1

13 Waters, 'Operating,' 94

14 Ibid., 104; NAC, Privy Council, 7 June 1917, RG 2, vol. 1170, reel 1779 v 918

15 NAC, RG 33, series 55, vol. 1, Canada, Royal Commission on Horse Racing
   (Rutherford Commission), 9

16 NAC, RG 13, Department of Justice, vol. 2176, 289–1923, To Senator
   Casgrain from E.W. Ferguson, 23 March 1923; Clapson, *A Bit*, 37

17 Shearer, 'Canada's,' 151; CBA, *Baptist Yearbook* for Ontario and Quebec and
   Western Canada 1919, passim

18 Canada, 'Royal Commission in Racing Inquiry, Report of J.G. Rutherford,
   CMG' (Ottawa 1920), 10 Geo. V, *Sessional Paper* 67 A, 1920, 5. Harness
   racing, or trotting, was popular in the Maritimes, but the commission
   found no public betting connected with this sport. Commercialized betting
   on harness racing would develop later.

19 Weinstein and Deitch, *Impact*, 13

20 Canada, 'Rutherford Report,' 60

21 Shearer, 'Canada's,' 151; AO, MU 7031, Rev. H.J. Cody Papers, Additional
   Pamphlets 1883–1929, 'Argument of Mr. John M. Godfrey to the investiga-
   tion conducted by Dr. Rutherford, the commissioner appointed by the
   Dominion Government to Investigate Racing and Race Track Gambling,'
   Social Service Council of Canada, 30 Jan. 1920, 14–15

22 NAC, RG 13, Department of Justice, vol. 2176, 289–1923 correspondence,

To Lomer Gouin, Minister of Justice, 9 April 1923; BCARS, GR 1323, AG, Correspondence 1902–37, M 251057, Race Tracks, To Federal Minister of Agriculture Motherwell from BC AG, 8 Sept. 1924; Israel, 'Montreal,' 58

23 PAM, GR 950, AG, Central Registry, K/4/6/4, 'Horse Racing, Horse Track Gambling, Ice Racing, 1946.' *Winnipeg Morning Free Press*, 6 July 1932; *Winnipeg Evening Tribune*, 4 July 1932; *Winnipeg Evening Free Press*, 15 Feb. 1928; to Major, AG, from 'A Protector of Boys,' 9 Aug. 1932. Dog races re-emerged in Manitoba and Saskatchewan after the Second World War. To J.G. Gardner, Minister of Agriculture, from James McLenaghen, Manitoba AG, 17 July 1946. O'Hara, *A Mug's Game*, 186–7. For the class bias against greyhound racing, see Baker, 'Going.'

24 *Montreal Herald*, 7 June 1920, 7; 'Racing to Be Reviewed by Ottawa,' *Saturday Night*, 10 May 1919, 1

25 'Horse Racing and Gambling,' *Saturday Night*, 31 Jan. 1920, 1; 'Making the Sinner Pay,' *Saturday Night*, 24 April 1920, 1; 'Mr. Raney and the King of Sports,' *Saturday Night*, 3 June 1922, 1; Rutherford Report, 5

26 Colin S. Campbell, 'Canadian,' 187–9; Waters, 'Operating,' 148–9, 136

27 BCARS, GR 1323, AG, Correspondence 1902–37, M 251-57, Race Tracks, 7 Sept., 6 Oct. 14 Dec., 2 Dec., 17 Nov. 1924; letter from B.C. Woodworkers Association, 20 Nov. 1924; PAM, GR 950, AG, Central Registry, K/4/6/4, 'Horse Racing, Horse Track Gambling, Ice Racing, 1946.' *Winnipeg Tribune*, 30 June 1925; *Winnipeg Evening Free Press*, 29 Nov. 1927, reported the sums bet at parimutuel machines as Quebec, $6,345,957; Ontario $30,379,960; the Prairies, $6,878,330; and British Columbia, $4,311,581; *Winnipeg Morning Free Press*, 5 March 1928. Betting, especially control and distribution of continental racing information, was the most commercialized aspect of interwar gambling, but because of its integration into organized crime, I discuss it in chapter 6.

28 Social club charters were virtually unattainable for Chinese-Canadians, as we see below in chapter 5.

29 AO, RG 23, Ontario Provincial Police, Series E-107, f. 4.62, Report, 2 Sept. 1958

30 *Victoria Colonist*, 27 Nov. 1936

31 *Vancouver Daily Province*, 25, 26 Nov. 1936, 31 May 1938; *Vancouver Sun*, 31 May 1938

32 NSARM, RG 42, Magistrates Court, Series C, Halifax Police Court, vol. 31, no. 449, *The King v. Quigley*; Parnaby, "The Red Hand under the White Glove,' noted Conn Jones's as a meeting place for returned veterans of the Spanish Civil War.

33 AO, RG 4-02, AG, Blackwell-Porter, Box 46.5, Crime Investigation, Papers

of the Select Committee of the Ontario Legislature Enquiring into the Administration of Justice in Ontario; RG 49, 126, Select Committee on Administration of Justice, est. 30 March 1951, vol. 4, 9 May 1951, testimony of Wm. H. Stringer (Commissioner of Police for Ontario), 504–5. The Combine Club was closed 13 April 1942; Coleman, 'Ten Bucks,' 46.

34 Cross, *Time*, 145–6
35 Best, *Nickel*, 29; NSARM, RG 42, Magistrates Court, Series C, Halifax Police Court, vol. 53, 1944, no. 12048
36 Best, *Nickel*, 29; Kelly, 'Slots'
37 Wetherell with Kmet, *Useful*, 367–70; PAM, GR 542, AG, Central Registry, J/13/2/5, 'Slot Machines,' to W.J. Major, AG, from J.K May, Sales Manager, Scott-Bathgate Co., 9 Oct. 1928
38 Kelly, 'Slots,' 37; PAM, GR 542, AG, Central Registry, J/13/2/5, 'Slot Machines,' AG to Christopher Newton, Winnipeg Chief Constable, 15 Oct. 1928; AO, RG 4-32, AG, Central Registry, 1927, f. 3347; 1928, f. 1028, 18 April 1928; *Halifax Citizen*, 8 Nov., 6 Dec. 1935; *Vancouver Sun*, 28 Nov. 1936
39 'Benevolent Games of Chance,' *Saturday Night*, 26 Nov. 1927, 26. For the role of the fair in western Canada, see David C. Jones, *Midways*.
40 NAC, RG 13, Department of Justice, vol. 2192, 1522/1927, CC S 236, Games of Chance at Agricultural Fairs, 23 April, 12 Feb. 1923; clipping, *Saskatoon Daily Star*, 26 Nov. 1924; AO, RG 4-32, AG, Central Registry, 1946, f. 1170
41 NAC, RG 13, Department of Justice, vol. 2192, 1522/1927, CC S 236, Games of Chance at Agricultural Fairs, clipping *Calgary Albertan*, 31 July 1928; *Wampus*, 25 July 1928
42 NAC, RG 13, Department of Justice, vol. 2205, 726/1930, 'That fraternal, Charitable and religious bodies be allowed to enjoy games of chance,' to Ernest Lapointe from S.S. Savage, 27 April 1930
43 Ibid., to K.A. Blatchford, MP, from S.S. Savage, 9 April 1930
44 Ibid., to Ernest Lapointe, Minister of Justice, from S.S. Savage, 11 May 1930; to Hugh Guthrie, Minister of Justice, from A.J. Costigan, Chairman, Grand Judiciary, 27 Feb. 1931
45 'Benevolent Games of Chance,' *Saturday Night*, 26 Nov. 1927, 26; *Halifax Citizen*, 25 Sept. 1936
46 Leonoff, 'Harry L. Salmon,' 344–7; NAC, RG 13, Department of Justice, A.2 1920 1313/1911, 11 Oct. 1911; *Victoria Daily Times*, 12 Dec. 1924; *Vancouver Daily Province*, 8 May, 29 Oct. 1931; *Victoria Daily Times*, 13 March 1934
47 NAC, RG 13, Department of Justice, vol. 2205, 726/1930, 'That fraternal, charitable and religious bodies be allowed to enjoy games of chance' correspondence, To R.B. Bennett, Prime Minister, from C.A.L. Ross,

30 March 1931; vol. 2012, 557/1933, United Kingdom, *Royal Commission on Lotteries and Betting 1932–33 Final Report*, Selection from Statements and Summary of Gambling Legislation in other Countries – Newfoundland, 564–5

48 ANQ-Q, E-17, Correspondance du Procureur-Général, 1927, f. 977, 2 Feb. 1927. There were many other similar examples, such as the tickets being sold outside Montreal for the Montreal Association for the Blind/L'Institut des Aveugles de Nazareth 1931, f. 2383

49 Brenner with Brenner, *Gambling*, 17; HC, *Debates*, 22 May 1934, 3286 (J.A. Mercier, Laurier-Outremont); Ewen, *Lotteries*, 345–50; Mildre Walle, of Prince Rupert, BC, won $50,000 in Army and Navy Sweepstakes, *Vancouver Daily Province*, 28 Oct. 1931; Clyde Horne of Dartmouth, Nova Scotia, won $123,000, *Daily Province*, 31 May 1932; Miss Inez Stewart, K.E. Luckhurst, and Ching Ong of Cobalt, Ontario, won. *Porcupine Advance*, 28 Oct. 1937; all Canadian winners have 'noms-de-plume,' *Welland–Port Colborne Tribune*, 30 Oct. 1934. This was also noted by W.B. Common, director of public prosecutions for the attorney general of Ontario during the JCSHC, *Minutes*, no. 7, 31 March 1954, 309.

50 Luce, 'There's a Way,' 16; Ewen, *Lotteries*, 348; *Vancouver Daily Province*, 11 Oct. 1931; *Globe and Mail*, 14 May 1938. In 1941 the population of Toronto was 667,457. The newspaper report suggested that 200,000 people had bought tickets; *Saturday Night*, 23 May 1931, 5 Nov. 1932; *Toronto Telegram*, 13 Nov. 1935. The commission from the sales of lottery and sweepstakes tickets was probably a source of supplemental or informal income for unemployed men and women. See Ayers, 'Hidden,' 274; United Kingdom, *Royal Commission on Lotteries and Betting, 1932–33*, 47; AO, RG 4, AG, 32–4, 1940, f. 62, re: arrest of professional sales.

51 Clotfelter and Cook, *Selling Hope*, 41. Contests and premium promotions antedated the inter-war period, with American national brands such as Jello and Bon Ami running contests before the First World War. See Strasser, *Satisfaction*, especially chaps. 5 and 6; AO, RG 4-32, AG, Central Registry, 1935, f. 1053, 30 Jan. 1930

52 AO, RG 4-32, AG, Central Registry, 1925, f. 2894, 1926, f. 1148, f. 1565, and f. 2850

53 *New Liskeard Speaker*, 13 May 1937; *Porcupine Advance*, 7, 14 Oct. 1937

54 Concern was also expressed about the 'unethical method of marketing' aimed at children, as in the complaint against the Try Your Luck chocolate bar in 1925. This item offered nickels in selected candy bars to attract consumers: AO, RG 4-32, AG, Central Registry, 1925, f. 1103, 2 April 1925.

55 Ibid., 1926, f. 2323, 21, 27 Oct. 1926; 1927, f. 1371, 30 May 1927. See, for

example, *Canadian Magazine*, Jan. 1928, 46–7. *Family Herald* and the *Weekly Star* of Montreal. Even the *Worker* offered prizes to correspondents, such as a copy of Gustavus Myers's *The History of Canadian Wealth*; *Worker*, March/April 1926. In Calgary, a privately owned weekly paper, the *Joker*, also ran a similar coupon game based on football results in England and Scotland. NAC, RG 13, Department of Justice, vol. 2176, 289–1923, To Lomer Gouin, Minister of Justice, from James Short, Office Alberta AG, 14 June 1923

56 PAM, MG 10, OBU Central Labour Council, Winnipeg, A 14-2, no. 17, 22 and 29 Nov. 1921; no. 15, Central Labour Council 1919–21, 2 Dec. 1921; *OBU Bulletin*, 8 Dec. 1921; Bercuson, *Fools*, 217–19

57 *OBU Bulletin*, 12 March 1925; NAC, RG 13, Department of Justice, vol. 2226, 126/1934, 'Guessing Games' correspondence, R.W. Lowe, Postmaster Winnipeg, to Postmaster General, 23 May 1922; correspondence Commissioner RCMP to E.L. Newcombe, Minister of Justice, 20 June 1922. The historian of the OBU, David Bercuson, claimed that by April 1922 over 150,000 weekly entries were arriving at the *Bulletin*'s office in Winnipeg. Bercuson, *Fools*, 218

58 NAC, RG 13, Department of Justice, vol. 2226, 126/1934, 'Guessing Games' correspondence, A.B. Hudson, Winnipeg, to Lomer Gouin, Minister of Justice, 18 April 1922; *OBU Bulletin*, 5 Feb., 12 March 1925

59 *OBU Bulletin*, 16 July, 20 Aug. 1925, 30 April, 20 Aug. 1931, 10 March 1932, 14 Sept., 19 Oct. 1933, 28 May 1934

60 NAC, RG 13, Department of Justice, vol. 2226, 126/1934, 'Guessing Games' correspondence, Charles F. Roland, Employers' Association of Manitoba, to Lomer Gouin, Minister of Justice, 10 June 1922

61 *Social Welfare*, 1 April 1922, 149; *Vancouver Daily Province*, 31 Jan. 1928; *Victoria Daily Times*, 31 Jan. 1928; AO, RG 4-32, AG, Central Registry, 1928, f. 2314, to Parry Sound CA from E. Bayly, Ontario Deputy AG, 20 Aug. 1928

62 AO, RG 4-32, AG, Central Registry, 1928, f. 2409, to CA Niagara District from Ont. Deputy AG, 14 Aug. 1928, memo AG of Ont., 15 Aug. 1928

63 Ibid., 1930, f. 2158; *Worker*, 26 Nov. 1927; AO, RG 4-32, AG, Central Registry, 1931, f. 1407, 6 June 1931; 1932, f. 385, 3 Feb. 1932; 1933, f. 2221, 24 Aug. 1933; 1935, f. 1521; f. 2208; 2671, 29 Oct. 1935; 1936, f. 65; re: priest, 1938, f. 49, 3, 17, 21 Jan., 3 Feb. 1938

64 See, for example, *Victoria Colonist*, 25 Nov. 1930; NAC, RG 13, Department of Justice A.2 2012, 557/1933, 'Royal Commission on Lotteries and Betting 1932–33 Final Report' to W. Stuart Edwards, Deputy Minister of Justice, from O.D. Skelton, 21 Feb. 1934.

65 Brenner with Brenner, *Gambling*, 18; Labrosse, *The Lottery*, 108; *Winnipeg Morning Free Press*, 18 May 1934

66 *Vancouver Sun*, 13 Jan. 1934; HC, Debates, 22 May, 3277 (J.A. Fraser, Cariboo); Vance, *Analysis of the Costs*, 57. Alexandre Taschereau, *The Lottery Issue*, Text of Speeches delivered before the Quebec Legislative Assembly on March 14, 1934, 4; Devereux, *Gambling*, 1023

67 ANQ-Q, E-17, Correspondance du Procureur-Général, 1930, f. 3917; 1936, f. 1034 and f. 437; 1930, f. 3500; Justice, 2072–5, Saisies relative aux loteries, ver. 1934–36

68 Ezell, *Fortune's*, 276; but Burnham cites this as 1931, *Bad Habits*, 154; Ponte, 'Religious Opposition,' 57

69 PAM, MG 10, OBU Central Labour Council, Winnipeg, A 14-2 Central Labour Council no. 20, 23 Dec. 1924; *Victoria Colonist*, 10 May 1931; *Vancouver Daily Province*, 24 April 1931; *Vancouver Sun*, 31 March 1939

70 HC, *Debates*, 11 April 1933, 3937; Almost the same words were also stated by A.M. Carmichael, Progressive Party member for Kindersely, in ibid., 3936.

71 Gilbert E Jackson, interview, *Canadian Magazine*, Jan. 1934, 42–3

72 *Vancouver News-Herald*, 2 June 1938

73 AVM, P 43, Enquête Caron, Box 54-06-02-01, 1952–46, testimony Harry Ship, 21 July 1952, 9, 209, 63–4

74 Baillargeon, 'If,' 220; Snow, *Snow*, 113

75 VCA, series 208, Police Department Tucker Report (1936), Letter of complaint, 5 Nov. 1936

76 Waters, 'Operating,' 180–2

77 ANQ-Q, E-17, Correspondance du Procureur-Général, 1936, f. 5292, 28 July 1936

78 AO, RG 4-32, AG, Central Registry, 1926, f. 1565, 5 July 1926; 1927, f. 1019; 1929, f. 2907; 1931, f. 1407, 29 May 1931; 1935, f. 2208; 1935, f. 2451; 1935, f. 2761; 1936, f. 65; 1940, f. 62, 26 Feb. 1940; 1931, f. 1407, 7 April 1936; 1935, f. 1521, 18 June 1935

79 *Porcupine Advance*, 12 July 1937. AO, RG 4-32, AG, Central Registry, 1931, f. 1407, 29 May 1931; 1939, f. 422, 13 Feb. 1939, 24 April 1939, 30 May 1939. This was a rare exception, as highly respected groups and communities regularly operated bingo, lotteries, and raffles contrary to the law and apparently immune to prosecution.

80 Luce, 'There's a Way'

81 VCA, Mayors' Papers – General Correspondence, series 1, vol. 47, to Minister of Finance, Ottawa, from Mayor Telford, 25 July 1940; Mayor Telford to Minister of Finance, 26 July 1940; AVM, P 43, Enquête Caron, Box 54-03-03-01, A-1, To F.R. Simms, Dominion Appraiser, Department of National Revenue, from J.-O. Asselin, 26 Feb. 1942; *Winnipeg Tribune*, 29 March 1944

82 PAM, GR 950, AG, Central Registry, K/4/6/4, 'Horse Racing, Race Track Gambling, Ice Racing 1946'; *Senate Debates*, 26 March 1946, 48; *Winnipeg Free Press*, 27 Dec. 1944

83 NAC, MG 28, Canadian Welfare Council, 1 10, vol. 70, 515, 1941–71, A.G. Harvey, Vancouver, to Canadian Welfare Council, 19 Aug. 1943

84 Plante, 'Shame,' part II, 8; *Vancouver Daily Province*, 11 Dec. 1945

85 Chubby Power and A.L. Beaubien, HC, *Debates*, 18 April 1933, 4040

86 *Halifax Star*, 16 May 1938, letter to editor

87 Zulaika, *Terranova*, 68–9, 75

3: Gambling, Respectable Masculinity, and Male Sporting Culture

1 AVM, P43, Enquête Caron, box 054-06-02-01, f. 1952–32, testimony of Jacqueline Sirois, 3 July 1952, 16; Box 43-04-02-01, testimony of Izzie Litwack, 6 Oct. 1950, 696

2 Burnham, *Bad Habits*; Peiss, *Cheap Amusements*, 21

3 Lancaster, *Life*, 191–6. See Nye, *Masculinity*, for another historically specific conception of ideal masculinity that shaped cultural discourse. Downes et al., *Gambling*, 132–3

4 Lears, *No Place*, 222

5 Rotundo, 'Manhood,' 426

6 See, for example, JCSHC, *Minutes*, no. 9, 29 April 1954, 395; see also Englander, 'Booth's,' 557, 563. The anglophone media regarded gambling as a particular problem in Montreal.

7 Israel, 'Montreal,' 195

8 Ryan, *Women*; Walkowitz, *City*; Stansell, *City*; and Chauncey, *Gay*

9 White, *First*, 12

10 Walden, *Becoming*, 250; Gilfoyle, *City*, 81, 98–9, 102, 104; Gorn, *Manly*; Walkowitz, *City*

11 Montreal gamblers in the 1940s had close connections to boxing and the operation of city nightclubs, restaurants, and cabarets. Despite some links between organized gambling and narcotics in the 1930s, with a few significant exceptions, most Montreal gamblers seemed to distance themselves from illegal narcotics and prostitution in the 1940s. In the testimony of Alderman Frank Hanley, a former jockey, he acknowledged a connection with two of the city's most prominent gamblers through boxing. AVM, P43, Enquête Caron, box 054-06-02-01, f. 1952-22, testimony of Frank Hanley, 27 June 1952, 20, 56. For taverns, see Robert A. Campbell, 'Ladies.'

12 Americans Kathy Peiss and Roy Rosenzweig have explored this in a

working-class context. Peiss, *Cheap*; Rosenzweig, *Eight*.

13 Valverde, *Age of Light*; Strange, 'Modern Babylon'; Rosecrance, *Gambling*, vii

14 Mabel L. Walker, 'Civic,' 350; HC, *Debates*, 22 May 1934, 3311 (J.L. Brown, Lisgar); McIlroy, 'Is Gambling Ethical?'; Knox, *Land*, 71

15 JCSHC, *Minutes*, no. 11, 29 March 1955, 340; translation, Plante, *Montréal*, 11

16 Rogers, 'Serving'; Marquis, 'Working'

17 AO, RG 49-126, Committee on the Administration of Justice, vol. 3, 6 May 1951, 337, testimony of William Stringer, Commissioner of the Ontario Provincial Police

18 *Montreal Herald*, 17 June 1921; Baillargeon, *Ménagères*, 202

19 JCSHC, *Minutes*, no. 11, 29 March 1955, 340, 366

20 *Vancouver Sun*, 28 Nov. 1936; *Windsor Star*, 7 Nov. 1935, 7 Feb. 1936; *Toronto Telegram*, 14 Aug. 1922; *Halifax Mail*, 14 May 1938; NAC, RG 13, Department of Justice, vol. 2192, 1522/1927, CC S 236, Games of Chance at Agricultural Fairs, to W.L.M. King from J. Phillips Jones, Social Service Council of Canada, 1 June 1925; UCA, fonds 3384, Hugh Wesley Dobson Papers, A.9, General Correspondence, 1924–5, file D, reel 23, Hugh Dobson to P.G. Drost, Vancouver, 5 Jan. 1925

21 JCSHC, *Minutes*, no. 7, 3 March 1954, 278, no. 11, 29 March 1955, 327, 375

22 AO, RG 23, Ont. Provincial Police, series E-107, f. 3.15, 21 May 1957, to AG Roberts from Mrs M.M., Superintendent of Law enforcement of Bruce's Woman's Christian Temperance Union, emphasis added

23 NAC, RG 13, Department of Justice, vol. 2226, 126/1934, Guessing Games, to Lomer Gouin, Minister of Justice, from Charles F. Roland of Employers' Association of Manitoba, 10 June, 28 April 1922

24 AO, RG 23, Ontario Provincial Police, series E-107, f. 1.1, Gambling GHQ file, 1938–1956, memo dated 28 April 1952, To W.B. Common, Director of Public Prosecutions, from Tomlinson, Staff Inspector of Anti-Gambling Squad

25 For examples of ruinous stories, see Duncan, *The Imperialist*, 41; NAC, RG 13, Department of Justice, vol. 226, 126/1934, Guessing Games, to Lomer Gouin, Minister of Justice, from F.R. Hyde, Acme Amusement Associates Limited, Winnipeg, 1 June 1922; vol. 2192, 1522/1927, 'Games of Chance at Agricultural Fairs,' to Ernest Lapointe, Minister of Justice, from W.G. Wallace, clerk Presbyterian Church in Canada, 9 July 1925

26 Women's role as consumers and mothers was reflected in the particular criticism surrounding women and gambling.

27 AO, MU 7018, H.J. Cody Papers, Cody, *Why?*, 7–8

28 AO, RG 4-32, AG, Central Registry, 1928, f. 2337, 21 Aug. 1928; *Toronto Telegram*, 14 Aug. 1922

29 Another example of the link between sexuality and gambling was suggested by Charlotte Olmsted in 'Heads I Win, Tail You Lose,' which claimed that 'sex-substitution is a prime reason for gambling's popularity in male preserves such as lumber camps and army barracks, where it helps reduce tension and a certain amount of homosexuality,' cited in Waller, *Gamblers*, 16. Recent work by Forestell has portrayed gambling as a vital element in homosocial culture. See her 'Bachelors.'

30 AO, RG 23, Ontario Provincial Police, series E-107, f. 3.6, April 1957; f. 7.47, Report Nov. 1961; Lacasse, *Prostitution*, 70

31 Fabian, *Card Sharps*, 3

32 Smith, 'Where'; Smith, 'When,' 105

33 Smith, 'When,' 106

34 Ownby, *Subduing*, 117–18; Burnham, *Bad Habits*, 278

35 Ken W. MacTaggart, 'Ideal Workingman's Home Embodies Many Ideas,' *Globe and Mail*, 15 June 1944, in AO, RG 4, AG, series 4–02, Minister's Office Files, 1926–1978, f. 22.1, 'Gambling 1943–44'

36 One of the city councillors representing the predominantly English-speaking suburb of Notre-Dame-de-Grâce, which itself never reported gambling activity, claimed that 'most of the bookies' in Montreal lived in his district with their families. According to the councillor, 'They do business in town and they live in the suburbs.' AVM, P43, Enquête Caron, box 054-06-02-01, f. 1952-24, testimony of John Edward Lyall, 27 June 1952, 64; for example, AO, RG 23, Ontario Provincial Police, series E-107. f. 3.3, Oshawa bookmaker, April 1957. This man was working from home, yet his wife denied any knowledge of the operation. A similar case occurred in Sarnia (f. 3.9, April 1957).

37 AO, RG 23, Ontario Provincial Police, series E107, f. 4.64, report dated 16 Sept. 1958; AVM, P43, Enquête Caron, box 054-04-02-01, testimony of Sidney Shorr, 2 Nov. 1950, 2917

38 AVM, P 43, Enquête Caron, box 054-04-02-01, testimony of Edgar Bruce Murdoch, 29 Sept. 1950, 182; testimony of Samuel Hyams, 2 Oct. 1950, 232; box 054-04-03-01, E-420, Inspection reports for 286 Ste-Catherine ouest (operated 1932–46); box 054-05-02-01, testimony of Albert Hotte, Sanitary Inspector, Food Division, re: 327 Ste-Catherine est, 6 Feb. 1951, 17; box 054-03-03-02, E-95, photos from 1455 Bleury taken 5 Sept. 1946

39 AVM, P 43, Enquête Caron, box 054-06-03-02, E-791; *Pic*, March 1950; Palmer, *Montreal Confidential*

40 Cooke, *Mayor*; Runyon, *Guys and Dolls*. This Montreal has also been captured in Weintraub's *City*.

41 Israel, 'Montreal,' 185; Linteau, *L'histoire*

42 McCormick, 'Gambling,' 7; Thomason, 'Men's.' This district in nineteenth-century Nashville was marked by tailors, tobacco shops, saloons, and barbershops.

43 AVM, P43, Enquête Caron, box 054-05-02-01, testimony of Palma Gauthier, constable, 2 Feb. 1951, 41; box 054-01-03-01, f. 1952–94, testimony of Albert Langlois, Chief of Police, 15 Sept. 1952. Inquiry witnesses verified this absence of gambling establishments in Westmount, Outremont, and Notre-Dame-de-Grâce. Montreal's geographical distribution of gambling conforms with the organizational characteristics observed by David C. Johnson in his study of American cities, which noted that the 'bright light districts' were embraced by criminal entrepreneurs. Illicit activities operated beside legitimate enterprises, lending the illegal neighbours an air of legitimacy and respectability. Proximity to train stations and hotels, along with theatres, restaurants, and nightclubs, generated a steady flow of sidewalk traffic that might be greeted on the streets by employees trying to hustle men inside. Johnson, 'Origins,' 596; Strong-Boag, 'Home'

44 AVM, P43, Enquête Caron, box 43-04-02-01, testimony of Izzie Litwack, 11 Oct. 1950, 874

45 Ibid., Barney Shulkin, 28 Sept. 1950, 363. A parallel example of a billiard parlour with only one table for its legitimate activity but many tables for card games was brought to the attention of the Coderre Inquiry in 1925. *Montreal Star*, 14 March 1925; AO, RG 23, Ontario Provincial Police, series E-107, f. 8.35, report, Sept. 1964

46 *Montreal Star*, 14 March 1925

47 AVM, P 43, Enquête Caron, box 054-05-02-02, f. 1951–78, testimony of Raymond Taillefer, 10 April 1951, 28; box 054-06-02-01, f. 1952–46, testimony of Harry Ship, 22 July 1952, 357

48 McCormick, 'Gambling,' 7; AVM, P 43, Enquête Caron, box 054-03-03-01, D-147. Handwritten note from Captain O'Neill; see, for example, *Montreal Standard*, 27 July 1946.

49 AVM, P 43, Enquête Caron, box 054-03-02-02, complaints re 6968 St-Denis

50 VCA, Police Inquiry 1928, series 209, before R.S. Lennie, Commissioner, vol. 1, 79

51 Ville de Montréal Bylaw 1103 (12/1/1931)

52 Phillips, 'Gambling,' 15

53 Allan, *Love Is a Long Shot*, 29

54 Ehrenreich, *Hearts*

4: Bingo, Women, and the Critics

1 *Montreal Gazette*, 26 Oct. 1945, 9 Sept. 1946

2 *Le Messager/The Messenger* (Verdun), 5, 12 Jan. 1950

3 Frayne, 'Biggest,' 33–4; DeLind, 'Bingo,' 153; Peiss, *Cheap*, 21–2; Schellenberg, 'Bingo.' During the Second World War, at least twenty radio stations in Ontario operated their own bingo games, which did not require women to leave their homes.

4 *Vancouver Sun*, 7 May 1953

5 BCARS, GR 2966, AG, Correspondence from C 95 (criminal prosecutions), 1966–70, vol. 5, f. 3, Bingo, gambling – general, *Bingo News*, 6 Oct. 1969, 1

6 JCSHC, *Reports*, 63. Lotteries none the less also operated illegally in late-nineteenth-century Ontario. Lynne Marks notes that a religious bazaar in Thorold in 1882 advertised throughout the United States and raised over $6,000 for the parish. Marks, 'Ladies,' 179

7 Frayne, 'Biggest,' 16; Grun, *Time Tables*, 439; AO, RG 4-32, AG, Central Registry, 1920, f. 3067; Methodist minister re gambling at Agricultural Fairs; *Catholic Register*, 14 Oct. 1934; *Porcupine Advance*, 16 Sept., 28 Oct., 8 Nov. 1937; *Toronto Telegram*, 14 Aug. 1922; Lemelin, *The Town Below*, 55 (Housie-Housie was the British name, and bingo, the U.S. appellation.)

8 VCA, series 211, Police Department, Chief Constable's Office Correspondence with City License Inspector, 10 Sept. 1936; PAM, GR 542, AG, Central Registry, J/13/2/4l, 'Slot Machines 1935–36,' *Winnipeg Free Press*, 21 Oct. 1935

9 *Victoria Daily Times*, 12 Feb. 1937

10 AO, RG 4-32, AG, Central Registry, 1937, f. 434, 14 Jan. 1937; *Hamilton Spectator*, 9 Jan. 1937; *Winnipeg Free Press*, 7 Feb. 1937; *Victoria Daily Times*, 12 Feb. 1937; Luce, 'There's a Way'; AO, RG 4-32, AG, Central Registry, 1935, f. 2671, 14 Dec. 1935

11 Joe Corrie, 'The Gambler,' *OBU Bulletin*, 28 June 1928. Ayers and Lambertz, in 'Marriage,' claim that women who participated in gambling and playing pools 'fell into a grey area between legitimate and not respectable,' 202–3. Clapson, *A Bit*, 47; *Montreal Gazette*, 11 Sept. 1946; *Le Messager/The Messenger* (Verdun), 15 Dec. 1949

12 HC, *Debates*, 22 May 1934, 3297 (H.A Mullins, Marquette); Rishell, *Bingo*, 9; JCSHC, *Minutes*, no. 11, 29 March 1955, 355; No. 8, 27 April 1954, 492; no. 13, 13 May 1954, 556

13 Nova Scotia, *Journal of House of Assembly*, 1920, Appendix 28, 'Report of the Superintendent of Neglected and Delinquent Children,' 15; *Halifax Evening Mail*, 14 Jan. 1926

14 JCSHC, *Minutes*, no. 9, 8 April 1955, 375. This connection continues today in the media portrayal of working-class mothers; *Le Messager/The Messenger* (Verdun), 8 Dec. 1949, 5 Jan. 1950; BCAR, GR 2966, AG, Correspondence from C 95 (criminal prosecutions), 1966–70

15 AVM, P 43, Enquête Caron, box 054-01-03-02, f. 1953–9, testimony of J-O Asselin, 28 Jan. 1953, 14–5; *Le Messager/The Messenger* (Verdun), 15 Dec. 1949, 12 Jan. 1950; JCSHC, *Minutes*, no. 15, 28 April 1955, 469

16 Brenner with Brenner, *Gambling*, 83. Best, *Nickel*

17 *Le Messager/The Messenger* (Verdun), 29 Dec. 1949

18 AO, RG 4-32, AG, Central Registry, 1937, f. 434, 2, 3, 8, 16 Feb. 1939

19 Ibid. 1935, f. 2671, 2 Nov. 1935; 1937, f. 434, 19 March 1939; *Kitchener Daily Record*, 18, 20 Jan. 1939; JCSHC, *Minutes*, no. 8, 15 March 1955, 219

20 *Victoria Colonist*, 1 Oct. 1957

21 PAM, GR 542, AG, Central Registry, J/1/2/8 no. 102–L, 'Lotteries 1957–60,' clipping *Ottawa Journal*, 30 March 1953

22 *Hamilton Spectator*, 15, 16, 18, 20 June 1938; AO, RG 4-32, AG, Central Registry, 1937, f. 434, 2 Nov. 1938

23 Best, *Nickel*, 84

24 AO, RG 4-32, AG, Central Registry, 1937, f. 434; PAM, GR 542, AG, Central Registry, J/1/2/7, 'Lotteries,' E.G. Porter to O.M.M. Kay, 8 Oct. 1955; To Cecil Rhodes Smith, from 'A.J.,' n.d.; to Cecil Rhodes Smith from 'G.H.,' 10 Nov. 1951; to O.M.M. Kay, Deputy AG, from C.W. Tupper, Crown Prosecutor, Winnipeg, 8 Feb. 1952; to O.M.M. Kay, Deputy AG, Man., from John A.Y. MacDonald, Deputy AG, N.S., 27 Feb. 1952, and 'Lawyer's Letter,' 18 Feb. 1952. In Winnipeg, there were accusations that, in order to attract crowds with a large jackpot, theatres padded ledgers with names from the city directory and telephone book. In an anonymous note to the attorney general, a women complained that although she had 'not been out for a long time' her name was drawn at a local theatre. The use of non-attenders was said to explain why a College Avenue theatre ran a 'foto-Nite' for thirty-five weeks before a winner emerged to claim the prize of $2,700.

25 NAC, RG 13, Department of Justice, vol. 2192, 1522/1927, 'Criminal Code S 236 Games of Chance At Agricultural Fairs,' from G.C. Lindsay, Motion Picture Association of Manitoba, to Ernest Lapointe, Minister of Justice, 27 Nov. 1924

26 NSARM, RG 39, Halifax County Supreme Court, C, vol. 857, f. 6647, *The King v. Aubrey Risser*, Halifax Police Court, 4 June 1936; vol. 869, f. 7268, Halifax Police Court; Minutes of Evidence, *The King v. William Lynch*; series C, Halifax County Supreme Court, 1935–45, vol. 869, case 7267; 4 June 1936, Minutes of Evidence, 5

27 AO, RG 4-32, AG, Central Registry, 1937, f. 434, memo re bingo in Hamilton, 28 Oct. 1938; Metropolitan Toronto Police, *Annual Report of the Chief Constable of the City of Toronto for the Year*, 1938, 43; 1939, 43; *Halifax Mail*, 10, 14, 16 May 1938; *Halifax Star*, 11, 16 May 1938

28 *Halifax Herald*, 21 May 1938; *Halifax Star*, 16, 17, 18 May 1938

29 *Halifax Herald*, 19 May 1938; *Halifax Star*, 18, 19 May 1938

30 Quote from Dr Curran in St Joseph Parish Bulletin, *Halifax Star*, 23 May 1938

31 *Vancouver Sun*, 12 Feb. 1937; *Le Messager/The Messenger* (Verdun), 19, 26 Jan. 1950

32 *Halifax Mail*, 23 May 1938; AO, RG 4-32, AG, Central Registry, 1937, f. 434, quoted by lawyer G.E. Williams, Hamilton, Ont., 17 Oct. 1938

33 *Halifax Mail*, 23 May 1938; Stanké and Morgan, *Pax*, 157–65; *Gazette*, 11, 13 Sept. 1946 Eight years later, Plante told a slightly different tale that injected much more drama into the struggle between the heroic law enforcer and the defiant curé. Plante claimed that the renegade priest announced from his pulpit that 'Next Saturday night we will have the biggest bingo ever held in this church. I will be there and my priests will be there. I invite all my wardens to be present. It is not a small lawyer from St James St who will dictate to me.'

The aborted Thursday night raid became a Saturday night standoff in Plante's embroidered description. As a parade of Black Marias approached the church with bells clanging, the hall emptied itself of all 1,500 patrons, who wanted to avoid the approaching conflict. Johnstone, 'Plante,' 106–7. In his testimony to the JCSHC on Capital Punishment, Corporal Punishment and Lotteries, Plante changed the night of the confrontation to Friday evening and claimed that there were 2,000 players in attendance: *Minutes*, no. 15, 28 April 1955, 479–80.

34 Josie, 'Social,' 31; Tremblay, 'Bingo,' 14

35 JCSHC, *Minutes*, no. 15, 3 May 1955: 480, quoted by Pax Plante as 17 March 1953

36 Mann, 'Lower,' 56

37 Brenner with Brenner, *Gambling*, 83; Ponte, 'Religious Opposition,' 59

38 PAM, GR 542, AG, Central Registry, J/1/2/, 8 no. 102-L, 'Lotteries 1957–60,' to Deputy AG, Nfld. from Deputy AG, Man., 18 June 1958

39 Ibid., Memo to Ivan Schultz, AG, Man., re: Right of Appeal by the Crown in Indictable Offenses, 3 Nov. 1953; to R.A. Gilroy, CA, Portage la Prairie, from O.M.M. Kay, Deputy AG, 6 May 1959; to O.M.M. Kay, Deputy AG, from Deputy AG, N.B., 6 Aug. 1956

40 Frayne, 'Biggest,' 16

41 AO, RG 4-32, AG, Central Registry, 1946, f. 1170; Manning, 'Is Bingo Bad?'
    12
42 *Vancouver Sun*, 7 May 1953, 1 April 1955; *Vancouver Daily Province*, 6 Nov.
    1954
43 *Vancouver Sun*, 17, 23 Aug. 1955, 1 Sept. 1955, 19 Aug., 14 Sept. 1956; 8, 9,
    10 May 1957; *Daily Province*, 18, 19 Aug., 14 Sept., 26, 29 Nov. 1956
44 AO, RG 23, Ontario Provincial Police, series E-107, f. 6.42, 43–2177,
    Article by Chief Constable J.D. Burger of Sudbury City Police written in
    spring 1962 to be published in *RCMP Gazette*. For additional contem-
    porary responses, see McNeil, 'What Comes,' 51–6, and Little,
    'Manhunts.'
45 Tremblay, 'Bingo,' 15; J. Dingman, 'Bingo Value,' *Chatelaine* 43 (Oct. 1970),
    6, 8
46 BCARS, GR 2966 AG, Correspondence from C 95 (criminal prosecutions),
    1966–70, vol. 5, f. 49, Victoria – Bingo, Letter from Chief Constable Gregory
    [Victoria] to the AG's office, 18 May 1966; f. 2, Bingo, gambling – general,
    Memo from Neil McDiarmid, Director of Criminal Law, to Deputy AG,
    10 April 1968; f. 48, Vancouver Bingo, E.A. Chambers, Vancouver, to AG,
    22 Dec. 1969; f. 3, Bingo, gambling – general, A. Menzies, Vancouver, to
    AG, 12 Sept. 1966
47 VCA, series 211, Police Department, Chief Constable's Office Correspond-
    ence with City License Inspector, 10 Sept. 1936
48 *Halifax Star*, 17 May 1938; Manning, 'Is Bingo Bad?' 11. Of course not all
    bingos were a financial success. A radio bingo operated by Kinsman in
    Vancouver in 1963 lost a great deal of money. BCARS, GR 2966, AG,
    Correspondence from C 95 (criminal prosecutions), 1966–70, vol. 5, f. 47,
    Vancouver Bingo Correspondence, Vancouver Bingo

5: Gambling 'Others': Race, Ethnicity, and Religion

1 Anthony B. Chan, *Gold Mountain*, 79–80
2 See Anderson, *Vancouver's Chinatown*, and Swyripa, *Wedded*.
3 See Berger, *Sense*; Ezell, *Fortune's*, vii.
4 *Vancouver Daily Province*, 24 April 1931; Canada, *Senate Debates*, 17 June
   1931, 279
5 NAC, RG 13, Department of Justice, vol. 2192, 1522/1927, CC S 236,
   Games of Chance at Agricultural Fairs, To Ernest Lapointe, Minister of
   Justice, from G.C. Lindsay, Motion Picture Association of Manitoba,
   27 Nov. 1927
6 Bell, 'Crime,' 111

7 Taschereau, 'Les petits commerçants.' In Chicago, several Black gambling entrepreneurs were considered respectable citizens and community leaders. Haller, 'Policy,' 722; Wolcott, 'Culture'

8 Garry and Sangster, 'Gambling,' 286

9 CUL, 'The Montreal Chinese Community: Oral History Project,' interview with Jack Leung by Kwok B. Chan, 7, 9 July 1975, 20

10 AVM, P 43, Enquête Caron, box 054-01-03-02, f. 1953–28, testimony of Frank Hanley, 25 Feb. 1953; *Victoria Colonist*, 14 June 1939

11 Culin, *Gambling*, 15; Robert, 'Dufferin District'; Anderson, *Vancouver's Chinatown*, 92–3; Light, 'From Vice'; Nipp, 'Chinese,' 155–6; Baureiss and Dreier, 'Winnipeg's Chinatown'; E.I. Hart, *Wake Up! Montreal!* (Montreal 1919), 14

12 *Dai Han Gung Bao*, 29 June 1928 (translated). Certain sections of the Black community were also associated with gambling in the minds of some Montrealers. Israel, 'Montreal,' 84

13 VCA, Mayors Papers – General Correspondence, series 1, vol. 47, 19 July 1940, statement by Vancouver Mayor Lyle Telford; *Vancouver Daily Province*, 18 July 1940

14 AO, RG 23, Ontario Provincial Police, series E-46, f. 1.5, 14 Oct. 1917, Reports from Undercover Policeman; AVM, P 43, Enquête Caron, box 054-05-02-02, f. 1951–75, testimony of Joseph Tremblay, 10 April 1951; box 054-05-02-01, testimony of Omer Dufresne, 2 Feb. 1951, 75

15 CRLG, P 47, Fonds du Comité de moralité publique, B.2, Comité exécutif, 19 Sept. 1951; B.4, 17, 27 Oct. 1951. The CMP decided to ignore Anglo-Canadian and Jewish groups. (However, Plante met with the YWHA in November 1952 and thanked the St-Laurent Kiwanis Club in December 1952.)

16 Mutchmor, *Mutchmor*, 124

17 'On Trying to Make Betting Illegal,' *Saturday Night*, 17 June 1922, 1; 5 Nov. 1932, 1

18 Metropolitan Toronto Police, *Annual Report of the Chief Constable of the City of Toronto* 1918, 3; 1924, 8; see ANQ-Q, E-17, Correspondance du Procureur-General, 1929, f. 4923; 1931, f. 692, f. 691, f. 3084, f. 3135; AVM, P 43, Enquête Caron, box 054-03-02-01, Morality Squad Reports. According to the 1941 census, there were few Chinese living on the Island of Montreal, whose population was 1,116,800. In 1951 the figure was 1,142 men and 292 women out of a total of 1,320,232. Canada, *Census* 1941, vol. 1, table 32, 'Population by Principal Origins for Census Sub-districts.' *Census*, 1951, vol. 1, table 34, 'Population by Origin and Sex for Counties and Census Divisions, 1951,' 34.9–34.10

19 'When Fictitious Names Come in Handy,' *Saturday Night*, 24 Aug. 1918, 1

20 Marquis, 'Vancouver,' 246; ANQ-Q, E-17, Correspondance du Procureur-General, 1929, f. 4923; 1930, f. 2947, 13 Sept. 1930; *Montreal Gazette*, 3 June 1946

21 Brailey, *Gambling*, 3. On the board, see Paul, 'Board.'

22 Rosecrance, *Gambling*, 34

23 Dodds, *Canadian*, 17–8; Waters, 'Operating,' 54; AO, RG 49-63, Press Clippings, 775, reel 25, 480, *Toronto Telegram*, 23 March 1927; Israel, 'Montreal,' 84

24 UCA, fonds 510, United Church of Canada, Board of Evangelism and Social Service, series 1, subject files Secretary, 1925–71, Public Morals, box 55, f. 197, Mutchmor to Rev. F.E. Barrett, 10 April 1945; *Halifax Citizen*, 8 Nov., 6 Dec. 1935

25 Tumpane, 'Breakdown,' 8–9

26 AVM, P 43, Enquête Caron, box 054-06-02-02, testimony of Harry Ship, 22 July 1952, 371, 365–70

27 *Vancouver News-Herald*, 1 March 1951

28 On the presence of Jews and sport gambling, especially bookmaking, see Riess, 'Sport,' 12–4. For Montreal's Jewish community, see Oiwa, 'Tradition'; Charbonneau, *La filière*, 19

29 AVM, P 43, Enquête Caron, box 054-06-02-02, f. 1952–108, testimony of Richard Quinn, 13 Nov. 1952. 18–19

30 *Victoria Colonist*, 8 Mar. 1939; Englander, 'Booth's,' 557

31 For examples from fiction, consider the father's hero worship of Jerry Dingleman in Richler's *The Apprenticeship of Duddy Kravitz*. See also Rockaway, 'Hoodlum'; Sarna, 'Jewish'; Ruth, *Inventing*.

32 *Canadian Jewish Chronicle*, 25 Aug. 1950; AVM, P 43, Enquête Caron, box 054-05-03-01, E-376, complaints Station 20, St-Louis-de-Mile-End; Joselit, *Our Gang*, 7, 20; AVM, P 43, Enquête Caron, box 054-03-03-01, vol. 3, D-145, Criminal Record of Eddy Baker alias 'Kid,' b 15 Apr. 1899 Odessa, Russia

33 Joselitt, *Our Gang*, 95

34 *Le Patriote* (Montreal), 11 May 1933. My thanks to Lisa Caplan for this reference.

35 'Montreal Becoming Second Chicago,' *Keneder Adler* (Montreal), 23 Aug. 1934 (translation)

36 'Amazing Sights and Bad Publicity,' ibid., 30 July 1946 (translation)

37 Rosenberg, *Canada's Jews*, 294

38 Ibid., 208

39 In the early 1920s, a Vancouver newspaper stated boldly that 'one-third of the Chinese population in Vancouver, variously estimated at 8,000 and

9,000, make a living as proprietors, employees or professional habitues of gambling houses.' VCA, series 181, Police Board General Files, To Board of Police Commissioners from 'A Fair Play Chinese,' 13 April 1925; Robert, 'Dufferin District,' 106

40 Ng, 'Ethnicity,' 54
41 Yee, *Saltwater City*, 16
42 McDonald, *Making Vancouver*, 187
43 Chong, *The Concubine's Children*, 34, 63
44 Robert, 'Dufferin District,' 80
45 Basu, 'Profit,' 228, 248, 251, 244, 246
46 UCA, fonds 122/12, Records Pertaining to Mission to the Chinese in Canada, box 3, f. 82, R. Duncanson to Rev. A.E. Armstrong, 10 Sept. 1914; CTA, Papers and Theses Collection, Valerie Mah, 'The "Bachelor Society": A Look at Toronto's Early Chinese Community from 1878–1924' (1978), 61; Yee, *Saltwater City*, 17–18
47 CUL, 'Montreal Chinese Community,' interview with Roger Ayotte by Kwok B. Chan, 11 Sept. 1983, 5; Basu, 'Profit,' 245
48 Kwok B. Chan, *Smoke*; Helly, *Les Chinois*; Anderson, *Vancouver's Chinatown*. Chinatown held its own particular dangers related to opium and mixed-race prostitution. For a parallel discussion of New Zealand, see David Grant, *On a Roll*; CUL, 'The Montreal Chinese Community,' interview with Roger Ayotte by Kwok B. Chan, 11 Sept. 1983, 3; VCA, series 199, Vancouver City Police, Gambling, Liquor Morality Branch, to Mayor re gambling, 30 March 1939.
49 *Dai Han Gung Bao* (Vancouver), 20 June 1928 (translated); Roy, *White*, 16; VCA, series 209, Vancouver Police Inquiry 1928, before R.S. Lennie, vol. 1, 450; *Verdun Messenger*, 15 Dec. 1949, 1. This was not strictly true – the presence of white women in Montreal's Chinese gambling establishments was noted by Jack Leung in CUL, 'Montreal Chinese Community,' interview, 7, 9 July 1975, 21
50 *Vancouver Daily Province*, 24 Aug. 1939
51 VCA, series 181, Police Board General Files, From 'A Fair Play Chinese,' to Board of Police Commissioners, 13 April 1925
52 VCA, series 181, Police Board General Files, 26 Sept. 1930, from lawyer Ian Cameron re: Sang Wing Society; 1 June 1932, to Chief of Police from same lawyer. The same practice existed in Toronto. See CTA, Papers and Theses Collection, Mah, '"Bachelor Society,"' 62–3; *Vancouver Sun*, 20 Feb. 1948
53 *Vancouver Sun*, 27 Feb. 1954
54 *Dai Han Gung Bao*, 14 Feb. 1924
55 UCA, fonds 510, United Church of Canada, Board of Evangelism and

Social Service, series 1, Subject Files Secretary, 1925–1971, Public Morals, box 55, f. 200, A Statement by Representatives of the Christian Social Council of Canada, 25 Feb. 1949

56 UCA, fonds 122/12, Records Pertaining to Mission to the Chinese in Canada, box 4, f. 124, R.G. MacBeth, 'Social Centre for Chinese in Vancouver,' 30 Sept. 1921; VCA, series 209, Vancouver Police Inquiry 1928, before R.S. Lennie, vol. 8, testimony of Mayor L.D. Taylor, 3416. Taylor openly identified with the workingman and was not above using anti-Asian rhetoric. McDonald, *Making*, 176; Dave Scott, 'Gambling Fines for Chinese, Price of Stopping Loneliness,' *Toronto Star*, 20 Jan. 1972

57 VCA, Mayor's Papers, vol. 35, 1939, 'Police-Gambling,' 14 July 1939, report of fines collected in the police court from 1936 to June 1939

58 *Dai Han Gung Bao*, 6 June 1928; *Vancouver Sun*, 19 Aug. 1933

59 UBC Special Collections, Chinese Canadian Research Collection, *Chinese Times*, 21 May, 20 July 1918

60 *Victoria Daily Times*, 15 April 1919; UCA, fonds 3384, Hugh Wesley Dobson Papers, B.13, reel 64, f. 11, 'Is Gambling Legalized in Vancouver?' *Information*, 15 Dec. 1927; *Dai Han Gung Bao*, 6 June 1928; *Vancouver Sun*, 28 Nov. 1936; *Liberty*, 3 Nov. 1945, 49

61 AO, RG 49-126, Committee on the Administration of Justice, vol. 8, 22 May 1951, 1042–3, testimony of John Chisholm, Chief Constable, City of Toronto; PAM, AG, Central Registry – series ATG, 0132, reference no. 542, box J/1/2/7, 8 Oct. 1945, From M.J. King to James McLenaghen, AG; UCA, fonds 3384, Hugh Wesley Dobson Papers, B.24, reel 92, f. 10. Gambling, Lotteries, sweepstakes, etc. (I), 1932–1950. 'Chinese Gambling,' *Vancouver Herald*, 17 Aug. 1949

62 *Victoria Daily Times*, 16 Aug. 1921; Huzel, 'Incidence,' 234

63 Williams, *Mayor*, 80–1; Marquis, 'Vancouver,' 246–52; *Daily Times*, 26 Nov. 1936

64 *Vancouver Sun*, 13 June 1939; VCA, series 199, Vancouver City Police: Gambling – Liquor – Morality Branch, Report on Clubs, Gambling and Lottery Conditions in the City of Vancouver, 1938, 12 Feb. 1939; AVM, P 43, Enquête Caron, box 054-01-03-02, f. 1953-28, testimony of Frank Hanley, 25 Feb. 1953

65 Chu, 'Chinese,' 22–3

66 Yee, *Saltwater City*, 84, re: Vancouver murder, 15 Oct. 1936, of a police informer

67 *Montreal Star*, 14 Dec. 1933; *Montreal Gazette*, 15, 16 Dec. 1933

68 *Dai Han Gung Bao*, 29 June 1928; VCA, series 199, Vancouver City Police: Gambling, Liquor, Morality Branch, Report on Clubs, Gambling and Lottery Conditions in the City of Vancouver for 1938, 12 Feb. 1939

69 Ng, 'Ethnicity,' 70

70 Ibid., 63–4; *Chinese Voice*, 12–13 Sept. 1955; for an earlier period see Howell, *Northern Sandlots*.

71 *Victoria Colonist*, 14 Dec. 1950

72 AO, RG 49-126, Committee on the Administration of Justice, vol. 8, 22 May 1951, 1042–3, 1045, testimony of John Chisholm, Chief Constable, City of Toronto

73 *Vancouver Sun*, 14 March 1949; *Vancouver Daily Province*, 12 April, 29 Nov. 1950, 10 March 1951

74 *Daily Province*, 29 March 1950; BCARS, GR 2966, AG, Correspondence from C95 (criminal prosecutions), 1966–1970, box 5, f. 47, C95.8 Vancouver – Bingo; Detective J.C. Horton, Vancouver Police, to N.A. McDiarmid, Departmental Solicitor, 10 July 1963

75 BCARS, GR 2966, AG, Correspondence from C95 (criminal prosecutions), 1966–1970, box 5, f. 49, C95.8 Victoria – Bingo; Police Chief Gregory, Victoria to AG, 23 Dec. 1969; *Victoria Daily Times*, 28 Oct. 1953; *Vancouver Daily Province*, 6 May 1965

76 *Vancouver Sun*, 25 Oct. 1966; *Vancouver Daily Province*, 7 Nov. 1966

77 *Dai Han Gung Bao*, 18 April 1962; the article was Phillips, 'Criminal.'

78 Bell, 'Crime,' 110; AO, RG 49-63, Press Clippings, MS-755, reel 589, 'Ottawa and Gambling,' editorial, *Toronto Mail*, 14 July 1922

79 No. 7 Circulaire de Mgr L'Administration Apostolique de clergé de son Diocèse, 21 nov. 1922, *Mandements, Lettres Pastorales, Circulaires et Autre Documents*, vol. 7 (Montreal 1926), 104

80 Ibid., no. 25, 29 Jan. 1951, vol. 21 (Montreal 1952), 410–2. Josie, 'Social,' 31; Manning, 'Is Bingo Bad?' 11

81 UCA, fonds 510, United Board of Evangelism and Social Service, series 1, Subject Files Secretary, 1925–71, Public Morals, box 565, f. 209, Brailey to Mutchmor, 23 March 1963

82 AO, RG 49-63, Press Clippings, MS-755, reel 585, *Toronto Mail*, 17 Aug. 1922

83 AO, RG 4-32, AG, Central Registry, 1929, f. 2907, Lindsay CA to Deputy AG, 21 Sept. 1929, and reply

84 ANQ-Q, E 17, Correspondance du Procureur-Général, 1930, f. 3613, 24 July 1930

85 AO, RG 4-32, AG, Central Registry, 1933, f. 2221; 1938, f. 49. At least once, an Anglican priest also faced charges for bingo, ibid., 1935, f. 2671, 29 Oct. 1935. PAM, GR 542, AG, Central Registry, J/1/2/20, f. 106, Betting Houses 1952–54, to O.M.M. Kay, Deputy AG, from Crown Prosecutor re alleged lottery at 915 Boyd, 22 Oct. 1952

86 BCARS, GR 2966, AG, Correspondence from C95 (criminal prosecutions),

1966–1970, box 5, f. 9, C95.8, 'No Name Given,' Letter from G.A. Gerrie, RCMP Supt in charge of Criminal Investigation, to J.A. Knox, Administrative Officer, 22 Aug. 1967

87 AO, RG 4-02, AG, Minister's Office Files, 1926–1978, L.E. Blackwell, f. 22.2, 'Gambling' letter dated 29 Dec. 1945 re legion; BCARS, GR 2966, AG Correspondence from C95 (criminal prosecutions), 1966–1970, box 5, f. 3, C95.8, 'No Name Given,' Letter from Mrs W.T.L. from Fort St John to AG, 20 July 1966

88 AO, RG 4-02, AG, Minister's Office Files, 1926–1978, L.E. Blackwell, f. 22.2, 'Gambling,' letter dated 20 Dec. 1945

89 Ibid., A.K. Roberts – F.M. Cass, f. 196.36, 'Criminal Matters – Gambling and Organized Crime, 1962,' letter dated 26 March 1963; Iacovetta, *Such Hardworking*

90 UCA, fonds 196, United Church of Canada Board of Evangelical and Social Service, box 55, 83.52C, Office of Secretary, Mutchmor to Louis St Laurent, 9 Nov. 1944

91 Ibid., Mutchmor to St Laurent, 15 Nov. 1944

92 AO, RG 4-02, AG, Minister's Office Files, 1926–1978, L.E. Blackwell, f. 22.2, 'Gambling,' letter dated 8 Sept. 1945. See Brailey, *Gambling*; UCA, fonds 510, United Church of Canada, Board of Evangelism and Social Service, series 1, subject files Secretary, 1925–71, Public Morals, box 55, f. 197, Mutchmor to Rev. F.E. Barrett, 10 April 1945

93 'Roman Catholics and Bingo,' *United Church Observer* 26, no. 9 (July 1964), 6

6: Professional Gambling and Organized Crime under Scrutiny

1 AO, RG 4-2, AG, Minister's Office Files, L.E. Blackwell, f. 36.4, Slot Machines (1943), 'Rackets and the Attorney General,' *Ottawa Journal*, 15 Oct. 1943

2 *Vancouver News-Herald*, 31 Dec. 1943

3 On Weber, see Corrigan and Sayer 'Afterthought,' 182–4.

4 Braden, 'More Dangerous,' 79

5 Boudreau, 'Crime'; AVM, P 43, Enquête Caron, box 054-01-02-01, E-829, *Rex v. Harry Ship*; *Halifax Mail*, 9 Oct. 1946; *Halifax Herald*, 19 Oct. 1946; PAM, AG Central Registry, GR 542 j/1/2/20, f. 106, Betting Houses, 1952–54, *Winnipeg Free Press*, 24 Nov. 1952; 23 Jan. 1953; *Winnipeg Tribune*, 24 Nov. 1952

6 AO, RG 4-41, Assistant Deputy, AG, Civil Law Correspondence Files, f. 13.9, Gambling Activities in Ontario, Memorandum to AG from Frank L.

Wilson, solicitor in Department of AG, 28 June 1961; Burnham, *Bad Habits*, 156–7; Bell, 'Crime,' 111

7 Bell, 'Crime,' 112

8 Ibid., 115–16; Reuter and Rubinstein, 'Illegal,' 52–5; Haller, 'Bootleggers,' 102–43. For the earlier period, see Johnson, 'Origins'; Kefauver, *Crime*, 35–52; Metropolitan Toronto Police, *Annual Report of the Chief Constable of the City of Toronto for the Year 1939*, 44; AO, RG 4-2, AG, Minister's Files, A.K. Roberts – F.M. Cass, f. 151.8, Criminal Matters: Gambling and Organized Crime 1961, 'Syndicated Gambling in New York State. A Report of the NY State Commission of Investigation, Feb. 1961,' 37–45

9 Devereaux, *Gambling*, vol. 1, 455–65. The horse racing research is particularly relevant to a Canadian study, as Devereaux worked in Toronto during the research and writing of this section.

10 'Padlock System Might Serve,' *Saturday Night*, 19 Dec. 1931, 1; VCA, series 207, Police Department, MacDonald Inquiry 1936, Inquiry by Hon. W.A. MacDonald arising out of the Tucker report, 21 Nov. 1936, Final Report, 15 Dec. 1936, 29. It read, 'When circumstance arose in Toronto requiring the appointment of a Chief of Police in that City, it was deemed advisable to go even outside the Province of Ontario and choose Brigadier General Draper from Quebec, with no previous police experience.'

11 Thomas, *From Police*, 51–5. Another large downtown bookmaking operation on Mercer Street was raided in 1939; police found twelve women and two men operating thirty-five telephones connected to fifty-seven lines and two switchboards. Toronto Police, *Annual Report*, 1939, 44

12 Higley, *O.P.P.*, 288; AVM, P 43, Enquête Caron, box 054-02-02-01, E-902, *Standard*, 18 April 1942; AO, RG 49-126, Committee on Administration of Justice, vol. 3, testimony of William Stringer, Commissioner OPP, 297; *Toronto Evening Telegram*, 13

13 *Vancouver Sun*, 6 Nov. 1944; AO, RG 4-41, Assistant Deputy, AG, Civil Law Correspondence Files, f. 13.9, Gambling Activities in Ontario, Memorandum to AG from Frank L Wilson, solicitor in Department of AG, 28 June 1961; AO, RG 4-2, AG, Minister's Office Files 1926–78, L.E. Blackwell, f. 22.1, Gambling 1943–44

14 Coleman, 'Ten Bucks'

15 AO, RG 49-126, Committee on Administration of Justice, vol. 1, testimony of Clifford R. Magone, 137, vol. 2, testimony of Magone, 149–50; Higley, *O.P.P.*, 282

16 Devereaux, *Gambling*, 475–6

17 Swan, *Century*. A similar situation existed in Victoria. In 1921, its chief of

police was charged with failing to enforce the law against Chinese lottery houses. *Colonist*, 17 Aug. 1921

18 VCA, series 209, Vancouver Police Inquiry 1928, vol. 2, 626; Swan, *Century*, 56–7; Marquis, 'Vancouver'; see also Huzel, 'Incidence.'

19 Swan, *Century*, 62; VCA, MacDonald Inquiry 1936, Exhibit 73, Report to the Chairman and Members of the Vancouver Police Commission from new Chief of Police, 18 Jan. 1935, 2; Williams, *Mayor* (Deputy Chief Murdoch was reinstated in 1937 after McGeer left office.) *Vancouver Sun*, 28 Nov. 1936; VCA, MacDonald Inquiry 1936, Final report, 15 Dec. 1935, 33

20 *Victoria Colonist*, 28 Aug. 1939; AVM, P 43, Enquête Caron, box 054-03-02-02, *Canadian Police Bulletin*, Dec. 1939, 5

21 VCA, Add. Ms. 54, Louis Denison Taylor Papers, vol. 9, no. 1, clippings, 11 March 1932; *Vancouver News-Herald*, 5 Jan. 1939. See also Robert A. Campbell, *Sit Down*, 39–41, on bookmaking in Vancouver's licenced beer parlours.

22 *Montreal Star*, 14 March 1925; Brodeur, *La délinquance*; Lévesque, *Making*, chap. AVM, P 43, Enquête Caron, box 054-02-03-01, *Montreal Star*, 12 Dec. 1952

23 *Montreal Herald*, 4 June 1921

24 AVM, P 43, Enquête Caron, box 054-06-03-01, E-710, Harold Dingman, 'What's Behind Montreal's Crime Clean-Up?' *Liberty*, 12 Oct. 1946, 10

25 AVM, P 43, Enquête Caron, box 054-03-03-01, D-145 (Eddy Baker) and D-146 (Harry Davis). Davis's record sheet contradicts the *Montreal Gazette*, 26 July 1946, which claimed that 'During his early years – that is to say, until the time he was about 28 – Harry Davis operated like any industrious, ambitious immigrant boy in a great country that promises a living to all who wish to work.' There is no mention of his charge for fencing in 1920. When Davis was twenty-eight he faced his first narcotics charge. See also D-144, RCMP to F. Dufresene, 20 Nov. 1941, re: Max Shapiro. Shapiro returned to Canada from Ohio in 1922 after bootlegging charges and thereafter was found guilty only of customs violations. Charbonneau, *La filière*, 22

26 *Montreal Star*, 2–7 Oct. 1933. Davis denied having any interest in the White House Inn or 1403 Peel.

27 Ibid., 22–23 Aug. 1934; Charbonneau, *La filière*, chap. 1. Davis allegedly kept quiet about the real culprits and earned $300 a week while in jail, accumulating $60,000 by the time he was released. AVM, P 43, Enquête Caron, box 054-06-03-02, E-35, *Montreal Standard*, 27 July 1946; *Montreal Star*, 24 Aug. 1934

28 *Montreal Star*, 6 Oct. 1933; see Penny Ante cartoon about poker, *Montreal Herald*, 21 Jan. 1922; Ruth, *Inventing*.

29 Moore, *Kefauver*, 25; Valverde, 'Building'; Adams, *Trouble*; AO, RG 49-126, Committee on Administration of Justice, vol. 3, testimony of William Stringer, Commissioner OPP, 297

30 Brodeur, *La delinquance*; CRLG, P 47, Fonds du Comité de moralité publique, B, 6–7, Comité exécutif, 26 Nov. 1952, 25 Feb. 1953. Kefauver declined the invitation; Rosecrance, *Gambling*, 96.

31 Bell, 'Crime,' 117; *Globe and Mail* quoted in Tumpane, 'Breakdown,' 9. JCSHC, *Minutes*, no. 7, 30 March 1954, 288; Ontario AG's Department, *Report of the Attorney General's Committee on Enforcement of the Law Relating to Gambling* (Toronto 1961); J. Ruddy, 'You're Buying a Dream – and Not Much Else – When You Bet on the Sweeps,' *Maclean's*, April 1967, 59–62; NAC, MG 28, Canadian Council on Social Development, I, 10, vol. 70, 515, 1941–71, to Kitchener Lions Club from W.T. McGrath, Executive Secretary, Canadian Corrections Association, 13 Dec. 1963

32 Davies, 'Police'; Luce, 'There's a Way,' 16; JCSHC, *Reports*, 65–6

33 Strange, 'Pain'; Vance, *Analysis*, 68; JCSHC, *Minutes*, no. 11, 29 March 1955, 314; Peterson was prominent in anti-gambling circles from 1942 on and former head of FBI offices in Boston, St Louis, and Milwaukee; Moore, *Kefauver*, 35.

34 UCA, fonds 510, United Church of Canada, Board of Evangelism and Social Service, series 1, Subject Files Secretary, 1925–1971, Public Morals, box 55, f. 200, A Statement by Representatives of the Christian Social Council of Canada, 25 Feb. 1949; AO, RG 4-2, AG, Minister's Office Files, Blackwell–Porter, f. 51.1, Gambling 1948–49, 'Proceedings of 26 Jan. 1948 re: New Toronto law enforcement,' 13; *Vancouver Daily Province*, 8 Dec. 1953; Coleman,' Ten Bucks,' 7; Ronald Williams, 'Gambling Octopus Grabs of $150 Millions a Year,' *Financial Post*, 30 April 1949, 13; AO, RG 49-126, Committee on Administration of Justice, vol. 8, testimony of Albert Lee, Inspector Toronto City Police in charge of Morality squad, 1136–7

35 McCaffrey, 'Putting,' 9

36 AO, RG 49-126, Committee on Administration of Justice, vol. 2, testimony of Clifford R Magone, 157; vol. 3, testimony of William Stringer, Commissioner OPP, 330. The important exception to this 'pretty clean' image was the Windsor Police Department. Accusations of corruption there emerged in 1950 resulting in the dismissal of both the chief of police and his deputy. Higley, *O.P.P.*, 347–8; AO, RG 49-126, Committee on Administration of Justice, vol. 12, testimony of William Stringer, Commissioner OPP, 1793–4

37 AO, RG 49-126, Committee on Administration of Justice, vol. 5, testimony of William Tomlinson, Chief of OPP anti-gambling squad, 662–6; vol. 9, testimony of Harold Young, General Manager of the Western Area of the Bell Telephone Company, 1237–73; ibid., vol. 8, testimony of Norman Munnoch, General Counsel for Bell Telephone Company, 1155–62

38 Ibid., vol. 10, testimony of Harold Young, General Manager of the Western Area of the Bell Telephone Company, 1341–8. This issue also emerged in Montreal and Vancouver. In Montreal, Bell would not disconnect or cancel telephone service unless 'that very person would have been condemned as such by a proper Court and with proper evidence.' AVM, P 43, Enquête Caron, box 054-06-02-02, f. 1952-59, testimony of William G. Bell of Bell Telephone Co. of Canada, 4 Aug. 1952, 16; AO, RG49-126, Committee on Administration of Justice, vol. 10, testimony of Harold Young, General Manager of the Western Area of the Bell Telephone Company, 1368, 1390

39 AVM, P 43, Enquête Caron, box 054-06-02-02, f. 1952-59, 1402, Bell President, 5 June 1947, posted memo

40 Ibid., testimony of Munnoch, General Counsel of the Bell Telephone Company, 1476–7

41 AO, RG 23, Ontario Provincial Police, E-107, f. 1.2, Gambling G.H.A. files, 1938–1956, Fred Baker, 'Fight Gamblers at Polls Too, Frost's Pledge,' *Toronto Telegram*, 31 Oct. 1951; f. 1.1, Gambling G.H.Q. file, 1938–1956, 'Circle-Bar Fourth Column,' by J.V. McAree, sponsored by Circle Bar Knitting Co. *Toronto Globe and Mail*, 30 Dec. 1953

42 AO, RG 23, Ontario Provincial Police, E-107, g. 1.1, Gambling G.H.Q file, 1938–1956, Howard Rutsey, 'An Old Foe Returns ... and Big-Time Gambling Ring Is Threatened,' *Toronto Telegram*, 28 April 1954; AO, RG 4-41, Assistant Deputy, AG, Civil Law Correspondence Files, f. 13.9, Gambling Activities in Ontario, Memorandum to AG from Frank L. Wilson, solicitor in department, 28 June 1961; AO, RG 4-02, Minister's Office Files, A.K. Roberts–F.M. Cass, f. 196.2, 'Criminal Matters – Gambling and Organized Crime, 1963,' Legislature of Ontario Debates, 29 Nov. 1961, Speech by Mr. J.J. Wintermeyer, Leader of Opposition, on Organized Crime and the Necessity of a Royal Commission to Expose all aspects of organized crime in Ontario; a direct appeal to Premier to establish a Royal Commission, 89–90, 101–5

43 AO, RG 4-41, Assistant Deputy, AG, Civil Law Correspondence Files, f. 13.9, Gambling Activities in Ontario, Memorandum to AG from Frank L.Wilson, solicitor in department, 28 June 1961; AO, RG 4-02, Minister's Office Files, A.K. Roberts–F.M. Cass, f. 196.2, 'Criminal Matters – Gambling and Organized Crime, 1963,' 'Mafia in Ontario? A-G Orders Probe,' *Toronto*

Telegram, 21 Aug. 1963; *Vancouver Sun*, 18 March 1963. Feeley and McDermott were associated with the Cooksville Club (known also as the Centre Road Club), the Riverdale Club in Toronto, the Rosland Club in Sandwich, the Frontier Club in Bertie Township near Fort Erie, and the Tisdale Club in Peterborough. Higley, *O.P.P.*, 403–6, 415–16

44 Marquis, 'Early' and *Policing*, 305

45 *Vancouver News-Herald*, 22 June 194; *Victoria Colonist*, 28 Sept. 1946; *Vancouver Sun*, 27, 28, 30 Sept. 1946; Macdonald and O'Keefe, *Mulligan*, 22. There were even allegations made by detective who was dismissed when Mulligan assumed responsibility for the Criminal Investigation Branch that Wismer was linked directly to prominent local gamblers: Macdonald and O'Keefe, *Mulligan*, 31; *Vancouver News-Herald*, 28 Sept. 1946

46 Swan, *The Vancouver Police*, 71; *Vancouver Sun*, 11 May 1951

47 The charge read that Harry and Louis Tisman, between 1 January 1937 and 31 March 1946, 'did unlawfully conspire each with the other and with divers other persons unknown to commit an indictable offense, to wit, to corruptly offer the following persons, Alexander G. Neill (former chief), Norman Corbett (former Deputy chief), Walter Bell, William Veitch, and William Bartlett, then being police officers of the city of Vancouver police force, employed for the detection of offenders, money to facilitate the commission of the crime of operating a gambling house.' *Vancouver News-Herald*, 21 April 1947; *Vancouver Sun*, 21 April 1947. The *Chinese Times* reported this affair in great detail as an example of a gambling scandal that did not involve any member of its community. *Chinese Times*, 20–24 March 1947

48 *Vancouver Daily Province*, 7 May 1947; *Vancouver Sun*, 7 Jan., 8 Sept. 1948; *Daily Province*, 19 July 1949

49 *Vancouver Sun*, 18 July 1940; no. 921 'By-Law to authorize the Recorder's Court of the City of Montreal to order the temporary closing of certain immoveables' (17 Jan. 1927), *By-laws of the City of Montreal: Compilation of All By-laws to Date* (Montreal 1931); AVM, P 43, Enquête Caron, box 054-04-02-01, testimony of Lionel Elie, 3 Oct. 1950, 305–14; box 054-03-03-02, E-19, E-20, E-21, E-22, Padlock Registers 1932–48; *Vancouver Sun*, 18 July 1940; AO, RG 23, Ontario Provincial Police, E-107, f. 1.2, Gambling G.H.Q., 1938–56(2), *Toronto Telegram*, 17 Apr. 1951; Weintraub, *City*, 60

50 *Vancouver Sun*, 19 May 1951; *Vancouver News-Herald*, 6 June 1951; *Vancouver Daily Province*, 10 March 1951; *Vancouver Sun*, 8 March 1951

51 *Victoria Colonist*, 13 May 1951; *Vancouver Sun*, 8, 11 May 1951; *Vancouver Daily Province*, 8 May, 17 July 1951; *Vancouver News-Herald*, 8 May 1951

52 Ibid., 24 Oct., 21–24, 27, 29–30 Nov., 3, 7–8, 11 Dec. 1951; *Vancouver Sun*, 24 Oct. 1951; *Vancouver Daily Province*, 22 Nov. 1951

53 *Vancouver News-Herald*, 24 Nov., 3 Dec 1951; *Vancouver Daily Province*, 1 Dec. 1951, 1, 20 March 1952; *Vancouver Sun*, 25 Nov. 1951

54 Macdonald and O'Keefe, *Mulligan*, 42

55 Swan, *Century*, 82. *Flash* began publishing in Toronto in the 1920s, and in 1947 it was bought by Lou Ruby, who also published the *Thoroughbred*. Macdonald and O'Keefe, *Mulligan*, 51–5; *Daily Province*, 15 Sept. 1955

56 *Daily Province*, 29 July 1955; *Vancouver Sun*, 26 Jan. 1956

57 *Vancouver Sun*, 26 Jan. 1956. Leo Bancroft also denied knowing Mulligan or ever paying protection money. *Vancouver Daily Province*, 15 Sept. 1955, 31 July 1956; Swan, *Century*, 82

58 *Vancouver Daily Province*, 31 July 1956, 18 May 1965, 15 Nov. 1961

59 Marquis, *Policing*, 254

60 Gilmore, *Swinging*, 90

61 Commend, 'De la femme'

62 McCormick, 'Gambling,' 5. This period is also described in Weintraub, *City*.

63 McCormick, 'Gambling,' 5–6; Dingman, 'Gambling;' 49

64 AVM, P 43, Enquête Caron, box 054-06-03-02, E-35; *Montreal Star*, 31 July 1945

65 AVM, P 43, Enquête Caron, box 054-06-03-01, E-705; *Montreal Gazette*, 20 July 1946

66 *Montreal Gazette*, 26 July 1946

67 Lacasse has written on the prostitution interests of this movement in *Prostitution*, 104. In 1943 the Ligue de vigilance sociale was formed to combat prostitution and venereal disease after the army had threatened to make Montreal off limits for all its soldiers.

68 *Gazette*, 20 July 1946

69 AVM, P 43, Enquête Caron, box 054-06-03-02, E-35, *Montreal Standard*, 27 July 1946; 'Amazing Sights and Bad Publicity,' *Keneder Adler*, 30 July 1946 (translated)

70 AVM, P 43, Enquête Caron, box 054-05-02-02, f. 1951–64, testimony of Able Nudleman, 29 March 1951; box 054-02-03-01, *La Patrie*, 25 July 1952; box 054-06-03-02, E-35, *Montreal Standard*, 27 July 1946; box 054-04-02-01, testimony of J. Rodrique Joly, 4 Oct. 1950

71 Keate, 'Unhorsed,' 6; see also 'Reformer's Return,' *Time*, 12 Dec. 1949, 19.

72 Stanké and Morgan, *Pax*, 32; Johnstone, 'Plante,' 12–4, 102–13; Plante's wife was successful partly because of a photo layout that had appeared in 1946 about a cruise that Plante took between Montreal and Burlington, Vermont, in the company of a friend and two women, after which he was named as an adulterer in one of the women's divorce proceedings. Keate,

'Unhorsed,' 44; AVM, P 43, Enquête Caron, box 054-02-03-01, *Le Canada*, 16 Sept. 1948

73 AVM, P 43, Enquête Caron, box 054-02-03-01, *Star*, 19 Sept. 1952

74 Ibid., box 054-06-02-01, testimony of Harry Ship, 21 July 1952, 6–7; box 054-06-02-02, f. 1952-108, testimony of Richard Quinn, 13 Nov. 1952, 18–19

75 Ibid., box 054-06-02-01, testimony of Harry Ship, 21 July 1952, 9, 30, 63–4, 122–3, 22 July 1952, 151–2, 275, 283; Weintraub, *City*, 61

76 Keates, 'Unhorsed,' 44; AVM, P 43, Enquête Caron, box 054-03-03-01, *Rex v. Harry Ship*; Plante, 'Shame,' part II, 10

77 Plante, 'Shame,' part I, 4; Johnstone, 'Plante,' 109. Plante later explained the lack of public support as being a result of blackmail. He claimed that Archbishop Carbonneau did not support him after his first firing because 'racketeers' claimed that they would publicize two brothels in Montreal that catered exclusively to priests and that he (Plante) had been painted as both 'a Don Juan' and a homosexual. Plante, 'Shame,' part III, 19

78 'Canada "Old Look,"' *Time*, 25 July 1949, 27; 'Reformer's Return,' *Time*, 12 Dec. 1949, 19; 'His Greatest Ally,' *Saturday Night*, 27 Dec. 1949, 36; Plante, 'The Shame of My City,' part I, 6. Plante identified Max Shapiro as the 'undisputed kingpin of the city's rackets.' Shapiro, who had links with Harry Davis and Charles Feigenbaum of Lachine's 'White House' Inn in the early 1930s, admitted to operating an exclusive book between 1942 and 1947/8 with only half a dozen clients and to having an interest in a members-only gaming house, 'The Wheel,' on Peel Street, with Harry Boris and McBurnie between 1939 and 1945. AVM, P 43, Enquête Caron, box 054-05-02-02, f. 1951-64, testimony of Max Shapiro, 30 March 1951, 5, 7, 9

79 Stanké and Morgan, *Pax*, 34; see Behiels, *Prelude.*

80 Lacasse, *Prostitution*, 106. The founding members were François-Albert Angers (future editor of *L'Action nationale*), Pierre DesMarais, Gérard Filion (editor of *Le Devoir*), Ruben Lévesque, J.-Z.-Léon Patenaude, Félix-Adolphe Senécal, and Lionel Vezeau. For example, the Ligues du sacré-coeur du Québec were founded in 1883 to 'propagate and conserve the Christian spirit in families and society' (Lacasse, *Prostitution*, 38); Special Collections, University of Ottawa, 'Les Ligues du Sacré-Coeur, Leur histoire, leur rôle,' speech by Paul-Émile Léger, 9 March 1958. Some form of the organization existed until the 1976 resolution of a libel and defamation suit by the estate of Police Chief Albert Langlois. Purcell and McKenna, *Drapeau*, 89

81 Hamelin, *Histoire*; Livernois, 'Monseigneur'

82 AVM, P 43, Enquête Caron, box 054-02-03-01, *Montreal Gazette*, 11 Sept. 1950

83 See also David, 'Le Comité'; de Champlain, *Le crime*; Purcell and McKenna, *Drapeau*; Plante, 'Shame,' part II, 11; Brodeur, *La délinquance*, 141.

84 AVM, P 43, Enquête Caron, box 054-02-03-01, *Le Devoir* (Montreal), 31 March 1951

85 AVM, P 43, Enquête Caron, box 054-04-02-01, testimony of George Vernot, chief assessor for city of Montreal, 28 Sept. 1950, 143; box 054-05-02-01, testimony of Albert Hotte, 6 Feb. 1951; box 054-06-02-01, f. 1952-23, testimony of Georges Godin, 27 June 1952; f. 1952-22, testimony of Frank Hanley, 27 June 1952; f. 1952-26, testimony of David Rochon, 28 June 1952. Dave Rochon denied his presence at Baker's funeral before the Inquiry; testimony of Harry Ship, 22 July 1952, 377-80. Ship explained that the phone number had been given to him and that when he approached the mayor about some 'personal trouble' Houde had slammed the telephone down; box 054-02-03-01, *Montreal Gazette*, 26 Sept. 1950.

86 Weintraub, *City*, 83. By the time of the Caron Inquiry, several of the accused members of the Montreal morality squad were moved to the anti-Communist, anti-subversive squad. For example, AVM, P 43, Enquête Caron, box 054-01-03-01, f. 1952-106, 12 Nov. 1952, Louis Champagne and Charles Senecal; f. 1952–122, 17 Nov. 1952, testimony of Jean-Marie Auger; box 054-04-02-01, 6 Oct. 1950, testimony of Armand Lefebvre; box 054-06-02-02, f. 1952-39, 9 July 1952; f. 1952-79, 26 Aug. 1952; f. 1952-82, 28 Aug. 1952; f. 1952-104, 1 Oct. 1952; f. 1952-118, 24 Nov. 1952; box 054-01-03-02, f. 1952(3)-2, 19 Jan. 1953; box 054–06–02–01, testimony of Harry Ship, 22 July 1952, 398

87 AVM, P 43, Enquête Caron, box 054-02-03-01, *Star*, 17 May 1951; AVM, Dossiers de Presse – Séries D, Enquête Moralité,' *Le Devoir* (Montreal), 6 Feb., 8 March 1952 (3.196–3.197), 16–17 April 1952 (3.202, 3.204–3.205); CRLG, P47, Fonds du Comité de moralité publique, B.6, Comité exécutif, 1 Oct. 1952; B.8, Comité exécutif, 28 Jan. 1953

88 Plante, 'Shame,' part I, 4; Purcell and McKenna, *Drapeau*, 99–100

89 Plante, 'Shame,' part I, 6; CRLG, P47, Fonds du Comité de moralité publique, G. 17 *Herald*, 15 March 1957; Plante, fired by Sarto Fournier in 1957, soon left Montreal after what he claimed were threats on his life and lived at a secret location in Mexico (Guadalajara) until his death in August 1976. In 1976 the Quebec Court of Appeal had awarded him $115,000 in back pay. *Le Devoir* (Montreal), 10 Aug. 1976; Plante, 'Shame,' part I, 4

90 AVM, P 43, Enquête Caron, box 054-04-02-02, testimony of Sidney Shorr, 2 Nov. 1950, 2926

91 AO, RG 23, Ontario Provincial Police, E-107, f. 1.2, Gambling G.H.Q., 1938–56(2), *Toronto Telegram*, 3 March 1951

92 *Toronto Star*, 5 March 1951; AO, RG 23, Ontario Provincial Police, E-107, f. 1.2 – Gambling G.H.Q., 1938–56(2), *Toronto Telegram*, 20 June, 5 March 1951; *Toronto Globe and Mail*, 27 June 1951; *Toronto Star*, 26 June 1951; *Toronto Telegram*, 26 June 1951

93 AO, RG 23, Ontario Provincial Police E-10, f. 1.2. – Gambling G.H.Q. 1938–56(2). *Toronto Telegram*, 17 April 1951; *Toronto Globe and Mail*, 18 April 1951

94 *Telegram*, 17 April 1951; AO, RG 23, Ontario Provincial Police, E-107, f. 1.2, Gambling G.H.Q., 1938–56(2), *Toronto Daily Star*, 17 April 1951

95 *Vancouver Daily Province*, 20 March 1952; 1 Oct. 1954

96 J.D. Morton, 'Gambling and the Law,' 16–17

7: Redefining the Public Interest: Gambling, Charity, and the Welfare State

1 HC, *Debates*, 26 Jan. 1962, 272

2 Ibid., 15 Feb. 1961, 896 (Doug Fisher, Port Arthur); AO, RG 4, AG, series 4-02, Minister's Office Files, 1926–78, f. 75.3, Lotteries, Raffles, and Bingo, news clippings, 'Opposes Plan for Lotteries, Wishart Says,' *Globe and Mail*, 27 Dec. 1967; AO, RG 4, AG, series 4-02, Minister's Office Files, 1926–78, f. 196.3, Criminal Matters: Gambling and Organized Crime, Lotteries, raffles, and bingo, 1963, P.F.W. to Fred Cass, AG, 29 Oct. 1963

3 *Victoria Colonist*, 22 Feb. 1962

4 'The United Church and Gambling' advertisement in *Maclean's*, 21 April 1962, 46; Ernest Marshall Howse, 'The Great Illusion,' *United Church Observer*, 1 April 1964, 19–20; BCARS, GR 2966, BC AG, correspondence from C95, 1966–70, vol. 5, f. 4, Bingo – Gambling, General, A.J. Gowland, Sec. of the Presbyterian Church of Canada, to AG, 19 Sept. 1963

5 BCARS, GR 2966, BC AG, correspondence from C95, 1966–70, vol. 5, f. 4, Bingo – Gambling, General, Rev. Fred N. Poulton, Sec of the Canadian Council of Churches, to AG, 16 Dec. 1963, 11; Mutchmor to AG, 10 Feb. 1966

6 UCA, fonds 200, United Church of Canada, Board of Evangelism and Social Service, Office Series 1, Subject Files, Secretary, 1925–1971, Public Morals, box 55, f. 200, Special Bulletin of *Lions Echo*; fonds 510, United Church of Canada Board of Evangelism and Social Service, series 1, Subject Files, Secretary, 1925–1971, Public Morals, box 56, f. 208, G.L Richardson (member of church and service club) to Mutchmor, 22 Nov. 1962; f. 206, Charlotte Whitton to Mutchmor, 20 April 1960

7 JCSHC, *Minutes*, no. 7, 30 March 1954, 283

8 UCA, fonds 200, United Church of Canada, Board of Evangelism and

Social Service, Office Series 1, Subject Files, Secretary, 1925–1971, Public Morals, f. 213, Jim Coleman, *Hamilton Spectator*, 29 July 196; f. 212, 'Churchmen Protest – Sunday Racing in Metro Could Start This Year,' *Toronto Star*, 28 March 1968; Rev W. Bothwell, Dean of Montreal, to Mutchmor, 23 May 1968

9 UCA, fonds 200, United Church of Canada, Board of Evangelism and Social Service, Office Series 1, Subject Files, Secretary, 1925–1971, Public Morals, f. 213, Controller Allan A. Lamport to Mutchmor, 15 Aug. 1968

10 Colin S. Campbell and Lowman, 'Introduction'

11 AO, RG 4, AG, series 4-02, Minister's Office Files, 1926–78, f. 22.2, Gambling 1945, W.A. Goodfellow, M.P.P., to AG, 28 Dec. 1945; HC, *Debates*, 26 Jan. 1962, 272 (J.F. Browne, Vancouver-Kingsway)

12 HC, *Debates*, 12 Jan. 1954. 1023 (E.D. Fulton, Kamloops)

13 BCARS, GR 2966, BC AG, Correspondence from C95, 1966–70, vol. 5, f. 4, Bingo – Gambling, General, Rev. Fred N. Poulton, Sec. of the Canadian Council of Churches, to AG, 16 Dec. 1963, 11. See also *Victoria Colonist*, 22 April 1954; *Vancouver Daily Province*, 20 Jan. 1944; Stein, 'Why,' 48; Josie, 'Social,' 30–1.

14 A similar position was taken by the Catholic church in Massachusetts. See Ponte, 'Religious Opposition,' 59; *Messenger* (Verdun), 15 Feb. 1951; J.V. McAree, 'Lotteries in the Air,' *Toronto Globe and Mail*, 4 May 1951

15 *Vancouver Daily Province*, 14 Aug. 1953; *Victoria Colonist*, 13 Aug. 1953

16 AO, RG 4, AG, series 4-02, Minister's Office Files, 1926–78, f. 375.2, Lotteries, Raffles and Bingo, 'Brief from the Canadian Council of Churches opposing any legislation to legalize lotteries in Canada,' presented to Prime Minister Trudeau and Minister of Justice John Turner, 9 Sept. 1968

17 *Vancouver Daily Province*, 6 March 1963; *Vancouver Sun*, 1 March 1963

18 Cronin, 'State Lottery,' 28; *Vancouver Sun*, 11 Oct. 1945; AO, RG 4, AG, series 4-02, Minister's Office Files, 1926–78, f. 22.2, Gambling 1945, Press Release Re: Lotteries, Raffles, and Bingo, 18 Dec. 1945; *Vancouver Sun*, 31 Aug. 1951; *Vancouver Daily Province*, 30 Oct. 1959

19 Ross, *Booming*, 11, 16. For a discussion of alcohol, see Robert A. Campbell, *Sit Down*; Marquis, 'Civilized.' On contraception, see Appleby, *Responsible Parenthood*.

20 *Vancouver Sun*, 19 Dec. 1964

21 AO, RG 4, AG, series 4-08, Advisory Committee on the Enforcement of Law Relating to Gambling (1961), 1

22 Owram, *Born*; George Grant, *Lament*, 56–7, 70–1

23 PAM, AG, Central Registry, GR 542, J/1/2/20, f. 106, Betting Houses, 1952–54, to AG from 'CRC' (pseudonym), 25 Nov. 1952

24 Dixon, 'Discovery,' 157

25 Chinn, *Better*, 175

26 Dixon, 'Discovery,' 162; Rosecrance, 'Compulsive,' 276; Michael Walker, 'Medicalisation,' 224

27 BCARS, GR 2966, BC AG, Correspondence from C95, 1966–70, vol. 5, f. 4, Bingo – Gambling, General, Rev. Fred N. Poulton, Sec. of the Canadian Council of Churches, to AG, 16 Dec. 1963, 11. See also *Victoria Colonist*, 22 April 1954; *Vancouver Daily Province*, 20 Jan. 1944; Stein, 'Why,' 48; Josie, 'Social,' 30–1

28 Rosecrance, 'Compulsive,' 277. Dunkely, *Gambling*, 7–9. Bergler is also credited with the phrase 'writer's block'; *Toronto Globe and Mail*, 18 July 1998.

29 Kisker, 'Mad,' 21, 32–3; Stearns, *Battleground*, 300

30 Valverde, 'Slavery'

31 Rosecrance, 'Medicalisation,' 279

32 HC, *Debates*, 21 April 1969, 7779 (Réal Caouette, Témiscamingue)

33 JCSHC, *Minutes*, no. 13, 13 May 1954, 559

34 Stearns, *Battleground*, 300–2

35 Collins, 'Pathological,' 71

36 *Vancouver Daily Province*, 4 June 1958

37 *Vancouver Sun*, 24 March 1956; 28 Oct. 1959

38 Ibid., 4 July 1966

39 *Vancouver Sun*, 30 March 1948; *Vancouver Daily Province*, 30 March 1948

40 *Daily Province*, 15 Sept. 1951

41 *Vancouver Sun*, 5 Sept. 1959, 7 April 1951, 15 Nov. 1952, 26 March 1960, 17 Oct. 1962

42 Ibid., 21 Oct. 1960, 25 March 1961; *Vancouver Daily Province*, 26 March 1965; 1 Oct. 1970; *Victoria Colonist*, 24 Oct. 1959

43 *Vancouver Daily Province*, 27 March 1969

44 UCA, fonds 3384, Hugh Wesley Dobson Papers, B.24, reel 92, f. 10, Gambling, Lotteries, Sweepstakes etc. (1) 1932–50 'Lotteries for War Met with Favor,' *Regina Leader*, 2 March 1944. In addition to the strong support that the idea received in Quebec, many British Columbians also joined the campaign. BC Labour MLA Tom Uphill declared in 1946, 'Let Eastern Canada do as it likes. Let us take care of our own.' Indeed, in 1959 a poll taken by the *Vancouver Sun* claimed that 85 per cent of British Columbians favoured sweepstakes as a means to raise money for charity and hospitals. *Victoria Colonist*, 28 March 1946; *Vancouver Sun*, 5 Sept. 1959

45 *Vancouver Daily Province*, 19 Dec. 1949

46 AO, RG 4, AG, series 4–02, Minister's Office Files, 1926–78, f. 311.8, Lotter-

ies, Raffles, and Bingo 1966, correspondence from Operation Sweepstake, CTV telepoll, 15 Dec. 1963

47 Ibid.

48 Ibid., f. 458.7, Lotteries, Raffles, Bingo 1970, Gallup Report, 7 May 1969, Canadian Institute of Public Opinion

49 Ibid., f. 151.8, Criminal Matters; Gambling and Organized Crime 1961, transcript, Channel 11, Norm Marshall's 'Capsule Comment,' 2 July 1961; *Victoria Colonist*, 17 April 1953; *Vancouver Daily Province*, 25 Sept. 1962; AO, RG 4, AG, series 4–08, Advisory Committee on the Enforcement of Law Relating to Gambling (1961), 1, 47; J.D. Morton, 'Gambling,' 16

50 *Vancouver Daily Province*, 3 Sept. 1959; *Vancouver Sun*, 7 Aug. 1959 (the author chose not to use his or her real name in this public forum).

51 *Vancouver Daily Province*, 23 Dec. 1946. It would be dangerous to extract generalizations on the basis of the exceptionalism of British Columbia, which offered the greatest support for liberalization of the law outside of Quebec. The *Province* can be identified as a culturally 'conservative' paper.

52 *Vancouver Daily Province*, 15 Sept. 1949

53 Ibid., 21 June 1958

54 *Vancouver Sun*, 1, 5 Aug. 1950; *Vancouver Daily Province*, 31 Jan. 1951

55 Canada, Royal Commission on Health Services, Eric J. Hanson, *The Public Finance Aspects of Health Services in Canada* (1964), 105; *Vancouver Sun*, 30 April 1963; HC, *Debates*, 16 Feb. 1961, 2099. New Hampshire became in 1964 the first state to introduce a lottery, followed by New York and Massachusetts. Vance, *Analysis of the Costs*, 46–8

56 J.D. Morton, 'Gambling,' 16

57 HC, *Debates*, 3 March 1967, 13746 (Georges Valade, Ste-Marie)

58 Ibid., 3 March 1967, 13748–9 (Georges Valade, Ste-Marie)

59 *Vancouver Sun*, 24 Aug. 1951

60 PAM, GR 542, AG, Central Registry, ATG 0132, box J/1/2/7, Deputy AG, New Brunswick, to O.M.M. Kay Deputy, AG, Manitoba, 6 Aug. 1956; *Vancouver Daily Province*, 21 June 1958, 25 Sept. 1962; Chaput and Graham, *Dear Enemies*, 58. The annual private members' bills for lotteries originated from Quebec MPs.

61 AO, RG 4, AG, series 4–02, Minister's Office Files, 1926–78, f. 22.1, Gambling 1943–44, F.W.L. Brailey to Leslie Blackwell, AG, 26 Dec. 1944

62 PAM, GR 542, AG, Central Registry, ATG 0132m J/1/2/8, Lotteries, 1947–48, CA, Minnedosa, Man., to AG, 11 July 1947. See also *Vancouver Sun*, 3 Sept. 1943.

63 *Vancouver News-Herald*, 13 Jan. 1947

64 AO, RG 4, AG, series 4-02, Minister's Office Files, 1926–78, f. 22.2, Gam-

bling 1945, Rev. R.H. MacKay, sec. of Toronto-Centre Presbytery of United Church of Canada, to Blackwell, AG, 20 Nov. 1945; Brailey to Blackwell, AG, 18 Oct. 1945, resolution of National Advisory Council of Service Clubs of Canada, 20 Sept. 1945; Brailey to Blackwell, AG, 15 Aug. 1945; Brailey, *Gambling*, 10; *United Church Observer*, 15 Feb. 1964, 9

65 CBA, *Baptist Yearbook for Ontario and Quebec*, 1945–6, 51; *Vancouver Daily Province*, 21 June 1950; AO, RG 4, AG, series 4-02, Minister's Office Files, 1926–78, f. 196.3, Criminal Matters; Gambling and Organized Crime, Lotteries, raffles, and bingo, 1963, Resolution of Kitchener Lions Club, 8 Nov. 1963; UCA, fonds 200, United Church Board of Evangelism and Social Service, Office Series 1, Subject Files, Secretary, 1925–1971, Public Morals, box 55, f. 200, Special Bulletin of *Lions Echo*

66 *Vancouver News-Herald*, 8 May 1948

67 *Vancouver Sun*, 24 April, 3, 4, 6, 18 May, 2 June 1948; *Vancouver Daily Province*, 3, 4, 11, 17 May; 7 July 1948; *Vancouver News-Herald*, 1 June 1948

68 *Vancouver Sun*, 18, 19 Aug. 1949; *Vancouver Daily Province*, 13 Sept. 1949; *Vancouver Sun*, 13 Sept., 31 Aug. 1949; *Vancouver News-Herald*, 10 Aug. 1951; *Vancouver Daily Province*, 26 Feb. 1955

69 PAM, GR 542, J/4/2/8, 102-L, Lotteries, 1947–48, Peter McSheffrey, Sec Treasurer, Trades and Labor Council, 14 June 1950; *Vancouver Sun*, 12, 14 Sept. 1949, 5 Nov. 1955, 14 Oct. 1965; BCARS, GR 2966, BC AG, Correspondence from C95, 1966–70, vol. 5, f. 47, Vancouver – Bingo, McDiarmid, Vancouver City Prosecutor, to AG Bonner, 25 Nov. 1965; *Vancouver Sun*, 19, 29 Aug. 1949; *Vancouver News-Herald*, 1 Feb. 1950

70 *Vancouver Daily Province*, 30 Jan., 1 Feb., 20 Sept. 1950, 31 May 1951

71 Ibid., 19, 20, 21 Sept. 1950; 21 Feb., 5 March, 26 April 1951; *Vancouver Sun*, 21 Feb., 5 March 1951; *Vancouver News-Herald*, 21 Sept. 1950, 21, 22 Feb., 27 April 1951

72 *Vancouver Sun*, 26 Oct. 1953

73 PAM, GR 5 42, AG, J/1/2/8, 102–L, Lotteries, 1957–60, Deputy AG Manitoba to Deputy AG Newfoundland, 18 June 1958; Memo to Ivan Schultz, AG Manitoba, 3 Nov. 1953; Court of Queen's Bench, Fall Assizes, Crown Evidence, 19, 20 Oct. 1953; *Vancouver Sun*, 19 Oct. 1957

74 HC, *Debates*, 10 March 1961, 2891 (L.J. Pigeon, Joliette-L'Assomption-Montcalm); 26 Jan. 1962, 272 (J.F. Browne, Vancouver-Kingsway); 'Bid Sad and Final Adieu to $150m Annually,' *Financial Post*, 56 (Nov. 1962), 17

75 *Vancouver Daily Province*, 21 June 1958, 21 Oct. 1963

76 Cronin, 'State Lottery,' 28; *Vancouver Daily Province*, 21 Sept. 1949, 10 Oct. 1950; *Vancouver Sun*, 17 March 1950

77 *United Church Observer*, 15 Feb. 1964, 41; Sainte-Marie, 'Gagnes,' 37; HC, *Debates*, 15 Feb. 1961, 2894 (J.P. Deschatelets, Maisonneuve-Rosemont); *La Presse* (Montreal), 15 Feb. 1961

78 *Victoria Colonist*, 27 Feb. 1962; HC, *Debates* (Montreal), 27 Feb. 1962, 1294 (Dubois, Richmond-Wolfe); *La Presse* (Montreal), 28 Feb. 1962

79 *Le Devoir* (Montreal), 14 March 1962 (translated); HC, *Debates*, 17 April 1964, 2327 (Réal Caouette, Témiscamingue); 28 April 1964, 2671 (L.J. Pigeon, Joliette-L'Assomption-Montcalm)

80 *Vancouver Sun*, 5 Feb. 1966, 4 (column by Gerald Waring); HC, *Debates*, 22 April 1969, 7826 (André Fortin, Lotbinière)

81 *Vancouver Sun*, 18 May 1954

82 Moss, 'Canada's,' 14; *Vancouver Sun*, 9 Oct. 1963; 'Spunky Mrs. English Ready to 'Sweep' up Parliament Hill,' *Financial Post* 57 (21 Sept. 1963), 27; AO, RG 4-02, AG, Minister's Office files, f. 311.8, 'Lotteries, Raffles, and Bingo, 1966,' 'Operation Sweepstake' pamphlet

83 *Victoria Colonist*, 13 Aug. 1965; *Vancouver Sun*, 19 June 1964

84 *Vancouver Sun*, 23 May 1951, 17; 14 June 1951, 38; Brenner with Brenner, *Gambling*, 18

85 *Winnipeg Free Press*, 18 May 1934

86 *Vancouver Sun*, 3 April, 28 May, 14 Aug., 11 Sept., 4 Oct., 2 Dec. 1968, 11 March, 5 June, 14 July, 15 Sept. 1969; AO, RG 4, AG, series 4-02, Minister's Office Files, 1926–78, f. 375.4, Montreal Lottery or Voluntary Tax Plan, Memo: State of Case; *Vancouver Daily Province*, 1 June, 4 July, 11 Sept., 4 Dec. 1968, 12 March 1969; *Victoria Colonist*, 4 Oct. 1968, 13 March 1969. In British Columbia, the post office delivered 1.5 million pieces of direct mail promoting the Montreal lottery to individual households.

87 *Vancouver Sun*, 27 April 1968; 5 June 1969; AO, RG 4, AG, series 4-02, Minister's Office Files, 1926–78, f. 375.4, Montreal Lottery or Voluntary Tax Plan, Memo W.C. Bowman to Arthur Wishart, AG, 3 May 1968; *Vancouver Daily Province*, 9 July 1969; Brenner with Brenner, *Gambling*, 18

88 HC, *Debates*, 8 Oct. 1963, 3324 (J.J. Greene, Renfrew-South)

89 Ibid., 15 Feb. 1961, 2893 (J P Deschatelets, Maisonneuve-Rosemont); 3 March 1967, 13750–1 (Henri Latulippe, Compton-Frontenac); 4 March 1963, 3179 (Ralph Cowan, York-Humber). See also AO, RG 4, AG, series 4–02, Minister's Office Files, 1926–78, f. 311.8, Lotteries, Raffles, and Bingo 1966, Allen A. Taylor, Brighton, to Arthur Wishart, AG, 14 March 1966; f. 22.3, Gambling 1946–7, Resolution passed Nov. 1947, Elgin County Council

90 AO, RG 4, AG, series 4-02, Minister's Office Files, 1926–78, f. 375.3, Lotteries, Raffles, and Bingo, news clippings, *Toronto Telegram*, 27 Dec. 1967

91 Ibid., f. 311.8, Lotteries, Raffles, and Bingo 1966, Arthur Wishart, AG, to J.C., District Governor of Lions International, 18 May 1966 (Personal and confidential); Howse, 'Legal Lotteries,' 30; *Victoria Colonist*, 16 Aug. 1953

92 Burnham, *Bad Habits*, 155; I am indebted to Shirley Tillotson for this point. Kennedy, 'Gambling,' 14

93 HC, *Debates*, 17 April 1955, 2818–9 (Roger Parizeau, Lac St Jean); 18 Jan. 1960, 35 (J.F. Browne, Vancouver-Kingsway, re: c-22 Hospital Sweepstake Board); *Financial Post*, 23 March 1949; HC, *Debates*, 19 July 1960, 6531 (L.J. Pigeon, Joliette-L'Assomption-Montcalm, re: C-23 Hospital & Universities); *Victoria Colonist*, 14 Sept. 1963

94 Howse, 'Legal Lotteries,' 30; La Filiale du Québec de L'Association des Médecins de Langue Française du Canada (17 April 1962) urged establishment of provincial lotteries to finance health. Canada, Royal Commission on Health Services, *Report*, vol. 1 (1964), 87

95 *Financial Post*, 12 Oct. 1963. See also *Victoria Colonist*, 21 Sept. 1951; Leslie K. Tarr, '"Something for Nothing" Just Doesn't Hold True,' *Toronto Star*, 21 June 1967

96 *Victoria Colonist*, 20 June 1964. See also Bonner's private correspondence: BCARS, GR 2966, BC AG, Correspondence from C95, 1966–70, vol. 5, f. 49 Victoria – Bingo, AG Bonner to C.A. Marcus, 20 June 1964; AO, RG 4, AG, series 4-02, Minister's Office Files, 1926–78, f. 311.7, Lotteries, etc. – Clippings, Rev. C.W. Cope, 'Lotteries Not the Answer to Needs of Municipality, Claims Minister,' *North Bay Nugget*, 18 June 1966

97 AO, RG 4, AG, series 4-02, Minister's Office Files, 1926–78, f. 343.6, Lotteries, Raffles, and Bingo, newspaper clippings 1967, 'The Tax Gamblers,' *Brantford Expositor*, 8 May 1967

98 *Vancouver Sun*, 11 Oct. 1962 (emphasis added); also 18 Oct. 1962

99 Ibid., 24 Nov. 1967; *Vancouver Daily Province*, 13 Oct. 1967

100 *Vancouver Sun*, 22 Dec. 1967; BCARS, GR 2966, BC AG, Correspondence from C95, 1966–70, vol. 5, f. 4, Bingo – Gambling, General, DAG Gilbert Kennedy to AG L.R. Peterson, 9 Aug. 1968; *Vancouver Daily Province*, 22 Dec. 1967

101 HC, *Debates*, 23 Jan. 1969, 4721 (John Turner, Ottawa-Carleton)

102 Ibid., 23 Jan. 1969, 4760 (David Lewis, York South)

103 Ibid., 11 Feb. 1969, 5377 (Stanley Knowles, Winnipeg–North Centre); 21 April 1969, 7785 (Les Benjamin, Regina–Lake Centre). Tommy Douglas expressed a similar concern: 22 April 1969, 7806 (T.C. Douglas, Nanaimo-Cowichan–The Islands).

104 Ibid., 27 Jan. 1969, 4842 (Gordon L. Fairweather, Fundy-Royal); 25 Feb. 1969, 5926 (John Gilbert, Broadview); 22 April 1969, 7806 (T.C. Douglas,

Nanaimo–Cowichan–The Islands); 22 April 1969, 7810–11 (Hon. W.G. Dinsdale, Brandon Souris); 27 Jan. 1969, 4860 (Robert McCleave, Halifax–East Hants); 11 Feb. 1969, 5377 (Stanley Knowles, Winnipeg–North Centre)

105 Ibid., 21 April 1969, 7782 (Andrew Brewin, Greenwood); 22 April 1969, 7810 (Hon. W.G. Dinsdale, Brandon Souris); 22 April 1969, 7817 (Giles Marceau, Lapointe)

106 Ibid., 13 Feb. 1969, 5471 (Henri Latulippe, Compton-Frontenac). See also 22 April 1969, 7808 (René Matte, Champlain); 21 April 1968, 7779–80 (Réal Caouette, Témiscamingue); 22 April 1969, 7831–2 (Bernard F. Dumont, Frontenac)

107 *Vancouver Sun*, 3, 16 July, 31 Aug. 1970, 29 Jan., 1, 4, 31 Dec. 1970; Osborne, 'Licensing without Law.' In 1985, British Columbia withdrew and formed its own corporation.

108 Files, '"Smocks and Jocks,"' 209, 217; *Ontario Lottery Corporation Annual Report 1975–76*, 4–5

109 *Ontario Lottery Corporation Annual Report, 1977–8*, 11, 14; *1978–9*, 17

110 Colin S. Campbell, 'Canadian Gambling Legislation,' 30, 247; Colin S. Campbell and Lowman, 'Introduction,' xvix; Vance, *Analysis*, 1. Ironically, the international growth of state lotteries eventually brought about the decline of the Irish Sweepstakes itself in the late 1980s, when it was replaced by an Irish national lottery. In the early 1970s it was estimated that the sweepstake had generated a gross income of $1.25 billion since it began in 1930. Vance, *Analysis*, 38; Weinstein and Deitch, *Impact*, 88

111 The adoption of the language of grassroots activism by such generally unsympathetic voices as *Brockville Recorder and Times* and the *Montreal Gazette* says much more about winning rhetoric and the state of class relations. AO, RG 4-02, AG, Minister's Office Files, f. 375.3, 'Lotteries, Raffles, Bingo clippings 1968,' *Brockville Recorder and Times*, 29 Dec. 1967

112 See Bryden, *Planners*. I am particularly grateful to Shirley Tillotson for this point.

113 See also Tillotson, 'A New Taxpayer.'

Conclusion

1 Lower, *My First*, 8

2 Brenner with Brenner, *Gambling*, 89; Vance, *Analysis*, 29

3 Fabian, *Card Sharps*, 11

4 Valverde, *Age of Light*, 105

5 Colin S. Campbell and Smith, 'Canadian Gambling,' 23–4

References

Adams, Mary Louise. 'In Sickness and in Health: State Formation, Moral Regulation, and Early VD Initiatives in Ontario.' *Journal of Canadian Studies* 28 (winter 1993–4), 117–30
– *The Trouble with Normal: Postwar Youth and the Making of Heterosexuality.* Toronto 1997
Allan, Ted. *Love Is a Long Shot: A Novel.* Toronto 1984
Allingham, Earl C. 'Is Speculation Destructive?' *Saturday Night*, 27 Dec. 1930
Anderson, Kay. *Vancouver's Chinatown: Racial Discourse in Canada, 1875–1980.* Montreal 1991
Ankli, Robert E. 'The North American Futures Market during World War I.' Pp. 172–91 in Donald H. Akenson, *Canadian Papers in Rural History*, vol. 6. Gananoque, ON, 1988
Appleby, Brenda. *Responsible Parenthood: Decriminalizing Contraception in Canada.* Toronto 1999
Armstrong, Christopher. *Blue Skies and Boiler Rooms: Buying and Selling Securities in Canada, 1870–1940.* Toronto 1997
Ayers, Pat. 'The Hidden Economy of Dockland Families: Liverpool in the 1930s.' Pp. 271–90 in Pat Hudson and W.R. Lee, *Women's Work and the Family Economy in Historical Perspective.* Manchester 1990
Ayers, Pat, and Jan Lambertz. 'Marriage Relations, Money, and Domestic Violence in Working-Class Liverpool, 1919–39.' Pp. 195–219 in Jane Lewis, ed., *Labour and Love: Women's Experience of Home and Family, 1850–1940.* Oxford 1986
Baillargeon, Denyse. '"If You Had No Money, You Had No Trouble, Did You?" Montreal Working-Class Housewives during the Great Depression.' *Women's History Review* 1, no. 2 (1992), 217–37
– *Ménagères au temps de la crise.* Montreal 1991

Baker, Norman. 'Going to the Dogs – Hostility to Greyhound Racing in Britain: Puritanism, Socialism and Pragmatism.' *Journal of Sport History* 23, no. 2 (summer 1996), 97–119

Baker, Paula. *The Moral Framework of Public Life: Gender, Politics and the State in Rural New York, 1870–1930.* New York 1991

Basu, Ellen Oxfeld. 'Profit, Loss and Fate: The Entrepreneurial Ethic and the Practice of Gambling in an Overseas Chinese Community.' *Modern China* 17 (April 1991), 227–59

Baureiss, Gunter, and Leo Dreier, 'Winnipeg's Chinatown: Demographic, Ecological and Organizational Change, 1900–1980,' *Urban History Review* 10, no. 3 (1982), 11–24

Behiels, Michael. *Prelude to Quebec's Quiet Revolution: Liberalism versus Neo-Nationalism, 1945–1960.* Montreal 1985

Bell, Daniel. 'Crime as an American Way of Life.' *Antioch Review* 50, nos. 1–2 (1992), 109–30

Bercuson, David. *Fools and Wise Men: The Rise of the One Big Union.* Toronto 1978

Berger, Carl. *The Sense of Power: Studies in the Ideas of Canadian Imperialism, 1867–1914.* Toronto 1970

Best, Gary Dean. *The Nickel and Dime Decade: American Popular Culture during the 1930s.* Westport, CT, 1993

Bouchier, Nancy. 'Strictly Honorable Races: Woodstock's Driving Park Association and Nineteenth Century Small Town Civic Holidays.' *Canadian Journal of History of Sport* 24, no. 1 (May 1993), 29–51

Boudreau, Michael. 'Crime and Society in a City of Order: Halifax, 1918–1935.' PhD thesis, Queen's University, 1996

Braden, Spruille. 'More Dangerous Than Spies.' *Reader's Digest,* June 1951

Brailey, F.W.L. *Gambling in Canada,* issued by the Board of Evangelical and Social Services of the United Church of Canada. Toronto, n.d.

Brenner, Reuven, with Gabrielle Brenner. *Gambling and Speculation: A Theory, a History, and a Future of Some Human Decisions.* Cambridge 1990

Brodeur, Jean Paul. *La délinquance de l'ordre. Recherches sur les commissions d'enquête.* Ville La Salle, QC, 1984

Brown, Douglas A. 'Thoroughbred Horse-Racing Receives an Imperial Nod: The Parliamentary Debate on Legalizing Gambling in Canada, 1910.' *International Journal of the History of Sport* 11, no. 2 (Aug. 1994), 252–69

Bryden, Penny. *Planners and Politicians: Liberal Politics and Social Policy, 1957–1968.* Montreal 1997

Burnham, John C. *Bad Habits: Drinking, Smoking, Taking Drugs, Gambling, Sexual Misbehavior and Swearing in American History.* New York 1993

Campbell, Colin S. 'Canadian Gambling Legislation: Social Origins of Legalization.' PhD thesis, Simon Fraser University, 1994

Campbell, Colin S., and John Lowman. 'Introduction.' In *Gambling in Canada: Golden Goose or Trojan Horse? Proceedings of the First National Symposium on Lotteries and Gambling.* Burnaby, BC, 1989

Campbell, Colin S., and Garry J. Smith. 'Canadian Gambling: Trends and Public Policy Issues.' *Annals: American Academy of Political Science and Sociology,* 556 (March 1998), 22–35

Campbell, Robert A. 'Ladies and Escorts, Gender Segregation and Public Policy in British Columbia Beer Parlours, 1925–1945.' *BC Studies* 105/106 (spring/summer 1995), 119–38

– *Sit Down and Drink Your Beer: Regulating Vancouver's Beer Parlours, 1925–1954.* Toronto 2001

Canada. *The King's Regulations and Orders for the Canadian Militia.* Ottawa 1939

Chan, Anthony B. *Gold Mountain: The Chinese in the New World.* Vancouver 1983

Chan, Kwok B. *Smoke and Fire: The Chinese in Montreal.* Hong Kong 1991

Chaput, Solange Rolland, and Gwethalyn Graham. *Dear Enemies: A Dialogue on French and English Canada.* Toronto 1963

Charbonneau, Jean-Pierre. *La filière canadienne.* Montreal 1975

Chauncey, George. *Gay New York: Gender, Urban Culture, and the Making of the Gay Male World, 1890–1940.* New York 1994

Chinn, Carl. *Better Betting with a Decent Fellow: Bookmaking, Betting, and the British Working Class, 1750–1990.* Hempstead 1991

Chong, Denise. *The Concubine's Children.* Toronto 1994

Christie, Nancy, and Michael Gauvreau. *A Full-Orbed Christianity: The Protestant Churches and Social Welfare in Canada, 1900–1940.* Montreal 1996

Chu, Yung-Deh Richard. 'Chinese Secret Societies in America: A Historical Survey.' *Asian Profiles,* 1, no. 1 (Aug. 1973), 22–3

Clapson, Mark. *A Bit of a Flutter. Popular Gambling and English Society, c 1823–1961.* Manchester 1992

Clotfelter, Charles, and Philip Cook. *Selling Hope: State Lotteries in America.* Cambridge, MA, 1989

Cody, H.J. *Why Is It Wrong to Gamble?* Moral and Social Reform Council of Canada, n.d.

Cohen, Stanley. *Rebellion against Victorianism: The Impetus for Cultural Change in 1920s America.* Oxford 1991

Coleman, Jim. 'Ten Bucks on the Nose, Joe.' *Maclean's,* 15 April 1944

Collier, James Lincoln. *The Rise of Selfishness in America.* New York 1991

Collins, Alan F. 'The Pathological Gamblers and the Government of Gambling,' *History of Human Sciences,* 9, no. 3 (1996), 69–100

Commend, Suzanne. 'De la femme dechue à la femme infectieuse: perception sociale et repression de la prostitution montréalaise pendant la Seconde guerre.' MA thesis, Université de Montréal, 1996

Cook, Ramsay. 'Henry George and the Poverty of Canadian Progress.' *Historical Papers*. Ottawa 1977, 142–57

Cooke, Ronald J. *The Mayor of Cote St Paul: A Harlequin Book*. Toronto 1950

Corrigan, Philip, and Derek Sayer. 'Afterthought.' In *The Great Arch: English State Formation as Cultural Revolution*. Oxford 1985

Cronin, Fergus. 'State Lottery May Become New 'Margarine Issue.' *Saturday Night*, 23 Aug. 1949

Cross, Gary. *Time and Money: The Making of Consumer Culture*. New York 1993

Culin, Stewart. *The Gambling Games of the Chinese in America*. Philadelphia 1891

David, François. 'Le Comité de Moralité Publique de Montréal.' *Cultures du Canada français* 8 (1991), 84–95

Davies, Andrew. 'The Police and the People: Gambling in Salford, 1900–1939.' *Historical Journal* 34, no. 1 (1991), 87–115

de Champlain, Pierre. *Le crime organisé à Montréal (1940–1980)*. Hull 1986

DeLind, Laura B. 'Bingo: Some Whys and Wherefores of a Popular Pastime.' *Journal of Popular Culture* 18 (fall 1984), 149–56

Devereaux, Edward C. *Gambling and the Social Structure: A Sociological Study of Lotteries and Horse Racing in Contemporary America*. New York 1980

Dingman, Harold. 'Gambling – Montreal's Biggest Business.' *Liberty*, 3 Nov. 1946

Dixon, Dave. 'The Discovery of the Compulsive Gambler.' Pp. 157–79 in Zenon Bankowski and Geoff Mungham, *Essays in Law and Society*. London 1980

Dixon, David. *From Prohibition to Regulation: Bookmaking, Anti-Gambling and the Law*. Oxford 1991

Dodds, E. King. *Canadian Turf: Recollections and Other Sketches*. Toronto 1909

Downes, D.M., B.P. Davies, M.E. Savid, and P. Stone. *Gambling, Work and Leisure: A Study across Three Areas*. London 1976

Duncan, Sara Jeannette. *The Imperialist*. Toronto [1907] 1966

Dunkely, John. *Gambling: A Social and Moral Problem in France, 1685–1792*. Oxford 1985

Eadington, William R., and James H. Frey. Preface. *Annals of the American Academy of Political Science and Sociology* 474 (July 1984), 9–11

Ehrenreich, Barbara. *The Hearts of Men: American Dreams and the Flight from Commitment*. New York 1983

Englander, David. 'Booth's Jews: The Presentation of Jews and Judaism in Life and Labour of the People of London.' *Victorian Studies* 32, no. 4 (summer 1989), 551–71

Ewen, Cecil L'Estrange. *Lotteries and Sweepstakes*. London 1932

Ezell, John Samuel. *Fortune's Merry Wheel: The Lottery in America*. Cambridge, MA, 1960

Fabian, Ann. *Card Sharps, Dream Books and Bucket Shops: Gambling in Nineteenth-Century America*. Ithaca, NY, 1990

Files, James. '"Smocks and Jocks": The Establishment of the Ontario Ministry of Culture and Recreation, 1974.' *Ontario History* 83, no. 3 (1991), 209–23

Fleming, James. *Merchants of Fear: An Investigation of Canada's Insurance Industry*. Toronto 1986

Forestell, Nancy. 'Bachelors, Boarding-Houses, and Blind Pigs: Gender Construction in a Multi-Ethnic Mining Camp, 1909–1920.' Pp. 251–90 in Franca Iacovetta with Paula Draper and Robert Ventresca, eds., *A Nation of Immigrants: Women, Workers, and Communities in Canadian History, 1840s–1960s*. Toronto 1998

Fox, Charlie. 'In Search of a Fair Bet.' Pp. 77–95 in Verity Burgmann and Jenny Lee, eds., *Constructing a Culture: A People's History of Australia since 1788*. Victoria, Australia, 1988

Fraser, Brian. *The Social Uplifters: Presbyterian Progressives and the Social Gospel in Canada, 1875–1915*. Waterloo, ON, 1988

Frayne, Trent. 'Biggest Bingo.' *Maclean's*, 1 Feb. 1946

Garry, Carl, and John Sangster. 'Gambling Isn't Necessarily Gaming in Ontario.' Pp. 279–93 in W.E. Mann, ed., *The Underside of Toronto*. Toronto 1970

Gilfoyle, Timothy. *City of Eros: New York City, Prostitution, and the Commercialization of Sex, 1790–1920*. New York 1992

Gilmore, John. *Swinging in Paradise: The Story of Jazz in Montreal*. Montreal 1988

Gordon, Linda. *Pitied But Not Entitled: Single Mothers and the History of Welfare*. New York 1994

Gorn, Elliot J. *The Manly Art: Bare-Knuckle Prize Fighting in America*. Ithaca, NY, 1986

Grant, David. *On a Roll: A History of Gambling*. Victoria, Australia, 1994

Grant, George. *Lament for a Nation: The Defeat of Canadian Nationalism*. Ottawa 1970

Grun, Bernard. *The Time Tables of History*. New York 1975

Haller, Mark. 'Bootleggers and American Gambling, 1920–1950.' Pp. 102–43 in Commission of the Review of National Policy toward Gambling, *Gambling in America*. Washington, DC, 1976

– 'Policy Gambling, Entertainment, and the Emergence of Black Politics: Chicago from 1900–1940.' *Journal of Social History* 24, no. 4 (1991), 719–39

Hallowell, Gerald. *Prohibition in Ontario, 1919–1923.* Ottawa 1972

Hamelin, Jean. *Histoire du catholicisme québécois: Le xxe siècle,* tome 2, *De 1940 à nos jours.* Montreal 1984

Harrison, Brian. *Drink and Victorians: The Temperance Question in England, 1815–1872.* London 1971

Helly, Denise. *Les Chinois de Montréal, 1877–1951.* Quebec 1987

Heron, Craig. 'Labourism and the Canadian Working Class.' *Labour/Le Travail* 13 (spring 1984), 45–75

Higley, Dahn D. *OPP: The History of the Ontario Provincial Police Force.* Toronto 1984

Homel, Gene Howard. '"Fading Beams of the Nineteenth Century": Radicalism and Early Socialism in Canada's 1890s.' *Labour/Le Travailleur* 5 (spring 1980), 7–32

Howell, Colin. *Northern Sandlots: A Social History of Maritime Baseball.* Toronto 1995

Howse, Rev. Ernest. 'Legal Lotteries Are Worse than Useless.' *Maclean's,* 25 July 1964

Hunt, Alan. *Governing Morals: A Social History of Moral Regulation.* New York 1999

Huzel, James. 'The Incidence of Crime in Vancouver during the Great Depression.' *BC Studies* (spring/summer 1986), 361–81

Iacovetta, Franca. *Such Hardworking People: Italian Immigrants in Postwar Toronto.* Montreal 1992

Israel, Wilfred Emmerson. 'The Montreal Negro Community.' MA thesis, McGill University, 1928

Itzkowitz, David C. 'Victorian Bookmakers and Their Customers.' *Victorian Studies* 32, no. 1 (autumn 1988), 7–30

Johnson, David R. 'The Origins and Structure of Intercity Criminal Activity 1940–1920: An Interpretation.' *Journal of Social History* 15, no. 4 (summer 1982), 593–605

Johnstone, Ken. 'How Plante and Drapeau Licked the Montreal Underworld.' *Maclean's,* 1 Dec. 1954

Jones, David C. *Midways, Judges and Smooth-Tongued Fakirs: The Illustrated Story of Country Fairs in the Prairie West.* Saskatoon 1983

Jones, Stephen G. *Workers at Play: A Social and Economic History of Leisure, 1918–1939.* London 1986

Joselit, Jenna Weissman. *Our Gang: Jewish Crime and the New York Jewish Community, 1900–1940.* Bloomington, IN, 1983

Josie, Svanhuit. 'The Social Effects of Gambling.' *Social Welfare,* 15 June 1953

Kavanagh, Thomas M. *Enlightenment and the Shadows of Chance: The Novel and the Culture of Gambling in Eighteenth-Century France*. Baltimore 1993

Keate, Stuart. 'The Unhorsed Galahad of Montreal.' *Maclean's*, 15 July 1948

Kefauver, Estes. *Crime in America*. Garden City, NY, 1951

Keller, Morton. *Regulating a New Society: Public Policy and Social Change in America, 1900–1933*. Cambridge, MA, 1994

Kelly, Jack. 'Slots.' *Invention and Technology* 16, no. 2 (fall 2000), 34–8, 40–1

Kennedy, John B. 'Gambling – the Ruling Racket.' *Saturday Night*, 6 June 1953

Kisker, George. 'Mad about Gambling.' *Maclean's*, 1 Sept. 1948

Knox, Gilbert (Madge MacBeth.) *The Land of Afternoon*. Ottawa 1924

Labrosse, Michel. *The Lottery ... from Jacques Cartier to Modern Times. Sidelights on the History of Lotteries in Québec*, trans. by Alan Brown. Montreal 1985

Lacasse, Danielle. *La prostitution féminine à Montréal, 1945–1970*. Montreal 1994

Lancaster, Roger N. *Life Is Hard: Machismo, Danger and the Intimacy of Power in Nicaragua*. Berkeley 1992

Lears, Jackson. 'Playing with Money.' *Wilson Quarterly* 19, no. 4 (autumn 1995), 7–23

Lears, T.J. Jackson. *No Place of Grace: Antimodernism and the Transformation of American Culture, 1880-1920*. New York 1981

Lemelin, Roger. *The Town Below* (English translation of *Au Pied de la pente douce*). Toronto [1944] 1948

Leonoff, Cyril E. 'Harry L. Salmon of Victoria.' *Western States Jewish History* 22, no. 4 (1990), 338–49

Lévesque, Andrée. *Making and Breaking the Rules: Women in Quebec, 1919–1939*. Toronto 1994

Light, Ivan. 'From Vice District to Tourist Attraction: The Moral Career of American Chinatowns, 1880–1940.' *Pacific Historical Review* 43, no. 3 (1974), 367–94

Linteau, Paul-André. *L'histoire de Montréal depuis la Confédération*. Montreal 1992

Little, Margaret. 'Manhunts and Bingo Blabs: The Everyday Concerns, Frustrations and Rebellions of Single Mothers in Ontario in the 1990s.' *Canadian Journal of Sociology* 19, no. 2 (1994), 233–48

Little, Margaret Hillyard. *No Car, No Radio, No Liquor Permit: The Moral Regulation of Single Mothers in Ontario, 1920–1997*. Toronto 1998

Livernois, Denis. 'Monseigneur Charbonneau. sixième évesque de Montréal (1940–1950.)' Pp. 107–12 in *L'Eglise de Montréal aperçus d'hier et d'aujourd'hui, 1936–1986*. Montreal 1986

Lower, Arthur R.M. *My First Seventy-five Years*. Toronto 1967

Luce, P.W. 'There's a Way to Make Any Lottery Legal.' *Saturday Night*, 27 April 1946

Macdonald, Ian, and Betty O'Keefe. *The Mulligan Affair: Top Cop on the Take.* Surrey, BC, 1997

McCaffrey, Gordon. 'They're Putting the Squeeze on Gambling.' *Saturday Night*, 18 April 1950

McCormick, Ted. 'Gambling in Montreal.' *Maclean's*, 15 Sept. 1945

McDonald, Robert. *Making Vancouver: Class, Status and Social Boundaries, 1863–1913.* Vancouver 1996

McIlroy, Kimball. 'Is Gambling Ethical?' *Saturday Night*, 6 Dec. 1947

McKibbon, Ross. 'Working-Class Gambling in Britain, 1880–1939.' Pp. 101–38 in *Ideologies of Class: Social Relations in Britain, 1880–1950*. Oxford 1990

McMillen, Jan, ed. *Gambling Cultures: Studies in History and Interpretation.* London 1996

McMillen, Jan. 'Understanding Gambling: History, Concepts and Theories.' Pp. 6–42 in McMillen, ed., *Gambling Cultures*

McNeil, Jeannine L. '"What Comes Around, Goes Around": Bingo as a Cape Breton Subculture.' Pp. 51–6 in Carol Corbin and Judith A. Rolls, eds., *The Centre of the World at the Edge of the Continent*. Sydney, NS, 1996

McQueen, Rod. *Risky Business: Inside Canada's $86-billion Insurance Company.* Toronto 1985

Mann, W.E. 'The Lower Ward.' in W.E. Mann, ed., *The Underside of Toronto.* Toronto 1970

Manning, Herbert. 'Is Bingo Bad for Your Town?' *Maclean's*, 6 Aug. 1955

Marks, Lynne. 'Ladies, Loafers, Knights and "Lasses": The Social Dimensions of Religion and Leisure in Late Nineteenth Century Small Town Ontario.' PhD thesis, York University, 1992

Marquis, Greg. 'Civilized Drinking: Alcohol and Society in New Brunswick, 1945–75.' Paper delivered to Canadian Historical Association, Edmonton, 2000

– 'The Early Twentieth-Century Toronto Police Institution.' PhD thesis, Queen's University, 1987

– *Policing Canada's Century: A History of the Canadian Association of Chiefs of Police.* Toronto 1993

– 'Vancouver Vice: The Police and the Negotiation of Morality, 1904–1935.' Pp. 242–73 in Hamar Foster and John McLaren, eds., *Essays in the History of Canadian Law*, Volume 6, *British Columbia and the Yukon*. Toronto 1995

Marquis, Greg. 'Working Men in Uniform: The Early Twentieth-Century Toronto Police.' *Histoire sociale/Social History* 20 (Nov. 1987), 259–77

Metcalfe, Alan. 'Organized Sport in the Mining Communities of South Northumberland, 1800–1889.' *Victorian Studies* 25, no. 4 (summer 1982), 469–95

Moore, William H. *The Kefauver Committee and the Politics of Crime, 1950–1952.* Columbia, MO, 1974

Morton, Desmond. '"Kicking and Complaining": Demobilization Riots and the Canadian Expeditionary Force, 1918–19.' *Canadian Historical Review* 61, no. 3 (1980), 334–60

– *When Your Number's Up: The Canadian Soldier in the First World War.* Toronto 1993

Morton, J.D. 'Gambling and the Law: Can the Criminal Element Be Wiped Out?' *Saturday Night,* 27 May 1961

Morton, Suzanne. 'Men and Women in a Halifax Working-Class Neighbourhood in the 1920s.' PhD thesis, Dalhousie University, 1990

– *Ideal Surroundings: Domestic Life in a Working-Class Suburb in the 1920s.* Toronto 1995

– 'Labourism and Labor Politics in Halifax, 1919–1926.' MA thesis, Dalhousie University, 1986

Morton, W.L. *The Progressive Party in Canada.* Toronto 1950

Moss, Bill. 'Canada's Sweepstake Crusader.' *Weekend Magazine,* 25 Jan. 1964

Mutchmor, James R. *Mutchmor: The Memoirs of James Ralph Mutchmor.* Toronto 1965

Naylor, James. *The New Democracy: Challenging the Social Order in Industrial Ontario, 1914–25.* Toronto 1991

Ng, Wing Chung. 'Ethnicity, Community: Southern Chinese Immigrants and Descendants in Vancouver, 1945–1980.' PhD thesis, University of British Columbia, 1993

Nipp, Dora. 'The Chinese in Toronto.' Pp. 147–75 in Robert F Harney, ed., *Gathering Place: Peoples and Neighbourhoods of Toronto, 1834–1945.* Toronto 1985

Nye, Robert A. *Masculinity and Male Codes of Honor in Modern France.* New York 1993

O'Hara, John. *A Mug's Game: A History of Gaming and Betting in Australia.* Kensington, NSW, 1988

Oiwa, Keninousuke. 'Tradition and Social Change: An Ideological Analysis of the Montreal Jewish Immigrant Ghetto in the Early Twentieth Century.' PhD thesis, Cornell University, 1988

Osborne, Judith, and Colin S. Campbell. 'Recent Amendments to Canadian Lottery and Gaming Laws: The Transfer of Power from Federal to Provincial Governments.' Pp. 127–147 in Campbell and Lowman, eds., *Gambling in Canada*

Osborne, Judith A. 'Licensing without Law: Legalized Gambling in British Columbia.' *Canadian Public Administration* 35, no. 1 (spring 1992), 56–74

Ownby, Ted. *Subduing Satan: Religion, Recreation and Manhood in the Rural South, 1865–1920.* Chapel Hill, NC, 1990

Owram, Doug. *Born at the Right Time: A History of the Baby Boom Generation.* Toronto 1996

Palmer, Al. *Montreal Confidential.* Montreal 1950

Parnaby, Andy. '"The Red Hand under the White Glove": The Workers' Unity League on the Vancouver Waterfront, 1929–1935.' Paper delivered to the Canadian Historical Association, St John's, Nfld., June 1997

Paton, J.H. 'Gambling.' Pp. 163–7 in J. Hastings, ed., *Encyclopaedia of Religion and Ethics*, vol. 6. Edinburgh 1954

Paul, Gerald W. 'The Board of Evangelism and Social Service, the United Church of Canada, 1925–1960.' MTh thesis, 1974, Vancouver School of Theology

Peiss, Kathy. *Cheap Amusements: Working Women and Leisure in Turn-of-the-Century New York.* Philadelphia 1986

Petrow, Stefan. *Policing Morals: The Metropolitan Police and the Home Office, 1870–1914.* Oxford 1994

Phillips, Alan. 'The Criminal Society That Dominates the Chinese in Canada.' *Maclean's,* 7 April 1962

– 'Gambling: The Greatest Criminal Conspiracy of Them All.' *Maclean's,* 7 March 1964

Plante, Pax. *Montréal sous le règne de la pègre.* Montreal 1950

Plante, Pax, with David MacDonald. 'The Shame of My City.' *Star Weekly Magazine,* 24 June, 1, 8, 14 July 1961

Ponte, Susan. 'Religious Opposition to the Massachusetts Lottery.' *Historical Journal of Massachusetts* 20, no. 1 (winter 1992), 53–63

Porter, John. *The Vertical Mosaic: An Analysis of Social Class and Power in Canada.* Toronto 1965

Price, W.H. 'Investment and Speculation.' Pp. 47–56 in *Yearbook of the Canadian Life Insurance Officers Association. Proceedings of the 34th Annual Meeting.* Toronto 1927

Purcell, Susan, and Brian McKenna. *Jean Drapeau.* Toronto 1980

Raney, W.E. 'The Scandal and Curse of Legalized Gambling.' *Social Welfare* (1 October 1921), 12–8

Reuter, Peter, and Jonathan Rubinstein. 'Illegal Gambling and Organized Crime.' *Society* 20, no. 5 (July/Aug. 1983), 52–55

Richler, Mordecai. *The Apprenticeship of Duddy Kravitz.* Toronto 1959

Riess, Steven. *City Games: The Evolution of American Urban Society and the Rise of Sport.* Chicago 1991

– 'Sport and the American Jew: A Second Look.' *American Jewish History* 83 (March 1995), 1–14

Rishell, Paul W. *Bingo and Christian Ethics.* New York State Council of Churches and Protestant Council of City of New York, n.d.

Robert, Percy. 'Dufferin District: An Area in Transition.' MA thesis, McGill University, 1928

Rockaway, Robert A. 'Hoodlum Hero: The Jewish Gangster as Defender of His People, 1919–1949.' *American Jewish History* 82 (December 1994), 215–35

Rodgers, Daniel. *The Work Ethic in Industrial America, 1850–1920*. Chicago 1974

Rogers, Nicholas. 'Serving Toronto the Good: The Development of the City Police Force, 1834–1884.' Pp. 116–40 Victor Russell, ed., in *Forging a Consensus: Historical Essays on Toronto*. Toronto 1985

Rosecrance, John. 'Compulsive Gambling and the Medicalization of Deviance.' *Social Problems* 32, no. 2 (Feb. 1985), 275–84

– *Gambling without Guilt: The Legitimation of an American Pastime*. Pacific Grove, CA, 1988

Rosenberg, Louis. *Canada's Jews: A Social and Economic Study of the Jews in Canada*. Montreal: Bureau of Social and Economic Research, Canadian Jewish Congress, 1939

Rosenzweig, Roy. *Eight Hours for What We Will: Workers and Leisure in an Industrial City, 1870–1920*. Cambridge 1983

Ross, Alexander. *The Booming Fifties 1950/1960*. Toronto 1977

Rotundo, Edward Anthony. 'Manhood in America: The Northern Middle Class, 1770–1920.' PhD dissertation, Brandeis University, 1982

Roy, Patricia. *A White Man's Province: British Columbia Politicians and Chinese and Japanese Immigrants, 1858–1914*. Vancouver 1989

Runyon, Damon. *Guys and Dolls*. Harmondsworth 1956 [1931]

Ruth, David E. *Inventing the Public Enemy: The Gangster in American Culture, 1918–1934*. Chicago 1996

Ryan, Mary P. *Women in Public: Between Banners and Ballots, 1825–1880*. Baltimore 1990

Sainte-Marie, Gilles. 'Gagnes le gros lot! A quand la lotterie québécoise?' *Magazine Maclean*, Dec. 1963

Sangster, Joan. *Regulating Girls and Women: Sexuality, the Family, and the Law in Ontario, 1920–1960*. Don Mills, ON, 2001

Sarna, Jonathan D. 'The Jewish Way of Crime.' *Commentary* 78, no. 2 (1984), 53–5

Schellenberg, Michael. 'Bingo as Salvation? A Comparison of Michel Tremblay's *Les Belles Soeurs* (1968) and Tomson Highway's *The Rez Sisters* (1988).' MA thesis, Université de Sherbrooke, 1994

Shearer, John. 'Canada's Legalized Betting Houses: An Appeal for Their Suppression.' *Social Welfare*, 1 April 1922

Smith, James F. 'When It's Bad It's Better: Conflicting Images of Gambling in American Culture.' Pp. 101–15 in McMillen, ed., *Gambling Cultures*

– 'Where the Action Is: Images of the Gambler in Recent Popular Films.'

Pp. 178–88 in Paul Loukides and Linda K. Fuller, eds., *Beyond the Stars: Stock Characters in American Popular Film*. Bowling Green, Ohio, 1990

Snow, Hank, with Jack Ownbey and Bob Burris. *The Hank Snow Story*. Urbana, IL, 1994

Stanké, Alan, and Jean-Louis Morgan. *Pax: Lutte à finir avec la pègre*. Montreal 1972

Stansell, Christine. *City of Women: Sex and Class in New York, 1789–1860*. Urbana, IL, 1987

Stearns, Peter N. *American Cool: Constructing a Twentieth-Century Emotional Style*. New York 1994

– *Battleground of Desire: The Struggle for Self Control in Modern America*. New York 1999

Stein, D.L. 'Why the Odds Are Getting Shorter against Legal Sweepstakes in Canada.' *Maclean's*, 27 July 1963

Strange, Carolyn. 'From Modern Babylon to a City on a Hill: The Toronto Social Survey Commission of 1915 and the Search for Sexual Order in the City.' Pp. 255–77 in Roger Hall, William Westfall, and Laurel Sefton MacDowell, eds., *Patterns of the Past: Interpreting Ontario's History*. Toronto 1988

– 'Pain, Death, and Profit: Calculating Risk and Calibrating Canadian Character in the 1950s.' Paper delivered to the Canadian Historical Association, St John's, Nfld., June 1997

Strasser, Susan. *Satisfaction Guaranteed: The Making of the American Mass Market*. New York 1989

Strong-Boag, Veronica. 'Home Dreams: Women and the Suburban Experiment in Canada, 1945–60.' *Canadian Historical Review* 72, no. 4 (Dec. 1991), 471–505

Swan, Joe. *A Century of Service: The Vancouver Police, 1886–1986*. Vancouver 1986

Swyripa, Francis. *Wedded to the Cause: Ukrainian-Canadian Women and Ethnic Identity, 1891–1991*. Toronto 1993

Taschereau, Sylvie. 'Les petits commerçants de l'alimentation et les milieux populaires montréalais, 1920–1940.' PhD thesis, Université de Québec à Montréal, 1992

Thomas, Jacko. *From Police Headquarters: True Tales from the Big City Crime Beat*. Toronto 1990

Thomason, Phillip. 'The Men's Quarter of Downtown Nashville.' *Tennessee Historical Quarterly* 41, no. 1 (1982), 48–66

Tillotson, Shirley. 'A New Taxpayer for a New State: Charitable Fundraising and the Origins of the Welfare State.' Pp. 138–55 in Raymond Blake, Penny

Bryden and Frank Strain, eds., *The Welfare State in Canada: Past, Present and Future*. Concord, ON, 1997

Tremblay, Albert. 'Bingo: jeu anodin qui rapporte gros.' *Magazine Maclean*, 10 Nov. 1970

Tumpane, Frank. 'Breakdown in Morals.' *Saturday Night*, 4 Sept. 1951

Valverde, Mariana. *The Age of Light, Soap and Water: Moral Reform in English Canada, 1885–1925*. Toronto 1991

– 'Building Anti-Delinquent Communities: Morality, Gender and Generation in the City.' Pp. 19–45 in Joy Parr, ed., *A Diversity of Women: Ontario, 1945–1980*. Toronto 1995

– '"Slavery from Within": The Invention of Alcoholism and the Question of Free Will.' *Social History* 22, no. 3 (Oct. 1997), 251–68

Vance, Joan. *An Analysis of the Costs and Benefits of Public Lotteries*. Lewiston, NY, 1989

Voisey, Paul. *Vulcan: The Making of a Prairie Community*. Toronto 1988

Walden, Keith. *Becoming Modern in Toronto: The Industrial Exhibition and the Shaping of a Late Victorian Culture*. Toronto 1997

Walker, Mabel L. 'Civic Gambling.' *Survey* (Nov. 1934)

Walker, Michael. 'The Medicalisation of Gambling as an 'Addiction.' Pp. 223–42 in McMillen, *Gambling Cultures*

Walkowitz, Judith. *City of Dreadful Delight: Narratives of Sexual Danger in Late-Victorian London*. Chicago 1992

Waller, Adrian. *The Gamblers*. Toronto 1974

Wamsley, Kevin B. 'State Formation and Institutionalized Racism: Gambling Laws in Nineteenth and Early Twentieth Century Canada.' *Sports History Review* 29 (1998), 77–85

Waters, Gregory J. 'Operating on the Border: A History of the Commercial Promotion, Moral Suppression, State Regulation of the Thoroughbred Racing Industry in Windsor, Ontario, 1884–1936.' M. Human Kinetics thesis, University of Windsor, 1992

Weaver, John C. *Crime, Constables and Courts: Order and Transgression in a Canadian City, 1816–1970*. Montreal 1995

Weinstein, David and Lilian Deitch. *The Impact of Legalized Gambling: The Socio-economic Consequences of Lotteries and Off-Track Betting*. New York 1974

Weintraub, William. *City Unique: Montreal Days and Nights in the 1940s and 1950s*. Toronto 1996

Wetherell, Donald G. with Irene Kmet. *Useful Pleasure: The Shaping of Leisure in Alberta, 1896–1945*. Regina 1990

Whaples, Robert, and David Buffum. 'Fraternalism, Paternalism, the Family, and the market: Insurance a Century Ago.' *Social Science History* 15, no. 1 (spring 1991), 97–122

White, Kevin. *The First Sexual Revolution: The Emergence of Male Heterosexuality in Modern America*. New York 1993

Williams, David Ricardo. *Mayor Gerry: The Remarkable Gerald Grattan McGeer*. Vancouver 1986

Wise, S.F. 'Sport and Class Values in Old Ontario and Quebec.' Pp. 93–117 in W.H. Heick and R. Graham, eds., *His Own Man: Essays in Honour of Arthur Reginald Marsden Lower*. Montreal 1974

Wolcott, Victoria W. 'The Culture of the Informal Economy: Numbers Runners in Inter-War Black Detriot.' *Radical History Review* 69 (1997), 46–75

Yee, Paul. *Saltwater City: An Illustrated History of the Chinese in Vancouver*. Vancouver 1988

Zelizer, Vivana. *Morals and Markets: The Development of Life Insurance in the United States*. New York 1979

Zulaika, Joseba. *Terranova: The Ethos and Luck of Deep-Sea Fishermen*, Social and Economic Studies no. 25. St John's 1981

– 'Yee Ah Chong Remembers Vacaville Chinatown: An Oral Account of Life in a Town-within-a-Town.' *California History* (summer 1984), 247–51

Illustration Credits

Index